*Christopher J. Alexander*

# Growth and Intimacy for Gay Men
## *A Workbook*

*Pre-publication*
*REVIEWS,*
*COMMENTARIES,*
*EVALUATIONS . . .*

"**G** *rowth and Intimacy for Gay Men: A Workbook* is a welcome addition to the tools available to gay men in their quest for therapeutic self-examination. Both clients and their therapists will find the exercises a useful and concrete way of eliciting important information as well as attitudes that may have been hampering their desired growth and development."

**Michael Shernoff, MSW**
*Private Practice, New York City;*
*Adjunct Faculty,*
*Hunter College Graduate School*
*of Social Work*

*More pre-publication*
*REVIEWS, COMMENTARIES, EVALUATIONS . . .*

"*Growth and Intimacy for Gay Men* is an innovative and welcome resource not only for mental health practitioners, but for anyone seeking to enhance his understanding of himself in relation to both the personal and social context within which we live as gay men. Dr. Alexander skillfully synthesizes psychological theory, research, and clinical practice in order to present a clear and accessible overview of important influences on gay men's psychology while leaving room for the particular paths that each gay man follows as he grows and develops.

This book offers a range of chapters on family, friendships, romance, shame, addiction, AIDS, and aging. Each stands on its own as an important catalyst for discussion and self-discovery, and together, they guide the reader through key milestones in the gay male life cycle. The purposeful and generous integration of qualitative and quantitative research is a refreshing addition to the literature. The user-friendly exercises at the end of each chapter will provide therapist, patient, and interested reader alike with ample fuel on the road to personal understanding and life enhancement."

**Benjamin Lipton, MSW, ACSW**
*Psychotherapist and Coordinator,*
*Mental Health Services,*
*Gay Men's Health Crisis,*
*New York, New York*

The Harrington Park Press
An Imprint of The Haworth Press, Inc.

# Growth and Intimacy for Gay Men
## for Gay Men
### *A Workbook*

## *HAWORTH* Gay & Lesbian Studies
### John P. De Cecco, PhD
### Editor in Chief

New, Recent, and Forthcoming Titles:

*Homosexuality as Behavior and Identity: Dialogues of the Sexual Revolution, Volume II* by Lawrence D. Mass

*Sexuality and Eroticism Among Males in Moslem Societies* edited by Arno Schmitt and Jehoeda Sofer

*Understanding the Male Hustler* by Samuel M. Steward

*Men Who Beat the Men Who Love Them: Battered Gay Men and Domestic Violence* by David Island and Patrick Letellier

*The Golden Boy* by James Melson

*The Second Plague of Europe: AIDS Prevention and Sexual Transmission Among Men in Western Europe* by Michael Pollak

*Barrack Buddies and Soldier Lovers: Dialogues with Gay Young Men in the U.S. Military* by Steven Zeeland

*Outing: Shattering the Conspiracy of Silence* by Warren Johansson and William A. Percy

*The Bisexual Option, Second Edition* by Fritz Klein

*And the Flag Was Still There: Straight People, Gay People, and Sexuality in the U.S. Military* by Lois Shawver

*One-Handed Histories: The Eroto-Politics of Gay Male Video Pornography* by John R. Burger

*Sailors and Sexual Identity: Crossing the Line Between "Straight" and "Gay" in the U.S. Navy* by Steven Zeeland

*The Gay Male's Odyssey in the Corporate World: From Disempowerment to Empowerment* by Gerald V. Miller

*Bisexual Politics: Theories, Queries, and Visions* edited by Naomi Tucker

*Gay and Gray: The Older Homosexual Man, Second Edition* by Raymond M. Berger

*Reviving the Tribe: Regenerating Gay Men's Sexuality and Culture in the Ongoing Epidemic* by Eric Rofes

*Gay and Lesbian Mental Health: A Sourcebook for Practitioners* edited by Christopher J. Alexander

*Against My Better Judgment: An Intimate Memoir of an Eminent Gay Psychologist* by Roger Brown

*The Masculine Marine: Homoeroticism in the U.S. Marine Corps* by Steven Zeeland

*Bisexual Characters in Film: From Anaïs to Zee* by Wayne M. Bryant

*Autopornography: A Memoir of Life in the Lust Lane* by Scott O'Hara

*The Bear Book: Readings in the History and Evolution of a Gay Male Subculture* edited by Les Wright

*Youths Living with HIV: Self-Evident Truths* by G. Cajetan Luna

*Growth and Intimacy for Gay Men: A Workbook* by Christopher J. Alexander

# Growth and Intimacy
# for Gay Men
## *A Workbook*

Christopher J. Alexander, PhD

The Harrington Park Press
An Imprint of The Haworth Press, Inc.
New York • London

Published by

The Harrington Park Press, an imprint of The Haworth Press, Inc., 10 Alice Street, Binghamton, NY 13904-1580

Cover design by Monica L. Seifert.

ISBN 1-56023-901-8.

To my mother and father,
for all their love and support.


To David,
for your patience and guidance
during this endeavor.

# ABOUT THE AUTHOR

**Christopher J. Alexander, PhD,** works as a clinical psychologist. He currently lives in Santa Fe, New Mexico, where he writes and teaches courses on mental health. He is on the editorial boards of *Journal of Homosexuality* and the *Journal of Gay and Lesbian Social Services*. He also writes a syndicated column on gay and lesbian mental health, and offers training for professionals, groups, and agencies on working with sexual minorities.

Feedback regarding this book, as well as general questions on gay male mental health, may be mailed directly to Dr. Alexander at 981 Paseo Del Sur, Santa Fe, New Mexico 87501.

# CONTENTS

Finally, and perhaps most important, is the concept of coming out inside. To be a traveler on the inner path is an activity that all gay men should pursue. . . . Here, at the root of the soul, is where answers about the meaning of being gay are to be found.

*Mark Thompson*

# Introduction

In writing a book for gay men on mental health, I wanted to develop something that would do more than present the reader with concepts and ideas about psychological development. Rather, I wanted to create a book that would engage the reader and allow him to bring in his own life experience as he reads the chapters. Drawing from the popular use of workbooks for issues such as recovery from addictions or abuse, I thought it would be helpful for gay men and the therapists who help them to have a collection of exercises that can be used to further one's awareness of one's personal identity. Thus, this workbook was written with the idea of providing gay men with an overview of many of the common issues gay men confront in our development while supporting my philosophy that it is not enough to just read about gay mental health in order to understand ourselves better. This workbook, therefore, contains over forty assignments or exercises that you, the reader, can use to better understand your own growth and identity as a gay man.

Whether you are a therapist looking for ways to facilitate insight or disclosure in your gay male clients, or a gay man wanting to learn more about your psychological development, this book offers the guidance and structure that is often needed to achieve these goals. This workbook was developed to be a working tool for gay men who are seeking to understand themselves better, and to provide background on some of the key issues we each must deal with as sexual minorities.

My choice of content for the chapters and exercises is based on my experience as a clinical psychologist who has devoted much of my work to helping gay men. It is not possible to include in one volume all the psychological challenges gay men encounter in their lives. However, I feel that this book addresses some of the more common themes that gay men struggle with in an attempt to sort out their identity. I think you will find that the chapters are comprehensive and informative, and I trust you will find the exercises to be challenging and helpful.

## THE WORKBOOK AS AN ADJUNCT TO THERAPY

Though some of you may find it satisfactory reading the book and doing the exercises on your own, I strongly encourage that this workbook be used in conjunction with psychotherapy or other personal growth endeavors. For example, you may want to read a chapter and do some of the exercises at home. Then, when you have your next therapy session, you can take your workbook with you and share your answers with your therapist. He or she can then guide you through the process of exploring the feelings and reactions you have about doing the exercises. If you are in couples therapy, perhaps both you and your lover can do some of the exercises separate from one another and then discuss your responses together in therapy.

Therapists may also want to consider assigning chapters and/or exercises to clients for homework. If you do this, it is important not to shame your clients for not doing a particular exercise. Rather, it can be helpful to explore with your client why he did not choose to complete a particular exercise.

## USING THE WORKBOOK IN STUDY
## OR SUPPORT GROUPS

Being gay can be very isolating for some men. Because of where we live, issues of trust and intimacy, or how "out" we are to others, we may not feel connected with other gay men in satisfactory ways. This is why gay support groups can be of enormous benefit for many gay men. Such groups can help you break feelings of isolation and be with other gay men where you can talk about topics that are meaningful in your life.

Another option for developing closeness with other gay men is to form or participate in a study or peer group in which you read and discuss the chapters in this book. To whatever extent group members feel comfortable, you can share your responses to the exercises with one another.

If you use this workbook in a study or support group, consider the following guidelines:

- *Keep the group limited in size.* It is best if you have no more than eight members in order to allow each person the opportunity to share his thoughts and feelings.
- *Meet consistently.* Study groups work best if the group meets at the same time each week. This allows group members the opportunity to build the meetings into their schedules. However, you may want to take turns meeting at one another's home in order to help the group members be more a part of each other's lives.
- *Establish ground rules early on.* Even if there is not a group leader, each participant should commit to the other members that what is said between group members stays inside of the group. Thus, those in the group are discouraged from telling others what was said in the group. The group should also decide how they want to handle absences by group members, length of the meetings, and for how long the group will meet. It can also help group members feel safe if you do not make personal sharing mandatory because one or more members may need to not share all of their reactions to reading the chapters and/or doing the exercises.

## THE FORMAT OF THE WORKBOOK

Each of the eight chapters in this workbook begin with an overview of the subject matter. In each chapter, I attempt to identify why the content is applicable to the lives of gay men. By using writings of other clinicians, research, and my professional experience, I try to identify themes and challenges that gay men encounter concerning family of origin, self-esteem, forming relationships, addictions, aging, and other areas of our development and life experience.

At the end of each chapter, there are exercises you can do to identify how the chapter content applies to your own life. For example, the exercises in this book will assist you in the process of exploring your relationship with your father, quantifying your self-esteem, identifying your feelings and experiences concerning coming out, clarifying your relationship needs, coping with abusive experiences, and many other areas.

You do not need to read the chapters in any particular order. I do encourage, however, that you begin with Chapter 1 as it lays the foundation for our early development as gay men. As is made clear in the chapter, our experiences in our family of origin lay the foundation for most experiences later in life, including relationships, self-image, coping style, etc.

## WHAT YOU WILL NEED TO DO THE WORKBOOK

This workbook is designed to be interactive in nature. The exercises that are included can be done in the book itself, but there are some you may want to do in your own personal journal. Since many of the exercises ask you questions that might require lengthy answers, there may not be enough room in the space given for you to fully answer the questions. Rather than forcing yourself to be brief, it is best if you write your full answers elsewhere. A journal will also provide you with space to write any additional comments or feelings you have as you do the exercises. Writing your answers in a journal may also feel safer for you than writing your answers in the workbook itself.

Regardless of whether you do the exercises in the workbook or in a journal, it is important that you feel your answers are as private as you need them to be. Though some of you may choose to share some or all of your answers with a friend, lover, or therapist, it will help you be more open and honest if you do not feel obligated to share everything you have written.

## WHAT CAN I EXPECT AS I DO THE WORKBOOK?

Each person reading this book and doing the exercises will have a different experience from others. For example, let us say you read the chapters and/or do the exercises as part of a gay reading or support group. Each person in the group will have different life experiences, memories, or circumstances that affect how they answer the questions. No two gay men have the exact same life experience.

The important thing is that you read the book and do the exercises at a pace with which you feel comfortable. If you are in therapy, share your feelings about doing the exercises with your therapist on a regular basis. If you have a lover, let him know that you may be examining some painful or complicated issues in your life and therefore need extra support or encouragement.

## *SUMMARY*

I hope that you find this workbook useful and informative. As gay men, we each confront a whole variety of developmental and identity challenges as we go through the process of discovering who we are. This workbook is designed to assist you in this journey. Take your time, be open and honest as you do the exercises, and give yourself credit for furthering your effort toward understanding more of your gay identity.

# Chapter 1

# Growing Up Gay:
# Gay Men and Families of Origin

I think that you first uncover [the past] by suffering and causing a great deal of pain. Unconsciously, you repeat, in situation
after situation, the devastation of childhood. Again and again,
you find yourself running against the same spear, and the spear
keeps going right through the same wound, widening it and
making it more and more painful. Eventually, if you are lucky,
you come to understand that there is something very damaged
about the way you envision yourself and with the way you
love, and you begin the long process of healing.

Andrew Harvey

## INTRODUCTION

A former client of mine once asked if I could meet with him and
his mother during her upcoming visit. He had just recently disclosed to her that he had AIDS. She knew he was gay, but this had
never been discussed in any depth between the two of them. She
had flown in to see her son a few days prior to our meeting from the
Midwest where her husband, choosing not to deal with his son's
illness or sexuality, had stayed behind. Though the three of us
discussed many topics and feelings in our one hour together, what
made an impresson on me the most was her shock and surprise at
how many friends—good friends—her son had in his life. This
visit afforded her the opportunity to see a life her son had that she

knew little about. In addition to the grief of losing her son to AIDS, she was simultaneously confronted with the reality that her son had a surrogate family that was more loving, more supportive, and much closer and accepting of him than his real family was—or ever could be.

As gay men, many of us are familiar with viewing our friends as family—whether or not we have good relationships with our families of origin. The unconditional love and acceptance we receive from our friends is very important. Friends provide validation that we are OK as gay men, and our interactions with them do not have to entail countless hours of explaining, defining, and rationalizing who we are or *how* we got this way. For many of us, these friendships provide for us what others may receive from their own biological families.

Clearly, the role of family in our lives is tremendously important. In all my years of education and clinical training, more time was spent addressing matters pertaining to family of origin than to any other subject—and for good reason. Regardless of why clients initially come to me for psychological services, issues pertaining to parents, siblings, and/or other relatives inevitably become an important focus of the psychotherapy. Sometimes clients need to address early childhood experiences. At other times, current relationships with family members are of central concern, particularly concerning issues of coming out or other related self-disclosures. Some people achieve a feeling of resolution regarding these matters while others are unable to obtain relief from the pain they feel concerning family issues.

Why are families so important to us? We certainly know that families do not have a particular hold on us just because we are gay men. A look at the lives of the more famous people in our society, from politicians to entertainers, shows how family dramas get played out universally. Popular examples include former President Reagan's children and their public relationship struggles with their family. Other examples include entertainers Michael Jackson and Roseanne Barr, both who have tales of childhood torment and abuse.

In this chapter, I will discuss families and childhood experience from a psychological and developmental perspective. I think it is helpful to understand a little about family, child, and personal development in order to give broader meaning to the concepts and topics I will be discussing in this book. The end of the chapter includes some exercises you can do to help clarify and understand your own family structure, dynamics, and characteristics. For now, I will start by taking a closer look at early childhood experiences, particularly those first hours, months, and years that we enter this world.

### *EARLY MOTHERING*

We are born into this world totally helpless. Without the intervention of others, typically provided by our mothers, we would die. Our needs at this time require that someone feed us, clothe us, protect us from harm, provide nurturing touch, etc. Studies suggest that our vulnerability at this time of life is so pronounced that even temporary separations from our mother leave us susceptible to prolonged symptoms of depression. This period is a time in an infant's life when he is intimately engaged with his mother. Thus the term, *symbiosis* is often used to describe the close bond experienced by both. The infant recognizes that his mother is indispensable for his well-being, and knows that she will help him negotiate the world until he is able to do so himself. Psychologists often define this time as the beginning of personality development because the infant begins the task of establishing what is "me" from what is "not me."

As the infant grows, he is still highly dependent upon his mother but is eventually able to take his own initiative. This begins with being able to sit up, crawl across the floor, use sounds to communicate feelings and needs, reach for desired objects, and eventually walk and eat on his own. As infants make these strides, they do so with the notion of establishing independence from the mother. Yet, it is characteristic of the child to look back to make sure the mother is still there. You may have seen, for example, a young child leave the room only to rush back in with a look of accomplishment on his face. Eventually, the infant moves toward being away from his mother for longer periods of time.

The path toward autonomy is slow. It depends upon the mother encouraging such initiative while simultaneously providing assurance to the child that, in his efforts toward finding "me," she will not abandon him. *Good-enough mothering*, another psychological term, refers to the mother's capacity to meet the infant's developmental and changing needs, provide for feelings of safety and security, encourage appropriate levels of independence while setting necessary limits, and communicating to the child unconditional love and acceptance. When we experience this type of mothering in our infant years, we are generally prepared to master the various tasks and responsibilities that confront us in life.

This all sounds simple enough, but time and again there are mothers who cannot foster or allow independence on the part of a child. For them, the child's efforts at becoming a separate individual are very threatening, and they utilize verbal and nonverbal cues that communicate to the child that it is not OK to individuate. Such mothers may react to individuation on the part of the child with a look of disappointment, withdrawal, or with efforts toward preventing independence. Infants, being highly sensitized to the mother's emotions and fearing abandonment, will often yield to their mother's desires. These children, feeling that they have done something wrong, typically begin to manifest feelings of shame, a concept which will be explored in depth later in this book.

And so it is that the mother and infant engage in an intense relationship that entails much more than basic feeding and nurturing. Our early relationship with our mother lays the groundwork for our sense of self, our capacity for future intimate relationships, and our early experience of growing up in what we later come to know as our family. This does not mean that we are not affected by our fathers, siblings, or other important people in our early years. Rather, the mother-child relationship is unique in the way in which it provides us with our first experiences of trust and identity.

## *GENDER ROLE*

A unique dynamic for us as males is that this early mothering relationship occurs with someone of the opposite gender. Though it takes a while for us to become aware of sex differences, mothers are certainly aware of this from day one. Studies suggest that mothers treat male and female infants equally in the first six months of life. However, after approximately six months, mothers tend to touch their girl children more, talk to them more, and give them more nonverbal contact (Some psychologists suggest that this feels to the male infant as forced separation and sets males up to have a greater fear of abandonment throughout their lives). Mothers often have different expectations of boys than of girls, and studies indicate that mothers often treat boys differently. Curiously, this is a universal phenomena, common to all known human societies, much of it in response to the recognition by most cultures of stereotypical *masculine* and *feminine* behaviors.

Parents, being vulnerable to society's expectations of appropriate male and female behavior, spend a great deal of time eradicating unacceptable and encouraging acceptable behaviors in their children. Gender role is one of the first categories infants are exposed to and learn about. Thus, boys are taught at an early age not to cry, not to whine, not to play with dolls, and generally not to act in certain ways. In other words, boys are taught how not to be "feminine."

Though not every gay male was effeminate in childhood, many were. The extent to which we were effeminate in appearance, behavior, or thought in childhood probably dictated how rigorously our parents' efforts at modifying our behavior was. Thus, it is likely that those of us who were more effeminate in childhood grew up facing more challenges to our personality development both within and outside of our families.

As previously mentioned, infants are highly sensitive to the messages and feelings of their mothers, and they quickly learn to accommodate these perceived expectations in order to receive love and approval. Some mothers are more accepting of nontraditional gender behaviors in their children than others. A male child who feels he has to act a certain way in order to receive parental acceptance, however, is susceptible to feeling unsure of himself. He also learns that he is not loved for who he is but rather for what he does or how he acts. In turn, the stage is set for the child's learning to be who others expect him to be and not who he truly is, particularly if he acts differently than other children.

Naturally, the young person confronted with such feelings will fear rejection. However, there are actually few instances in which parents outright reject their young children based on effeminate behaviors. My experience is that parental rejection because of their son's homosexuality occurs later, usually from mid-adolescence on.

Usually parents find themselves confused over what, if anything, to do about such behavior, often deciding to let it continue.

## *FEELING DIFFERENT*

I have never seen formal studies done on the topic, but most of the gay men I have talked to about sexuality admit to recognizing, on some level, attributes or feelings we later identify as gay as early as five or six years of age. In addition, most gay men acknowledge being aware that, whatever these feelings are, they make us different from others. Thus, even though we do not have the vocabulary, experience, or self-awareness to realize we are gay, there lies within many of us the first indicators that maybe we are not who or what we are *supposed* to be, or who or what most others are. My view is that as we gain this awareness, consciously or unconsciously, it takes on the quality of a secret. We soon feel that if the secret were known, we would be seen as letting our parents down, or worse, risk rejection by them.

It is in our family of origin that we first recognize these feelings of being different. How our parents and siblings react to this difference sets up our first experiences and expectations of how the world feels about people like us. When others in the world treat us unfavorably for being different—based on effeminate behavior, choice of activities, etc.—we carefully gage the support we do or do not receive from our families. One client of mine, when he would tell his parents of being picked on at school, would be told by his father that he should "fight back like a man." Such reactions are very unsupportive and communicate to the person how his family might react to subsequent disclosures about his identity.

## *BOYS AND THEIR FATHERS*

Think about the stereotypes that exist about gay men's relationships with their fathers. What thoughts and images come to mind? Think about what friends have told you about their relationship with their fathers, and think about your relationship to your own father.

Perhaps one of the most popular stereotypes about fathers, particularly fathers of gay men, is that they were unavailable, distant, uncaring, aloof, and uninvolved in their male child's life. Though I have had gay male clients tell of such experiences with their fathers, I have heard the same complaints from several of my heterosexual clients, both male and female. Someone once said that if every child who had an unavailable father were gay, we would have more gay people than straight people.

But what of the role of father in our lives? What effect does our relationship with this other man in our early lives have upon our adult lives, regardless of whether we are gay or not? Is there anything unique about our relationship, as gay men, with our fathers that deserves any special emphasis? Let us start by examining the effect of our father on our early development.

As mentioned, it is a universal phenomena for male and female infants to establish their first affectional ties to their mother. Young girls, by nature of being female, can mirror their gender identity by observing and interacting with their mother in this close relationship. Boys on the other hand, either have to make their gender identification with their father or conversely, develop it by internalizing some image of the male ideal. Unfortunately, more boys today are growing up with no or absent fathers than was true for many men who are currently in adulthood; subsequently, these boys have to find other ways of learning about male behavior.

Fathers not only provide us with another male after which to model and with which to identify, but we are also able to use him to test our separateness from our mother. Boys' relationship with their fathers tend not to be as symbiotic as the mother-child relationship so fathers provide us with a bridge to a world separate from the mother-child dyad. Our father is typically the first masculine figure in our lives and he therefore shapes how we relate to the masculine side of ourselves.

Boys also learn, from observing and interacting with their father, one concept of manhood. One of the roles of a father is to lead us from the protected realm of the mother and home into the outside world, helping us to understand and cope with the realities of being a man. In some respects, this is a tremendous responsibility for the father, and rarely do we get a full or representative view of what it means to be a man from him. Some fathers internalize this role so dramatically that often it becomes difficult for them to accept their son's homosexuality, seeing it as some reflection of their failure at modeling manhood.

Proponents of what has come to be called *traditional family values* like to hold up an image of a father and mother who are mutually active in the family. In this view there is a mother who assumes primary responsibility for raising the children while the father earns the family income. Yet, in this model, no one is at a loss by the father's absence during the day because he comes home, plays with the children, kisses his wife, and weekends are spent having family picnics and going to church. The children, in turn, are supposed to identify with their respective parent and grow up modeling similar behavior. In this view, there is no family discord, no abuse or neglect, and certainly no homosexuality. Why should there be homosexuality in this model? Everyone is doing everything *right*.

In reality, this model is not very common in today's society, and I seriously question whether it ever existed in such a clean, neat form. Even in intact families in which the mother stayed home and father worked, boys rarely saw their fathers and when they did he was usually tired from working all day. Girls, on the other hand, traditionally had continuous exposure to the woman's role. Boys often knew what their father did all day, but rarely did the boy ever get to witness his father at work. Thus, boys then, and often still, grow up with this image of what a man does but rarely get to glimpse it outside of television and magazines.

Additionally, boys in our society learn that men are valued for what they do, not who they are. Most of us view our fathers as someone who is always *doing*, and we expect nurturing and compassion not from our fathers so much, but rather from our mothers. Thus, we also learn that women and men fulfill different needs, with women fulfilling our need for nurturing. Further, typical male conditioning engenders feelings of self-reliance, dominance, competition, power, control, and high needs for achievement.

## GAY MEN AND THEIR RELATIONSHIPS
## WITH THEIR FATHERS

In my clinical work with gay men, I have been surprised by the emphasis placed on father-son relationships. Though my clients have not been void of issues pertaining to their mothers, a greater focus on the father-son relationship has typically been warranted. Father-son relationships are usually discussed with feelings of helplessness, whereas mother-son relationships are more typically discussed with feelings of frustration. In many respects, the father-son relationships discussed with my clients carry more feelings of vulnerability than do mother-son relationships. A common scenario is that the client feels that he is or has been working through his struggles with his mother-son relationship, but that the father-son relationship feels unmovable.

Examples of issues and comments made by my gay male clients about their fathers include the following:

- I could never do enough to please my father.
- Nothing I ever do is right in my father's eyes.
- I never felt support from my father.
- I never felt OK to be who I am.
- My father teased me about my behaviors.
- He was never there for me.
- He is always right; I am always wrong. I cannot win.
- I feel like I compete with my father.
- I never feel like a man in my father's eyes.

What has also been noteworthy in my work with these clients is not so much their grief that their early relationships with their fathers were unfulfilling, but rather that the relationship they have always longed for with their fathers still seems unattainable.

Parents inevitably have hopes, dreams, and fantasies about their children's lives. Sometimes parents just want their children to have better lives than they did when they were growing up. Some fantasize about their child attaining great status and recognition. Others—and in my view this is more specific to fathers—want their children to accomplish more in life than they did. Again, as males, we are raised to achieve and accomplish a great deal, and rarely do we ever satisfy our expectations concerning this. Many of us constantly feel we could have done better. Thus, we feel pressure from our families and from ourselves.

Another common theme I hear from my gay male clients is feeling that their relationship with their father is a competitive one. Some remark that they feel their father rides them every step of the way, constantly insisting that they try harder and do better. Their father, in turn, feels like the abusive coach rather than a loving father. Some report feeling that if they could just achieve or accomplish more, then they would win their father's love and approval. Others report the perception that many of their self-destructive patterns are cries for help with the aim of getting their father's attention. One client of mine with AIDS, for example, reported feeling that becoming infected with HIV was a way to obtain more of his father's attention. And even that did not work.

For many men this dynamic continues throughout their adult years. Some maintain the competitive relationship, hoping someday to win. Others opt to change the way they relate to their fathers. I have had a few clients, for example, sever all ties with their fathers out of feeling that the competitive dynamic would otherwise continue. Though ceasing communication with their fathers was painful, it felt necessary for their own well-being.

Again, these dynamics are not specific to gay men. Many men in our society experience these same difficulties with their own fathers. Gay men, however, have the added struggle of feeling different—or at times, disadvantaged—because of our sexuality. Thus, some of us feel unworthy or unable to derive more from our relationship with our fathers because of our sexuality. In essence, many of us are vulnerable to feeling damaged or disabled because of who we are.

Psychoanalytic theory posits that gay men suffer in their masculine identity. This, the theory proposes, is because the father fails in his role of helping the son separate from his mother. Richard Isay (1989) proposes an alternative theory regarding gay sons and their fathers. He proposes that homosexual boys adopt feminine manners, in dress and behavior, in order to attract and sustain the attention of their father. Some of these fathers sense that their male child has a special need for closeness, as well as a erotic attachment to them. Because of their own anxiety, often rooted in their own homoerotic desires, the father withdraws from the child. To Isay, this is what accounts for low self-esteem, as well as the difficulty many men have in forming loving and trusting relationships with men. Though accepted by some mental health professionals, this is not a theory I find much credence in. I do not feel that most gay sons attempt to seduce their fathers, nor view them with romantic intent.

Rather, in my view, what the boy desires is to develop a nonsexual bonding and closeness that, unfortunately, most fathers find difficult to achieve with their sons, regardless of whether either is gay.

Regardless of the multitude of father-son dynamics in the lives of gay men, I feel it is helpful to explore our own relationships to our fathers. Thus, there are exercises at the end of this chapter that guide you through the process of examining your past and current relationship with your father.

### SIBLING RELATIONSHIPS

With the mother-child bond being so intense and exclusive, you can imagine the feelings infants have when they must share this attachment with a sibling. Sibling rivalry in childhood is more the norm than an exception. This is not to say that a certain closeness between siblings does not eventually develop, but in the early years, the competition and jealousy between siblings is immense.

Having more than one child is not easy for parents, either. As much as parents try to be fair and equitable in their treatment of their children, inevitably each child receives, at different times, more favors, attention, praise, admiration, or touch than the others. Those of us with siblings, in turn, are quick to identify how a brother or sister is a better ballplayer, runner, dancer, painter, student, etc. It always seems that the other child(ren) received more from our parents than we did.

Most children outgrow their sibling rivalry; however, studies show that siblings rarely discuss the rivalry that occurred in childhood (Ross and Milgram, 1982). Some people, however, never outgrow rivalry, and this dynamic continues in adult relationships with friends, lovers, and co-workers. All relationships feel as competitive to them as did the sibling relationships of childhood.

For the most part, I am unaware of any studies done on the relationships gay men have with their siblings. Homosexual research on siblings has focused on twin studies to determine whether or not there is a genetic component to homosexuality. From clinical data, however, I can attest to the fact that sibling relationships in the childhood of the gay men I have counseled have been intense. Often these are important relationships in the process of coming out.

Gay clients have reported various types of relationships with their brothers and sisters. Some had close relationships with their brothers while growing up, while others had very separate lives. Many have reported, however, much closer relationships with their sisters, particularly in their adult years. Several clients have said, for example, that their sister was one of the first people they ever told about their sexuality. Sometimes it is the sister who is the sole person in the family who knows of her brother's homosexuality. This then becomes a crucial tie as the gay man uses his sister as a reality check before disclosing his sexuality to other members of the family. It has been my experience that many gay men with AIDS disclose this information to a sibling before telling a parent. Unfortunately, for some gay men, contact with a sibling is the only family contact they have due to rejection or avoidance by parents.

Stanley Siegel and Ed Lowe, in their 1994 book on life passages of gay men, suggest that parents may compare the gay child unfavorably to his siblings because of unconventional behaviors, In turn, a good child/bad child split is set up with the worse consequence being total rejection of the gay child by the entire family. My experience suggests that even when parents have difficulty accepting the homosexuality of one of their sons, the siblings do not necessarily share this view. For those that do, however, the level of disapproval is not as intense as it is for the parents.

## FAMILY BALANCE

Families operate like many other interrelated systems. Think of the human body, for example. Each part and organ of the body has its own function or task, yet each is affected by the whole. A breakdown or change in one part of the body affects many other components. If you lose your eyesight, for example, you have to strengthen the use of your other senses in order to compensate. The operation of a family, just like the operation of the human body, requires the interconnectedness of several members. Thus, we often speak of families as *systems*.

Virginia Satir compares the family system to that of a mobile
(Figure 1.1). When a mobile is just hanging, it maintains a certain
equilibrium. If you blow on the mobile, it will bounce around, but
eventually it will return to its original balanced state. This is true of
families. Families operate with a variety of rules and patterns of

FIGURE 1.1. Families operate like a mobile. The hanging images represent the
family members and the sticks represent the family rules. When wind hits the
mobile, it will respond with movement, but it slowly brings itself to its original state
of balance.

responding. When a family experiences stress or disruption it will respond. However, the eventual goal is to return to the previous state of balance.

When a gay man discloses his homosexuality to the family, this serves as a blast of wind on the mobile. Thus, the disclosure is usually met with denial by most members. Parents often say, "How can you be gay? You always. . . . liked girls, liked sports, wanted kids, etc." Others will say, "You cannot be gay . . . You just have not found the right girl; You are still feeling stung from that last relationship; You just do not get out enough; Maybe you were molested."

Thus, the initial response from most family members to the son's disclosure of being gay is to try to return the family mobile to its equilibrium position. The challenge we experience when we come out is whether we allow the family mobile to return to its original position—which often means denial and compliance with patterns that may be unhealthy—or whether we attempt to change the status quo.

## ADULTS AND THEIR PARENTS

An interesting shift occurs as many of us get older. We typically assume more responsibility, and in turn, we experience more feelings of competency. Our parents, however, are getting older, and many have to deal with the economic and health realities associated with this. Oftentimes as we become more independent and self-sufficient, our parents become more dependent and vulnerable.

A unique dynamic for adults is that even as we take pride in our accomplishments and relationships in adulthood, we are still seen as children by our parents. Though most parents recognize that we are adults, they still strongly associate us as their children. Thus, they worry about us, question our decisions, and at times try to exert what can feel like undue control over our lives.

Just as raising a child requires constant limit-setting, dealing with parents in our adult years often requires the same. As adults we want to assert our independence, and most of us do not want others telling us what to do. Parents, however, are accustomed to being intimately involved in our lives, and often have been instrumental in key decisions we have made (e.g., moving out, choosing a college, etc.). Thus,

it is a delicate balance between living our own lives and accommodating our parents' interests and concerns about our lives.

Gay men often struggle with issues of self-disclosure with parents, and some find it so stressful that they avoid talking at all with
their parents. This is particularly noteworthy depending on how
much you want your parents to know about your sexuality. Adult
children commonly feel that they must tell their parents all or most
things about their lives. For the gay man who has not disclosed his
sexual preference to his parents, or who may not feel comfortable
discussing his dating or relationship patterns, talking to his parents
can feel like being on trial.

The reality is that we are not obligated to share all facets of our
lives with our parents. We are in control of how detailed we want to
be with them about a particular subject, and it is OK to say "That is
private," or "I do not want to discuss it." Some parents may balk at
this, but that is why I frame it in terms of limit-setting. At times we
have to say "No," and at times we have to determine how much of
our lives we want to share with our parents.

Some gay men may want to have more discussion about their
lives with their parents, particularly concerning sexuality and relationships. To have a new relationship that you are excited about and
to feel that telling your parents is off-limits can be very difficult. If
you have a long-term relationship, naturally you will want to talk
about the events, and projects that happen with your lover. However, some families are so uncomfortable discussing their son's
sexuality that implicit or explicit messages are given that it is not
OK for their son to talk about his private life.

Many parents feel as though they no longer know their child after
he comes out. Others sense that a barrier is raised after the child
comes out. Instead of seeing their child for all of who he is, many
can only focus on their son's homosexuality. In order to deal with
these feelings, some parents try to suppress all associations to and
discussions about homosexuality. By prohibiting their child from
talking about this aspect of his life, they, in turn, selfishly prevent
themselves from dealing with the reality that their child is gay (see
Figure 1.2).

In such instances, the person is confronted with some difficult
choices. You can take the stance that if your family wants to talk

FIGURE 1.2. A look at the research: How parents feel about having gay and lesbian children.

Barbara Bernstein (1990) surveyed sixty-two parents of gay men and lesbians regarding how they feel about their children. She found that for most of the parents she interviewed, the coming out of their son or daughter resulted in a significant family crisis. Bernstein writes the following:

> Shocked and devastated, they felt isolated and too ashamed to turn to family, friends, or religious leaders for support. They were angry with their gay son or daughter . . . ruminated about how they or the gay child's other parent might be to blame . . . continued to deny the reality . . . and worried that others would judge them to have been bad parents. (p. 39)

Bernstein found that the major obstacle to parental acceptance of their child's homosexuality was the fear of social stigma, both toward themselves as inadequate parents, and toward their son or daughter as sick and deviant. She adds that many parents' self-esteem had been lowered due to their child's homosexuality, and some lost an image of themselves as perfect parents. Many tried to keep their feelings suppressed, believing that they could not be both accepting and understanding of their gay child while simultaneously being angry, sad, or ashamed of their child.

Several parents in these interviews expressed the belief that their child would not have experiences that they believed are necessary for happiness, such as marriage and children. Instead, they believed their child would be lonely throughout life. Some felt that a gay or lesbian long-term relationship was not possible.

To help parents of gays and lesbians cope with these feelings, Bernstein suggests the following guidelines:

- Expect parents to feel anger, guilt, resentment, shame, embarrassment, and/or disappointment about having a gay or lesbian child.
- Parents will need to mourn the child they thought they had. Many parents end up feeling deceived, and may feel they do not know their child any longer.
- Parents often assume that "accepting" and "liking" are the same. Parents are often relieved to learn that they can both dislike their child's homosexuality and, at the same time, accept it.
- The majority of parents expressed the inability to expect grandchildren from their gay son or lesbian daughter as one of their major losses. This sadness needs to be expressed.
- Most parents believe that psychological factors cause homosexuality. Therefore, they need room to discuss their belief that gay and lesbian children can "change."
- Many parents are relieved to learn that some researchers have found that family backgrounds have little or no effect on a person's sexual orientation, and that no family background variable correlates with sexual orientation. To this end, educational materials can be highly beneficial when the parent is ready to read about the topic of homosexuality.

with you at all, they must be willing to hear about the important people or events in your life. Alternately, you can agree to go along with their wishes, though typically you will feel anger and resentment toward them. One answer to these dilemmas is never more right than another. The challenge is to find a way of communicating with your family while not sacrificing your principles or identity.

Some parents refuse to discuss the relationships in their gay son's life solely for the purpose of trying to exert control. In these instances, it can be helpful to make short references to your life in response to their inquiries.

For example:

Mother:   How are things going for you?
Son:      Good. I like my new job, and Rick and I are planning a trip to France for Christmas.
Mother:   I thought I told you that I do not want to hear about him.
Son:      As I said before, Rick is an important part of my life. If you want to know about my life, you will have to hear about Rick at times. I try not to tell you everything about his and my life together, but I cannot talk to you and pretend that he does not exist.

The important thing is that you not deny your life or relationship just because others might want you to. My experience is that most parents of gay men eventually allow some discussion of the topic of homosexuality. The challenge is to find the balance between pretending your gay life does not exist and having nothing else to discuss aside from gay-related topics.

## THE GAY FAMILY

Based on the prior discussion, it is easy to see how the gay man's relationship to his family faces additional dilemmas compared to those confronted by heterosexuals. Because of feeling different or being treated differently, many gay men isolate themselves from their families. Sometimes this manifests as a mental withdrawal in which the person disengages into fantasy, shyness, or avoidance behaviors. At other times, it manifests as a blatant physical withdrawal: the gay man, as a teenager or young adult, flees the ties of his family environment for the comfort of a larger community.

A gay client of mine who lived in San Francisco once said, "No one is born here. Everyone just comes here from somewhere else in order to get away from their families." Though this was an exaggeration, there is also an element of truth in the statement. Many gay men long for the camaraderie of San Francisco, New York, or other major metropolitan areas that have sizable gay communities. For these men, the hope of finally finding unconditional acceptance from others exists, as well as the desire to live life as an openly gay man.

Whether gay men seek larger cities or not, most find their way to a network of other gay men. The opportunities for doing this certainly increase as one moves to a larger community, but even smaller cities have bars, churches, and gay organizations. Through these channels, gay men find others who share similar backgrounds and life experiences, and eventually most find a network of friends.

These friendships develop added meaning as we find that we do not have to account for our sexuality or desires. It is no wonder that, for many gay men, the friendships we develop take on the role of family. It is not uncommon, for example, for a particular group of gay men to regularly gather for holidays, birthdays, and other times, which others consider occassions to spend with one's family of origin.

## SUMMARY

What I hope to have communicated in the previous discussion is how our early experiences in our family shape and prepare us for all subsequent relationships and life experiences. Through our family of origin we learn about trust, safety, and interpersonal skills, and have our first experiences of individuality. Some of us emerge from these early experiences with a healthy sense of who we and others are. Others, because of different experiences and challenges, find it difficult to trust other people, developing intimacy with others, and feeling good about who they are. Thus, as you read the following chapters and do the exercises, I encourage you to examine how your family experience has affected you in areas of relationships, intimacy, coping with loss, etc.

Though developing a strong support network of other gay men is necessary and important for our growth and gay identity, the truth is that rarely can these friendships compensate for our earlier years in our family of origin. I always tell my clients that I do not dwell on the past, but that much of what we discuss relates very directly to early family life. Thus, I always take a lengthy family history from each of my clients. The first exercise in this chapter will help you consolidate onto one page much of your own family history and experience.

# Exercises

## *CONSTRUCTING YOUR FAMILY GENOGRAM*

Shortly after meeting with a client for the first time I will construct with them, on a sheet of paper, what is called a genogram. Basically, a genogram is a family tree or family map that shows patterns and relationships which occur in families over time. The genogram is a construction of figures representing people and lines delineating their relationships. To be most useful, the genogram should include at least three generations.

My reason for using a genogram with clients is that it gives me an overview of all the significant family members in the client's life while also providing an avenue for identifying certain themes (divorce, abuse, family myths, cause of death, mental illness, personality traits, suicide, even homosexuality) that exist in the family through each generation. I rely upon the use of the genogram in therapy because of my observation that themes continually get repeated in families, generation after generation.

Each family member is represented by a box or a circle according to his gender (i.e., boxes for males, circles for females). You will include yourself in the genogram, making double lines around your box. For a person who is deceased, an X is placed inside the figure. It is helpful to also include in the box the age at which they died and how the death occurred.

## *Step 1*

Begin by drawing a box and a circle for your parents. Connect the two with a line as shown below. If either parent is deceased, place an X inside the box. If your parents divorced, indicate this by drawing a double line, as shown, through the horizontal connecting line. If either parent remarried, extend the horizontal line away from their box or circle and include the other spouse(s).

DIAGRAM 1

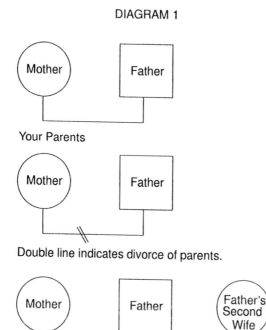

Your Parents

Double line indicates divorce of parents.

Extended horizontal line and circle indicate father's next marriage.

## Step 2

You will then make boxes and circles to indicate your parents' children. Include each sibling. In each box or circle include their age. Draw double lines around your own box. If your parents had children from other marriages, represent this under the horizontal line that shows their marriage to their other spouse.

DIAGRAM 2

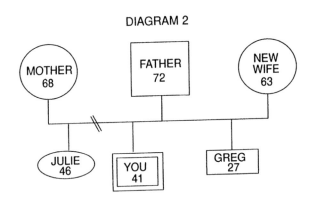

## *Step 3*

Next you will draw lines, circles, and boxes to indicate your grandparents and their children. As you became a box under the marriage line for your parents, your parents will respectively become children under the marriage line for your grandparents.

DIAGRAM 3

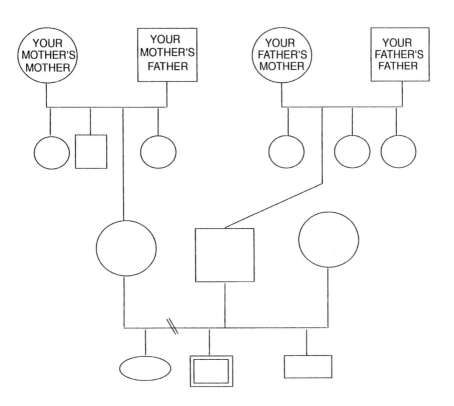

## Step 4

Now you will show the marriages and significant relationships of you and your siblings. I use a solid line to indicate that the relationship is one of marriage, and a dotted line to show that their relationship is not marriage. Indicate divorces as shown.

DIAGRAM 4

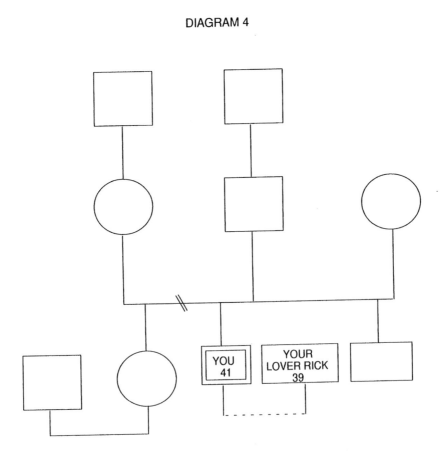

## Step 5

Include any children for each sibling, and for yourself if you have any.

DIAGRAM 5

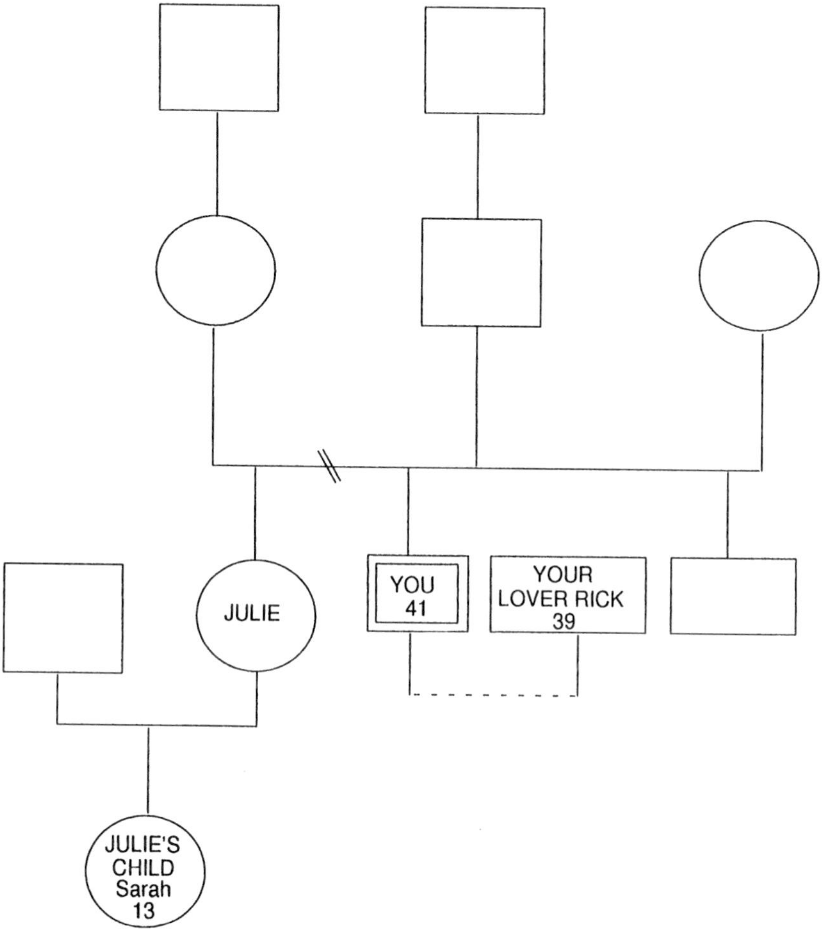

## Step 6

You will now designate on your genogram who had close relationships and who had stormy, or difficult, relationships. Beginning with yourself, draw a single line to the sibling(s), parent, or other family member you felt closest to growing up. Next, draw a lightning bolt to the person(s) you had challenging or conflictual relationships with. You do not have to do this with every family member. What is important is that you designate who you were closest to.

DIAGRAM 6

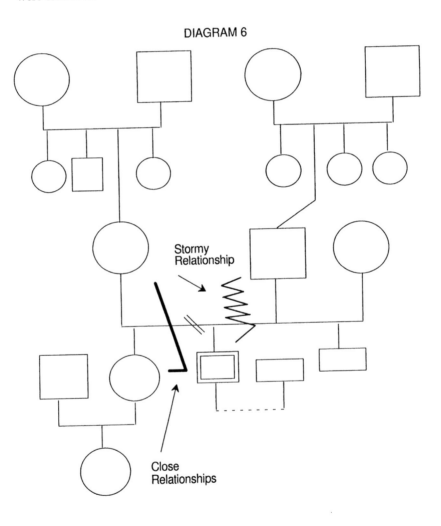

## Step 7

By now you should have about seven circles and boxes—perhaps more depending on the size of your family. If you choose, you can extend the genogram to include great-grandparents. Include the following information on your genogram, as applicable, either inside the box or circle or off to the side:

- The person's name and occupation
- How the person died and at what age (be sure to specifically note any suicides)
- Significant medical or psychiatric conditions for each member (diabetes, heart disease, obesity, stroke, depression, bipolar disorder, schizophrenia, etc.)
- Excessive use of alcohol or drugs
- Physically or sexually abused
- Gay or lesbian
- Other information you deem important (adoptions, abortions, criminal history, history of extramarital affairs, religious affiliation, etc.)

DIAGRAM 7

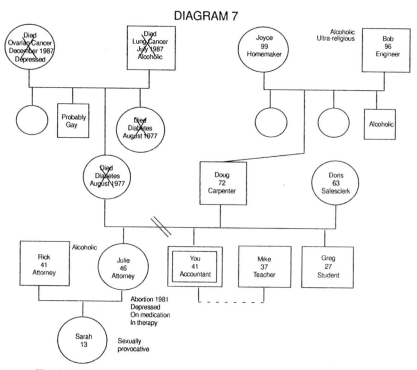

The X inside a box or circle indicates a deceased family member.

### Interpretation of Your Genogram

As mentioned, the purpose of the genogram is to help you identify themes and patterns that exist in your family of origin. Look over your genogram and try to identify three or four themes.

- Look for coincidences. For example, does the death of a family member occur at the same time some other family event was happening (a divorce, a childbirth, an illness)?
- Were there a lot of divorces in your family? What does this tell you about your own capacity for finding and maintaining a long-term relationship?
- Were there a lot of suicides in your family? This could be an indicator of depression or manic-depressive illness in your family. It could also be a warning to you not to let major issues in your life go unaddressed.
- Are there patterns of medical and/or psychiatric disorders in your family? Might you be at risk for the same?
- Who were you close with and with whom did you have conflictual relationships? How did these dynamics develop?
- Are you the only gay person in your family? Homosexuality has a genetic component to it, so it is likely you will see other gay family members identified—whether or not they were open about it.

### ASSESSING FAMILY FUNCTIONING

A feeling I often have is that, as chaotic and dysfunctional as many families may appear, ultimately most of the members are doing the best they can. Unless we study psychology and family systems in college, or read about the topic in a book, most of us do not get adequate education or training on how to be a father, mother, son, daughter, brother, sister, uncle, etc. In fact, the most I hear from people on the topic is, "I will do it differently from how my parents did it." Yet, when pressed for more specific details, few people can adequately say what they would do. Usually they will say, "Well, I will not abuse my children," or "I will listen to what my children have to say."

This exercise is designed to give you a visual overview of how your family dealt with common family dynamics. By answering and reviewing your responses, perhaps you can gain an understanding of styles of relating in your family of origin that you bring to current and future relationships.

1.  How often did people in your family share their feelings with one another?

    Always_____Never
    1                          2                          3

2.  How close were your parents to one another?

    Very _____Not Very
    1                          2                          3

3.  How much conflict was in your family?

    Not Much_____A Great Deal
    1                          2                          3

4.  How often did people get blamed for the actions of others in your family?

    Rarely_____Always
    1                          2                          3

5.  How often did people in your family act like they could read each other's minds?

    Rarely_____Always
    1                          2                          3

6.  How rigid were family rules?

Not Very_____Very
    1                        2                   3

7.  How supportive was your family during times of grief or crisis?

Very  _____Not Very
    1                        2                   3

8.  How often did you wish you had a different family?

Never_____Always
    1                        2                   3

9.  How many problems do you think your family had compared to most families?

The Same_____A Great More
    1                        2                   3

10. Were people accepted for who they are in your family?

Generally_____Never
    1                        2                   3

Scoring:

| | |
|---|---|
| 15 or less: | Healthy Family Functioning |
| 5 to 25: | Some Rigidity in Functioning |
| 25 or more: | Rigid, Unsupportive Family |

Based on your responses to the above questions, what do you feel are three main themes you learned about family functioning while growing up in your family?

_____

_____

_____

How do you now, or will you in the future, do things differently in your own relationships from how it was in your family? What are the clues to watch for that tell you you are repeating family patterns and behaviors that you hoped you never would?

_____

_____

_____

_____

_____

_____

_____

_____

## *THE PARENT INTERVIEW*

This exercise is for those of you who have parents with whom you can talk fairly openly about your homosexuality. At some point after coming out to our parents, we hear of their reactions to, feelings to, and thoughts about our disclosure. Rarely do we get a comprehensive perspective on how they feel about us being gay. This occurs for a variety of reasons including their feelings of shock, their emphasis on wanting to support us, or our tension regarding hearing what they have to say. Also, many parents may not know how they feel about this disclosure for quite some time. A friend of mine once told his parents, "It has taken me several years to cope with and accept who I am. I cannot expect the same from you in any less time."

This exercise entails interviewing your parents about your presence in their lives. Rather than just being a chance to discuss their feelings about you being gay, this exercise affords you the chance to understand more about who your parents are and about how you have affected them over your life span. Some of the questions suggested below may be on topics you have already discussed with your parents. Alternately, you may want to omit some of the questions, perhaps choosing to substitute questions of your own.

Tell your parent(s) that you would like to spend some time talking with them about your life as a child, and their feelings about your homosexuality. Try to cover as many of these questions as you can. You can conduct an interview or you can conversationally ask the questions. This exercise is best done well after you have disclosed your sexuality to your parents, as they will have a clearer perspective on their feelings about your homosexuality. Since this exercise is more about encouraging a dialogue between you and your parents, you may not want to take notes per se. Tape-recording the conversations might be a nice way of preserving some of your family history.

### Sample Questions

- Talk with me about the thoughts you had about what your lives would be like after my birth.
- What were your hopes and fantasies of what my life would be like? If my getting married and having grandchildren were part of that scenario, how important was this to you?
- What had been your experiences with gay people prior to my telling you that I am gay? If I was not gay, but a friend of yours had told you their son was, what advice would you have given? How

does this coincide with how you would or would not have judged or blamed them as parents?

- What has been the biggest sense of loss in knowing that I am gay? What is or has been your biggest hope and your biggest fear? What has been the biggest embarrassment?
- How often do you find yourself asking if there was not something you could have done to prevent my homosexuality? How often do you find yourself wondering or hoping that I might discover that I am not gay after all?
- Someone once remarked that as gay children come out of the closet their parents go into the closet. Has your experience been one of shame, trying not to talk about me with others, or fearing others will judge you because I am gay?
- Has my being gay been harder on Mother or Father? How much did the two of you talk about my being gay with one another after you found out? Did you feel the other blamed you? How much went unspoken between the two of you about the subject? Have you since discussed it together in any depth?

*Add your own questions below:*

_____

_____

_____

_____

_____

_____

_____

_____

_____

## IDENTIFYING YOUR COPING MECHANISMS

By nature of being human we all develop and use various defenses—or coping mechanisms—when faced with stressful or difficult circumstances. We employ these defenses in childhood as tools for survival; these tools were intended to be situational, not chronic. However, sometimes we deal with feelings or situations in which we continue to use these defenses to prevent ourselves from being overloaded with fear, sadness, or feelings of abandonment.

Naturally, our experience with these coping mechanisms develops in childhood, much of it in response to what is happening in our family of origin. These defenses afford us an opportunity to numb out, deny, or avoid dealing with uncomfortable feelings or situations. As we grow older, the continued use of some of these defenses are maladaptive in that they distract us from difficult memories, interpersonal encounters, or feelings. Thus, in childhood we become the class clown or the bully to avoid dealing with feelings of inadequacy. In adulthood we may use alcohol, drugs, or sex to cope with these same feelings.

In this exercise you will be able to identify the various behaviors, defenses, and coping mechanisms you have used in your life. Not all of these are maladaptive, though some (e.g., alcoholism) have more serious consequences than others. When you are finished, you are encouraged to write or talk with your therapist about how you feel you developed these coping styles, and whether you wish to keep or relinquish any of them.

### Instructions

Place a check mark after each statement if it was true for you in childhood and/or true for you now.

| DEFENSE BEHAVIOR | TRUE AS CHILD | TRUE NOW |
|---|---|---|
| • Crying to get my way | | |
| • Being violent to get my way | | |
| • Hiding when scared | | |
| • Denying the situation | | |
| • Hurting myself when angry | | |
| • Using humor to defuse my own or others tension | | |
| • Withdrawing from others when uncomfortable | | |
| • Eating excessively when experiencing stress | | |
| • Having sex to reduce tension (including masturbation) | | |

| DEFENSE BEHAVIOR | TRUE AS CHILD | TRUE NOW |
|---|---|---|

- Exhibiting perfectionism
  and control
- Avoiding intimacy with others
- Lying and manipulating
- Retreating into fantasy when
  a situation or feeling
  is uncomfortable
- Letting someone else run my
  life or tell me what to do
- Stealing
- Trying not to listen or remember
- Pretending something never
  happened
- Minimizing my feelings
- Feigning illness
- Blaming others

*From this list, identify:*

The top three characteristics that have helped you the most in life.

1. _____

2. _____

3. _____

The top three characteristics that have been most problematic for you.

1. _____

2. _____

3. _____

The top three characteristics you wish to change.

1. _____

2. _____

3. _____

## ASSESSING THE IMPACT OF DISCLOSURE

Earlier in this chapter I mentioned that most of the clients I see in psychotherapy spend a great deal of time talking about family-of-origin issues. Sometimes we talk directly about how being gay influences family relationships; at other times we talk about family dynamics and events that happened independent of the client being gay. One noteworthy theme that we eventually discuss is the ambivalence some clients feel toward their relationships with parents and/or siblings, and how much this stems from the the client's homosexuality. One client once remarked how he feels that he has little in common with many heterosexuals his age. Thus, aside from his work environment, he does not really socialize with them. However, he said he cannot understand why he feels so alienated from the lives of his two sisters and one brother, adding: "It seems that after growing up in the same house together for eighteen years, going to the same schools and the same church, we would have something in common now that we are adults."

I, too, wonder if my relationship with my siblings would be different if my life took a path similar to their own. It is not that we do not get along, but sometimes it feels that our lives are too separate. In turn, I share little with them about my friends, projects, and interests, and perhaps they do the same. Conversely, I have regular contact with my uncle who is gay, a man I hardly knew while growing up. Do he and I keep in contact because we are both gay or because of other reasons? I do not know.

The purpose of this exercise is to get you to examine your current relationship with your parents, siblings, and any other significant family members, and to assess the impact your disclosure had on the relationship. You will then be asked to consider if and how things might be different if you were not gay. Perhaps for you, the effect of telling a family member you are gay has been very positive. Thus, your experience is that your disclosure has altered the quality of the relationship in a positive manner.

Identify a family member whose relationship to you you would like to examine:

_____

How did this person learn that you are gay? How old were you? How long ago did this happen?

_____

_____

_____

What was your relationship with this person like prior to your disclosure? What did the two of you have in common? What was special between the two of you? In what direction were your lives headed?

_____

_____

_____

_____

Whether they are positive or negative, identify the subtle and obvious changes that occurred in your relationship with this person after they learned you are gay. Try to identify what both of you said or did that contributed to these changes. What other significant events occurred simultaneously in either of your lives (e.g., new relationship, marriage, children, moving, illness).

_____

_____

_____

Consider what they told you, and consider your perceptions about what they *did not* tell you of their feelings about you being gay. Write down what they told you (e.g., "It is OK"; "It does not matter"; "I love you any way"; "It is wrong"; "Could I have done anything different?"; "You need help"; "Why are you telling me this?"). Write down what you think they did not tell you, but thought or felt. What makes you think this? Would you ever ask them directly if your perceptions are correct? If no, why not? What is the worst that could happen by confronting them?

_____

_____

_____

_____

Finally, what would you want your relationship with this person to be like now? Do you think it would be the way you want it to be if you were not gay? If yes, why? What could you do to help the relationship become more of what you want it to be?

_____

_____

_____

_____

_____

_____

_____

_____

_____

_____

_____

_____

_____

_____

_____

_____

_____

_____

_____

## THE FAMILY LETTER

Sometimes it is not realistic or possible to express to your parents or family the full range of feelings you have about their role and presence in your life. Often, the appreciation, disappointments, hurts, and love we feel toward those in our family goes unexpressed. It is not necessary for each of us to express these feelings verbally or in writing. Sometimes things are better left unsaid. Some people also find other ways of communicating their feelings to their parents or family.

However, for some people, the ways family members exert influence, control, and negativity in their lives is very pronounced. In turn, the individual lives his life feeling like a caged animal—angry, resentful, and helpless. For him, the challenge is finding an avenue for communicating his full range of feelings. One option is psychotherapy. Another is writing a letter to the person(s), expressing all of these feelings. Even if the letter is never delivered to the person to whom it is written, the feeling of release that can come from writing such a letter can be highly beneficial. It can also help the person feel more in control.

The clues I look for when suggesting to a client to consider communicating his feelings to his family are indicators that he feels stuck. By stuck I mean that he believes he cannot move forward in his life because of family experiences or dynamics. For some, they still feel that their parents exert too much control and influence over their lives, even though they may be successful, grown adults. They live their lives believing that things could be better "If only my family would . . . "

This exercise entails you writing a letter to your family. The letter can be addressed to the family as a whole, or to one or two persons. The goal and challenge is to write every feeling and emotion—both positive and negative—you feel about this person or persons. Though you are encouraged to take full liberty and express all that you feel, stay aware of what you need to say as it pertains to you being gay.

The letter should address the past, but I encourage you to focus on the here and now. For example, keep the following thoughts in mind as you write the letter:

- Why do you want to write this letter now?
- How does your current relationship with this person or persons affect the quality of your life?
- What is it about your relationship with this person that leaves you feeling stuck, angry, resentful, controlled, or manipulated?
- Why does this person have so much influence over your life and emotions at this time?

As you write your letter, remember the following points:

- No one has to see what you have written, including your therapist, partner, friends, or family.
- Express all of your feelings. If you choose to send or share the letter with someone, you can revise, condense, and edit it later.
- Try not to think, "They do not care anyhow," or "They will just have an argument for why they are in the right." This might be true, but it is your letter and your chance to express your feelings.

The following words and sentences are offered for inclusion in your letter. Feel free to include them if they fit your feelings or situation, and try to expand on them in your letter:

- I do not have to justify who I am.
- I do not have to apologize for who I am.
- You are not better than I.
- I do not have to educate you about homosexuality.
- I am a survivor.
- Can you love me for who I am?
- I can no longer try to meet your expectations of who you want me to be.
- Who makes the rules?
- For once you will listen to me.
- Accept who is in my life.

- Perfection
- Damaged
- Unconditional love
- Shame
- Control
- God
- Self-righteous
- Punishment
- Abandonment
- Embarrassment
- Caretaking
- Religion

## *YOU AND YOUR FATHER*

This exercise provides you the opportunity to examine your relationship with your father, both past and present. The father-son relationship is very meaningful for all males; however, as gay men, we have a few added relationship dynamics that heterosexual males do not. The stereotype is that fathers of gay men were cold and distant. Maybe this is true in your relationship with your father, and maybe not. By completing this exercise, perhaps you can gain further clarity on what your relationship was like with your father.

What is your father's full name: _____

Where was he born: _____

How old is he (or if he is deceased, how old was he when he died): _____

What do you know about your father's relationship with his own father? Describe:

_____

_____

_____

_____

_____

_____

_____


How did your father meet your mother? Describe how their early relationship developed:

_____

_____

_____

_____

_____

_____

_____

Do you have any brothers? YES     NO
    If YES, are they older or younger than you? OLDER      YOUNGER

What was your father's occupation while you were growing up?_____
How many hours of each day was your father at work?_____
Did your father travel or work weekends as part of his job? YES    NO

What is your earliest memory of your father? Describe:

_____

_____

_____

_____

_____

How do you think your father felt about you during your early years (Birth-7)?

_____

_____

_____

_____

_____

Do you think your father had ideas or fantasies of what your life would turn out like? If YES, describe:

_____

_____

_____

_____

_____

_____

Describe the ways in which your father was active in your life (e.g., taking you camping, playing sports with you, attending school events, getting you ready for church, etc.):_____

_____

_____
_____
_____
_____

Describe the ways in which you wish your father had been more active in your life or had shown more interest in you. Cite examples:_____

_____
_____
_____
_____
_____

Did you ever fear your father while growing up? Describe:_____

_____
_____
_____
_____

Were you ever sexually attracted to your father? Describe:_____

_____
_____
_____
_____

Did your mother ever try to *protect* you from your father? Describe:_____

_____
_____
_____
_____

Was your relationship with your father a competitive one? YES   NO
    If YES, how did this develop? What is your role in maintaining the
competition:_____

_____

_____

_____

_____

_____


Describe how you have tried to get your father to pay attention to you,
both in childhood and adulthood. How successful have your efforts been?

_____

_____

_____

_____

_____


If your father was distant from you, why do you think this was?_____

_____

_____

_____

_____

_____


Do you think your father ever felt he failed or did something wrong
because you are gay? If YES, describe:_____

_____

_____

_____

_____

If you have brothers or sisters, did you perceive your father as having a closer or better relationship with them? If YES, why do you think this was?

_____

_____

_____

_____

_____

Very Good_____Very Poor
     10   9   8   7   6   5   4   3   2   1   0

Using the above scale, write the number that best reflects your feelings about the following:

- My overall relationship with my father while growing up _____
- My current relationship with my father _____
- The effort my father put into his relationship with me _____
- How well my father was at being a dad _____
- How my father would rate his job at being my dad _____
- How my father's parenting ability compares to most other fathers _____

When do you think your father first thought you might be gay? Describe:

_____

_____

_____

_____

_____

Have you come out or discussed being gay with your father? YES   NO
If YES, how old were you? _____

Describe this experience. Include your father's reaction to your disclosure:

_____

_____

_____

_____

_____

Write about the positive and negative consequences of telling your father you are gay:

_____

_____

_____

_____

_____

Overall, how good or poor of a job did your father do at raising you? How do you think he feels about his role as a father? How was this affected by your being gay? In what ways do you think your childhood and adult relationship with your father would have been different if you had not been born gay?

_____

_____

_____

_____

_____

# Chapter 2

# Self-Esteem and Shame
# in the Lives of Gay Men

| Mark Thompson: | As you travel around the country what is your reading of gay men today? What is the inner work we need to do collectively? |
|---|---|
| Will Roscoe: | Nothing is going to happen until we deal with self-esteem. I wish I could say, "Now it's time to address our relationships with our fathers," but that actually would be a second step. The first step is self-esteem, of taking yourself seriously. |

## *INTRODUCTION*

In Chapter 1, I noted that, regardless of why most gay men come to see me for psychotherapy, family-of-origin issues inevitably get discussed in great depth. However, if I were to classify the original reason most of these men contacted me, it would be to discuss and explore issues of self-image, self-esteem, and self-identity. Collectively, these terms comprise what is called our sense of self.

The development of our self-image—the positive and negative perceptions we have about ourselves—is very complex. A whole variety of individual, family, and societal factors interplay to shape how well we separate from our caregivers, and how we come to feel about ourselves as individuals. Gay male self-image and self-esteem do not develop differently from that of others, but as gay men we do confront unique circumstances, feelings, and challenges due to our sexuality.

Our early perceptions of feeling different from others, coupled with how our difference is reacted to by family and society, affect how we trust and relate to others and how we expect others to treat us. If we grow up feeling OK about being different, we are less likely to tolerate discrimination, condemnation, and misperception by others about who we are. If, however, we experience confusion over who we are, we tend to be unsure of ourselves and to have little self-confidence. Ultimately, our challenge as gay people is to recognize, on a very individual level, that we are OK and that we do not owe apologies or explanations for who we are (Figure 2.1).

FIGURE 2.1. Consequences of low self-esteem.

There can be many consequences of low self-esteem. When we feel bad about who we are, we do things to either make ourselves feel better or to disguise how poorly we feel. The following are some examples of how low self-esteem can negatively affect our lives:

- High substance abuse potential
- Less likely to practice safe sex
- Unable to assert one's needs to others
- Unsatisfactory relationships
- Feelings of underachievement
- Feelings of guilt and shame
- Fear of rejection
- Prone to depression
- Feeling inferior to others
- Suicidal feelings

## EARLY SELF-IMAGE

Our first sense of who we are develops as we start to separate from the symbiotic attachment to our mother. As we begin to explore our surroundings and see ourselves as separate from our mother, we begin to recognize that there are elements of the world that are outside of us. Children at this stage of development—from about six to nine months of age—are very excited about life. They love exploring their bodies, challenging their body movements, crawling, babbling, and touching and tasting everything they can.

Increasingly, the child explores his environment while using his mother as a safety zone. As mentioned in Chapter 1, the child is dependent on his mother to allow, or foster, this separation while simultaneously providing him with assurance that she will not abandon him. This is a crucial stage in our personality development as well as in the development of our sense of self. If our mother fosters our independence, yet remains available to us in the ways we require, we develop a healthy sense of autonomy and independence. If, however, we receive messages from her that expressing autonomy threatens her, or worse, poses the possibility of abandonment by her, we grow to be dependent, unsure of ourselves, overly cautious, and reluctant to take initiative. In short, these early experiences collectively help color our self-confidence and self-image.

People who do not have a complete and adequate sense of their identity often do amazing and sometimes careless things as they try to sort out who they are. Not having a healthy, autonomous identity, such people will often assume a fantasy identity, make decisions in the interest of others, lose sight of the needs of others, and engage in self-defeating or self-destructive activities or behaviors.

A common manifestation of this are eating disorders. People with eating disorders often have low self-esteem, which they try to mask with overeating. In turn, they feel guilty for overeating and begin to feel worthless, which they try to soothe by eating more. It becomes a self-destructive pattern that perpetuates the symptom of overeating. This scenario also occurs with other addictive disorders involving drugs, alcohol, relationships, sex, gambling, and a whole variety of other behaviors.

When a poor self-concept is intensified with feelings of guilt and shame, the person is unable to effectively manage life without resorting to self-destructive behaviors. In turn, they feel little enjoyment in life, feel like a fraud, and derive little satisfaction from almost any activity. Many would have us believe these feelings are synonymous with being gay. However, being gay does not mean having to experience these feelings. It is possible to be gay and have a healthy self-identity. Sometimes, however, we have to sort out and examine messages and experiences that came at a time when we had very little control over them. Unfortunately, many of us were on the receiving end of these messages when we were in the early stages of recognizing who we are.

## THE SECRET OF BEING DIFFERENT

There is no universal mother-son relationship for all gay men. Some gay men had mothers who handled the role of motherhood admirably; others had very challenging relationships with their mothers. The stereotype of gay men having overbearing and overprotective mothers has not been borne out in the clinical experience of those working with gay men. Although some gay men have had such mothers, many others have not.

It is also important to point out that our early relationship with our mother is not the sole factor determining our self-image. Rather, our relationship with our mothers prepares us for issues of trust and interpersonal relations, but there are other influential people and circumstances in our lives that shape our self-perceptions. One significant factor for gay men is how we, as children, reconciled our feelings with how we perceived family and public perception of people like us.

I mentioned in Chapter 1, many, if not most, gay men have some idea of being different at a very young age. This difference is what we later translate and recognize as the first realization that we are gay. Though as children we do not have the vocabulary or understanding of what these feelings mean, we realize that this sense of being different is best left unexpressed to others. Again, it takes on the quality of being a secret that even we do not fully comprehend.

Secrets can be unproblematic depending on the context in which they were communicated to us, as well as what they mean to us. Some gay men have told me that they understood to some extent their gayness at a very young age, and that these feelings presented very little conflict for them. Others, because of accompanying guilt, religious teaching, teasing from peers, or internalization of negative messages from family or society, felt an enormous burden because of their sexuality. For them, the secret was something they never asked for or wanted, and a great deal of energy went into trying to suppress any feelings associated with the secret.

Many gay men recall with horror the feeling that their secret was out as peers teased them because of nontraditional behaviors. Maybe some of them did not like sports; others may have had effeminate mannerisms. Some might even have tried to clue their friends into the secret. For example, I remember playing the game, Truth or Dare with a friend when we were twelve years old. I dared him to do sit-ups naked. He said to me, "Are you a fag?" I just repeated my dare and told him that the rules of the game allowed me to ask of him whatever I want. Again he asked, "Are you a fag?" I never answered his question because on some level I knew that yes, I was a "fag." Instead of retreating and refuting his question, I was testing the waters of adolescent sexuality, seeking from him an answer to questions about my own sexuality. In testing him, I was actually trying to learn more about myself.

As we enter late adolescence and early adulthood, most of us gain a clearer understanding of what I am labeling here "our difference." By this time some of us have acted on our sexual urges, perhaps with children our own age, though sometimes with older men. Similarly, many young men who later identify as gay engage in sexual relations with young women, for example in high school or college. This is all part of trying to identify who we are, how we feel about who we are, and how we define for ourselves and others who we are. Ultimately, we seek to relinquish responsibility for keeping our secret, to share with others who we are, and to find acceptance from those closest to us in light of our disclosure.

By the time this stage occurs, however, we are not only more familiar with our difference from others, but many of us are much more aware of how others perceive people like us. This is a fragile time in the development of our self-image and identity as we integrate feelings from within us with public perceptions of homosexuality. One client of mine, a gay man in his fifties, expressed feeling that it must be harder for gays of the current generation to come out than it was for him. He acknowledged going through both personal and social struggles with his own sexual identity but said it was mostly a private matter. Regarding all the recent talk of homosexuality, however, particularly from the Religious Right, he feels that younger gays are probably more aware of the oppression and hatred that can exist against homosexuals than what he was exposed to. For many of us, therefore, a major challenge is reconciling our stereotypes of gay men with who gay men really are.

## *COMING OUT*

Every gay person eventually makes a decision about when he will stop hiding his feelings and identity from others, and when he will share with others who he is. This process has become known as *coming out*, and it refers to the disclosures a gay man makes to others about his sexuality. Rather than being a single event, coming out is a process that continues throughout the lifespan. Richard Friedman (1988) says that coming out is our attempt as gay men to realign profoundly important relationships, such as those with parents, siblings, and employers, with our true selves.

Gay men tend to come out to others at a younger age than do lesbians. Interviews with gay men about coming out suggest that most gay men disclose their sexual identity to another person by the time they are in their early twenties. Thus, we develop more experience in coming out earlier than do lesbians.

By the time a gay man discloses his sexual identity to another person, he has usually had years of experience dealing with his feelings, attractions, and sense of difference. Just as coming out is a developmental process, so is self-acceptance. Thus, coming out to another for the first time provides us with more information about our identity. Usually, after coming out to someone, we are presented with questions or reactions that we may not have anticipated. These might include the following:

- When did you first realize you might be gay?
- Have you ever tried to change?
- Have you ever had a satisfying relationship with another man?
- Did I do something to cause this?
- Are you saying this to hurt me?
- Have you told anyone else?
- How do you know you are not bisexual?
- Are you really sure you are gay?
- How could you do this to me?
- Have you discussed this with a professional?
- Do you think this could change?
- You don't have AIDS, do you?
- I do not want to discuss this further.

Hearing some of these questions for the first time may surprise us. And the truth is that we may not have answers for many of the questions we are presented with. Over time, however, as we become more comfortable and familiar with our sexuality, we are better able to answer such questions and deal with some of the responses we receive from others when we come out to them.

Coming out can be an experience that is unpredictable and very stressful. Oftentimes we try to find what we feel is the "right time" to come out to someone, but the truth is that sometimes there is no such time. Also, even though we may be ready to come out to another person, they may not be ready or willing to hear it. Many gay men report having believed that the person they came out to already suspected he is gay, only to find out that they had no idea about this.

Our challenge is to assess our motives for coming out to another person. Are we doing it for ourselves, or are we doing it for them? Also, since coming out can cause the other person to experience feelings of grief or self-incrimination, it is helpful to ask if we are purposely trying to hurt them by coming out to them. It is not uncommon, for example, for a gay man to tell his parents he is gay during an argument. Coming out, in this example, is sometimes used as a weapon against them.

Finally, sometimes coming out may be in our best interest even though we would rather not disclose this information (Figure 2.2). For example, many gay men have difficulty telling their doctor they are gay even though they may have medical questions related to gay male sexuality. In this scenario, our motive for self-disclosure is to receive more comprehensive medical care, even though we know that we might be judged by telling our physician we are gay.

By examining what we feel we need by coming out to another person, we are in a better position to deal with the range of feelings both they and we will have. Some motives people have for coming out include the following:

- I want them to know the real me.
- Now they will stop trying to set me up with single women.
- They already suspect I am gay.
- To keep the secret any longer can only hurt them more.
- I need them to know in order to feel better about myself.

FIGURE 2.2. Gay men and the health care system: Exercising prudence when choosing and coming out to providers.

Martin Schwartz (1996), in an article on gay men and health care providers, points out that dealing with a physician as a gay man is similar to the lifelong process of coming out. That is, each encounter requires a decision about what, if anything, he will share with health care providers. Often, gay men cannot expect or anticipate that their physician is familiar with gay male sex practices. Thus, he may find himself in the uncomfortable position of having to educate his doctor about different sexual behaviors.

This means that some gay men may choose not to share their concerns about venereal disease, anal warts, or HIV exposure out of fear of being harshly judged or ridiculed. For those patients who are HIV positive, quality medical service, and open dialogue between provider and patient, is critical to his survival. Confidentiality is a sacrosanct tenet in all professional activities, yet many gay men tell stories of how their sexuality or HIV status has "leaked" to receptionists, clerks, and others who do not need to know this information.

The medical community has far to go in educating its members about the needs and behaviors associated with gay men. By being better informed about gay male sexuality, providers can reduce the tension felt by gay male patients by assuming more responsibility for asking the right questions and offering effective interventions. Until such time, however, gay men requiring medical care should consider the following:

- Check with your friends or local gay community center for referral to gay or gay-sensitive medical providers.

- Even though you are not HIV infected, calling a local AIDS service organization can help you identify providers who are skilled in gay men's health.

- It is in your best interest that your health care provider know you are gay. Therefore, anticipate in advance coming out and telling him or her you are gay. Ask him or her directly about their experience treating gay men and in addressing gay men's health concerns.

- Try not to feel ashamed of your sexual practices or of any questions you have related to gay male sexuality. You are hiring your provider to provide you with quality and informed care without judgment expressed about your preferences. If you do not feel he or she is providing such care, find another provider immediately.

- Report all homophobic comments or gestures made to you by health care providers to their licensing board and to the insurance company that authorizes them to treat you. Consider filing legal charges if the provider's homophobic attitudes constitute malpractice.

- I owe it to them to tell them.
- I do not like having this secret.
- I am tired of the facade.
- As my doctor, he needs to know this information.
- If he knows I am gay, he will understand why I am reacting this way.
- By knowing I am gay, perhaps he will change some of his biased views.

## GAY ROLE MODELS

In Chapter 1, I asserted that the male child looks to his father for cues on how to be a man. This is the concept of role models. Role models are important to us throughout our life span. Role models provide us with someone to admire and with which to identify. Often we use them as guides for our own actions and behaviors. One thing desperately lacking in the lives of many gay men are other gay men who can help shape our identity and concept of what it means to be gay. Thus, our self image is often left with a void as we wander around trying to figure out what persona to place on the aspect of ourselves we begin to know as gay. This is particularly true for gay men in the earlier stages of coming out.

Many gay male friends and clients have said that they wish they had known other gay people when they were first coming out. These men recognized they are probably gay but that the image they held of gay men, based solely on stereotypes and media images, did not fit with how they saw themselves. The confusion during this time is enormous as these men feel estranged not only from general society but also from the world of other gay men. Many feel that in order to be gay they have to assume an identity, personality, and behaviors that are inconsistent with who they are. This is why some people place so much emphasis on public figures coming out as gay. They feel that if more people saw gays and lesbians as *regular* people, then the popular myths about who gays/lesbians are might be diminished.

We use other males throughout life to learn about manhood. We use our peers to learn about age-appropriate behavior, we observe fathers to learn about being male, and we often use family or clergy to learn about morality. Without adequate gay role models, many gay men continually struggle with what it means to be gay. Because this is such a significant part of our identity, many gay men lack a complete image of themselves that integrates and includes their sexual identity.

It is heartening to see the development of programs for gay youth throughout this country. Many of these programs grow out of gay mental health agencies, but some develop from the efforts of people in the general community. One small town in Northern California, for example, has started a mentoring program that relies upon adults to provide individual and group support for adolescent gays and lesbians. A gay and lesbian professionals group in New Mexico offers college scholarships to young gays and lesbians. Though many of us did not have such support when we were growing up, it is tremendously beneficial to our community and to our own self-image to contribute to these efforts. It is not too late for us to become role models for others.

## SHAME AND SELF-ESTEEM

The concept of shame has received much attention in the media lately. Even one of the top two national weekly news magazines recently did a cover story on the topic. I suspect that the approach the media is taking with the subject of shame is that if more people felt it, we might have a less chaotic society. In other words, those prone to antisocial acts might be less inclined to take advantage of others if they feared reprisal.

Shame is a natural emotion and not all of it is bad. We first learn about shame when we are about one to two years old. As we explore our environment, we do so with a feeling of omnipotence. The world is our oyster, and we do not want anyone to prevent us from sampling all of it. In this new environment, however, we are bound to make mistakes. Children hit their heads on tables, fall off unsteady objects, run into streets, put pencils in light sockets, and try to touch animals with little awareness of how friendly they may or may not be.

As much as we do not want interference with our childhood explorations, we do require our caregivers to anticipate and prevent dangerous situations and to introduce us to the concept of boundaries. Someone once remarked to me that 95 percent of parenting is setting limits. This is where we first learn shame. If our mother, or other caregiver, can gently coax us away from certain situations, and do so in a way that communicates their desire to protect or teach us, we develop what is called healthy shame. Healthy shame keeps us aware of the fact that we are not omnipotent, and that we do require the intervention of others who *know better*. It reminds us that we rely upon the love and support of others at times. It also keeps us aware of our limitations, which is necessary in a communal society.

If, however, we are made to feel bad, stupid, or inferior because of our natural mistakes, we begin to develop unhealthy shame. You have probably seen those parents who ridicule and insult their children, often in public, as they pull them by their arm away from some activity. Sometimes the child will go down the wrong aisle in a grocery store, or approach the toy or candy rack. Then, before you know it, the mother or father is yelling, pulling, and blaming. You just know that the parent does the same when the child cries, when he wets his bed, when his grades fail, and at countless other times. Older boys are often made to feel shame with comments such as, "Big boys don't cry," "Be a man," "You sissy," "You are just like a girl," "You will never amount to anything," and "Act your age."

This is how unhealthy shame becomes instilled. We are given the message that our efforts toward independence or self-gratification are wrong, disruptive to others, and foolish. Feeling defective and damaged is the result of these experiences, particularly when they are repeated. Fortunately, most of us are resilient enough to tolerate periodic teasing, humiliation, or accusations. But when these are constant and repeated, we begin to internalize the message and intent, and shame is no longer a feeling, but rather a state of being. When people are repeatedly shamed, particularly in childhood, they lose a sense of their own personal value. They feel they do not matter and that no can ever be there for them.

The psychiatrist, Leon Wurmser (1987), defines shame in this way:

> Shame is first the *fear* of disgrace, it is the *anxiety* about the danger that we might be looked at with contempt for having dishonored ourselves. Second, it is the feeling when one is looked at with such scorn. It is, in other words, the *affect of contempt* directed against the self—by others or by one's own conscience. Contempt says: "You should disappear as such a

being as you have shown yourself to be—failing, weak, flawed, and dirty. Get out of my sight: Disappear!" (p. 67)

Shame leaves us feeling exposed. This is why we often see people who feel ashamed of some action cover their eyes or their faces. I can always tell when clients feel shame about a topic because of their tendency to keep their heads down, put their hands to their face, and look as if they wish they or I would just disappear. Wurmser says that to "disappear into nothing is the punishment for such failure" (p. 67).

Shame is different from guilt, though they often go hand-in-hand. Whereas shame refers to some weakness of the self, guilt refers to some violation of others. Guilt is usually not tied to our identity. Rather, guilt results when we have violated our own standards and principles. Guilt is what helps socialize us. Most of us tend to rebound from guilt more easily than from shame.

Underlying shame is the feeling that you have to apologize for yourself, justify your actions, or explain to others who you are or why you do the things you do. It leaves us with the feeling that we have to keep our lives and our inner experience hidden from the rest of society in order to be accepted. In many respects, persons feeling shame, be they gay or not, report not feeling "normal." Naturally, shame is a very isolating experience.

## SHAME AND SELF-PROTECTION

Considering the prior discussion, it makes sense that the individual feeling shame will go to great lengths to prevent others from knowing the real him. This protection of the self occurs not only with others but also with ourselves. Thus, the person distances himself from who he truly is and how he truly feels. Most men find it relatively easy to do this as society encourages productivity and accomplishment over emotion in men. This is why many men put all their efforts toward achievement, often at the expense of personal insight.

This becomes dangerous in how we treat other people. It is difficult respecting others when we neither respect nor feel good about ourselves. In turn, we take advantage of others without sensing what we are doing. Others are objectified in our minds and we use people for personal, social, sexual, or financial gain.

We also feel threatened by others when we are feeling ashamed of who we are, and it is natural to go to great lengths to protect ourselves from the potential hurts of others. For some people the reaction to this threat is "I will hurt you before you hurt me." Such a reaction helps the person feel more in control. For example, how often have you heard someone constantly belittle others for their looks, accomplishments, tastes, choices, etc.? A national gay magazine recently profiled several gay men and lesbians in Los Angeles who were considered to be among the top eligible unattached people. The profiles were accompanied by statements from each about their likes and dislikes, hobbies, favorite foods, etc. When asked what his favorite pasttime was, one man said that his was making fun of his friends in public. How sad, I thought, that a primary source of enjoyment for this person was belittling people—his friends, no less—in public. At times it can be fun to joke with those in our lives about their behaviors or comments. But how many people do you know who go to extremes with this? How must they feel about those they tease? More important, how must they feel about themselves?

## WHAT DID YOU DO WRONG?

One of the interventions I use as a psychologist is asking the client who is in the depths of shame, "What did you do wrong?" Often, the person feeling shame feels so guilty, disgusted, and dirty that they lose perspective on exactly what it is they think they should be held accountable for. If I am working with a parent who abused their child, I want to see shame. They should feel remorse. Too often I see clients, particularly gay men, who feel ashamed for being who they are, and again I pose the question, "What did you do wrong?"

Shame is a painful state and often a precursor to depression. Earlier I wrote of the distinction between guilt and shame. What I see clinically is that guilt-ridden persons rarely experience prolonged depression. Rather, remorse is the more common—and temporary—emotion. Persons feeling shame, however, tend to have a greater likelihood of depression and low self-esteem. Since shame is often instilled in us early in our lives, the depression many gay men feel is lifelong.

I also discussed the recognition of being different that many gay men feel in early childhood. I mentioned that this realization often acquires the feeling of a secret that should be carefully guarded. A balance many of us gay men need to achieve when we come to this realization is how to understand the meaning of our secret without falling prey to the shackles of shame. Given societal, religious, and family beliefs and stereotypes about homosexuality, this can be quite an endeavor.

I think it is important for each of us to assess to what extent we have been taught or conditioned to feel ashamed of being gay. Some men have internalized these messages more than others. Others have literally had the messages beaten into them. For some men, the message came through an upbringing based on a strong cultural prohibition against homosexuality, for example in many Asian or Middle Eastern cultures. Others grew up in religions that take a fear-based approach to discussion of the topic. Still others received negative messages from family, the media, friends, and unfortunately, the mental health profession. Some psychotherapists, well-intentioned or not, have done great harm to many gay men by equating homosexuality with poor parenting, fixations in childhood, abusive experiences, heterosexual inadequacy, or poor social conditioning. Furthermore, many women have fallen in love with the gay man who was counseled by his church leaders to marry only to find that the man discovers this solution to be temporary and short-sighted.

At the end of this chapter is an exercise that will guide you on how best to approach and assess this question of internalizing negative messages. Though many of the exercises in this book are meant to be done alone or as part of your therapy, it can be helpful to share your answers with others who have also answered the question. Because each of us takes in these messages in so many different ways, seeing how our experience compares with that of others is useful. Also, by sharing these experiences, we either start or continue to break the isolation that can result from shameful feelings.

One of the benefits of the way the gay community (e.g., bars, clubs, organizations, places for anonymous sex, community events, churches, etc.) is structured is that we can sample of variety of situations that put us in the presence of other gays and lesbians. Many of these are fairly noncommittal and thus provide an easy out if we are uncomfortable or dissatisfied. A negative aspect, however, is that it can become easy to feel alone while with others. How many times has your visit to a crowded gay bar felt like one of life's loneliest experiences? Too often many gay men take what appears to be an active role in the social part of gay life while simultaneously deriving little satisfaction or really getting to know other gay men. This is why I encourage sharing, on your part, pieces of your life experience with other gay men. It helps break the isolation, normalize your feelings and experiences, and decrease feelings of shame while helping you feel better about yourself.

## NARCISSISM AND GAY MEN

For reasons that are much too technical for this book to examine, psychoanalytic theory has traditionally seen a natural connection between homosexuality and narcissism. There is current debate in psychoanalytic circles regarding this topic, much of it due to differing conceptions of narcissism. Further, our understanding of the complexity of homosexuality has far to go, and we should be cautious about assigning blanket generalizations.

What is worth examining, however, is to what degree, if any, gay men are more susceptible to narcissistic disorders. Many gay men exhibit a "showy" quality; thus, it has been easy for laypersons to assign the label of narcissistic to us. Further, psychotherapists working with gay men often report witnessing narcissistic attitudes or defenses on the part of their clients. My premise is that narcissism and homosexuality do not go hand-in-hand as a matter of course, but that there are components of gay male development which make many gay men prone to developing or using narcissistic features or defenses. The result of this is that many gay men feel it necessary, consciously and unconsciously, to prove themselves to others—to show that they are not damaged goods, if you will.

Clinical psychologists generally see shame as being at the root of narcissism. Indeed, narcissism is often conceived of clinically as being founded on a pathological form of the regulation of self-esteem. In this view, the narcissistic individual has an exaggerated and unrealistic "yardstick" by which to measure his own view of himself, and thus requires the constant admiration and attention of others in order to undo feelings of inferiority. This runs counter to the image most narcissists portray, which is one of success, wealth, great attainments, and power.

Generally, most people with narcissistic personalities are not necessarily unlikable, and we would not consider them to be *disturbed*. Narcissism runs along a continuum with one end including those persons whose behavior is highly exploitative and sociopathic. This end contains those people who are charming but capable of criminal acts. Perhaps you have seen the charm of many high-profile criminals, such as the Menendez brothers (convicted in 1996 of killing both their parents).

The other end of the continuum holds those narcissists who are able to function in society in an appropriate manner. Many have good social skills and adequate impulse control, and frequently aspire to and attain great success politically, in business, and socially. These people rely upon the world—their friends, career, car, clothes, etc.—to reflect their exaggerated sense of importance and worth. Only when they are not receiving the attention of others do they become bored, restless, and prone to immersing themselves in grandiose fantasy. Having nothing to do is highly threatening to them, and many, as James Masterson (1988) points out, are workaholics.

The connection between shame and narcissism is that both are related to experiences in which the *self* is central. Whereas shame represents a negative view of the self, narcissism represents a positive view of the self. In narcissism, however, the positive view of the self is artificial: underlying it is intense self-hatred, humiliation, and depression. Narcissistic defenses are used to keep others from getting too close and from doing any more harm to an already fragile sense of self. Simultaneously, however, the narcissist requires the admiration and feedback of others to reassure him of his greatness. Though different theories address the development of narcissistic personality, most theories agree that the roots of narcissism are in early childhood experience.

Some theorists offer that narcissists have mothers who are highly narcissistic themselves. These mothers require that their children be perfect so that they can reflect to the world what great mothers they are. Other theorists propose that the mothers of narcissists are cold and withdrawn, perhaps even depressed, and thus require perfection in their children so that they do not have to work so hard. Some theorists suggest that the mothers of narcissists communicate to the child that he is in some way defective as a human being, and that the infant counters these shameful assaults with reactive grandiosity. Studies suggest that many narcissistic individuals often had talents in childhood that elicited admiration from others. The psychiatrist Richard Chessick (1985) notes that many were pivotal in their families, typically the only child, and thus carried the burden of fulfilling family expectations.

These theorists generally accept the notion that under normal circumstances most mothers teach their children about limits, boundaries, and frustrations in life—but not the mother of narcissists. Thus, the child never outgrows feeling the omnipotence and grandiosity associated with infancy. The infant's identity is never fully developed; in turn, he is reliant upon others to help him maintain some sense of self. Because the stage was set early on for perfectionism and omnipotence, the narcissist is highly dependent on others to provide this feedback.

Without adequate feedback from others, the narcissist is vulnerable to the feelings of depression that underlie the disorder. The infant-narcissist learned early to defend against depression lest he wither away and die because of it. Because depression is so threatening to him, he will do all he can to keep the admiration coming. Again, many narcissists do this quite well, achieving great accomplishments. However, narcissists do not seek accomplishment for its own worth, but rather for the recognition it brings.

To infer that the preceding descriptions apply to all gay men is where psychological theory can lose some of its credibility. To the extent that a gay man presents with indicators of narcissistic personality function, psychotherapists need to look beyond his sexual identity and into the other complexities of his development and life experience.

My own opinion is that there is no single cause of narcissism just as rarely is there a single cause for most psychological disorders. I believe that the theories mentioned here adequately outline the developmental antecedents of narcissism, though they are by no means the only theories. The important issue for us, however, is whether or not there is something about the childhood and/or personality development of gay men that make us more susceptible to narcissistic disorders.

## NARCISSISM AS DEFENSE, NOT JUST PERSONALITY

Many gay men do present with features of narcissism, but such presentation must be viewed as a form of defense rather than as a pervasive, inflexible, and unchanging personality characteristic. I do not believe that these features develop and manifest in gay men because of the parenting styles reflected in the theories I mentioned. Rather, I feel that many gay men recognize their difference early in life and subsequently take steps they feel necessary to prove to themselves and others that they are not deficient.

Unfortunately, the societal messages about homosexuality are pervasive, and some gay men feel the need to go to extremes to convince the world of their adequacy. Those who feel most damaged and insecure present to others with protective defenses that others easily translate as narcissistic. They continually attempt to make others feel helpless and intimated, and they incessantly try to obtain admiration from others.

When we recognize that we are not inherently damaged because we are gay, and when we feel less of a need to try to prove this fact to others, then a more genuine, less defensive presentation to the world occurs. Ultimately, one of our biggest challenges as gay men is coming to understand that being gay is a unique characteristic and not a disability.

## ACTUAL VERSUS IDEAL SELF

At about the age of two we develop the capacity to symbolically represent ideas and images. One of the images we create for ourselves during early childhood is an image of our *ideal self*. The ideal self is our fantasy of who we would like to be. It is based on past successes, feedback from important people in our lives, and a perception of what we think we are capable of becoming. In essence, the ideal self is a blueprint for ourselves that we attempt to approximate.

In reality, however, few of us ever attain our ideal self. Rather, there is an *actual self* that more adequately reflects our competencies and incompetencies. The actual self includes our accomplishments, our strengths and weaknesses, the good parts of our personality, as well as the bad. The actual self is closely related to self-image in that it is comprised of all the true features of who we are. Yet, we constantly strive to make our actual self reach the ideal self. Because we are constantly faced with new demands and experiences in life, the blueprint for the ideal self changes (Figure 2.3).

Between our actual self and ideal self lies shame. Some people have a healthy struggle with themselves whereby they work hard to better themselves and attain their ideal self. Others have such high or unrealistic expectations of themselves that the ideal self feels unreachable. For these people, they often feel the following sentiment: "I cannot measure up; I am trying, but I am helpless."

One of our challenges as gay men is developing and having an ideal self that is consistent with how we perceive our individual potential. If the Ideal Self is defined as: Do not be gay; Be more masculine; Do not act that way; Do not have those thoughts; Do not get close to men, etc., it is natural that the gap between our actual self and ideal self will be wide. Thus, we have even more shame (Figure 2.4).

If we choose to believe that we have already attained our ideal self—which no one ever does—we are more susceptible to narcis-

FIGURE 2.3. We try to make our actual self and our ideal self approximate each other.

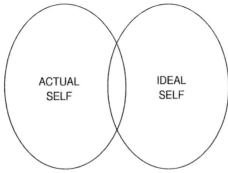

FIGURE 2.4. The further apart our actual self is from our ideal self, the more shame we are likely to have.

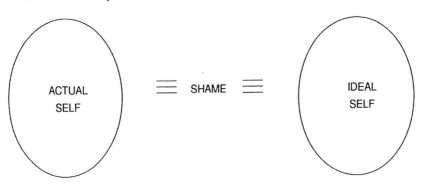

sistic presentation. We also find ourselves more removed from our actual self where all the good and bad features of our personality lie.

## HIV RISK AND SELF-ESTEEM

Contrary to extensive HIV education and prevention efforts targeted for gay men, studies suggest that upward of 26 to 66 percent of gay men engage in unsafe sexual practices (Martin and Knox, 1995; Ekstrand and Coates, 1990; Kelly, St. Lawrence, and Brasfield, 1991). What these studies point out is that those gay men who practice unsafe sex do not necessarily do so with every sexual encounter. Thus, sometimes their behavior is considered safe in terms of HIV risk while at other times it is unsafe. One point of view (Perkins et. al., 1993) proposes that fluctuating unsafe sex practices may correlate with fluctuating self-esteem.

It is natural that our self-esteem will change periodically. The reality of life is that sometimes we feel very good about ourselves while at other times we may not. A successful project, a good interaction with another person, or a failed test can have tremendous impact on our self-perception. When our self-esteem is low, we are prone to engaging in self-destructive or self-defeating behaviors (Figure 2.5). This might mean we drink a little more, exercise a little less, perhaps even get depressed. In extreme states

FIGURE 2.5. The final consequence of low self-esteem: Suicide in gay men.

---

Researchers have just recently begun to identify the high rates of suicide in sexual minority populations. Much of this research has focused on gay and lesbian adolescents, since we know that teenagers in general have an elevated risk of suicide attempt and completion. Studies of gay and lesbian youth estimate that suicide attempts in this population range from 21 to 42 percent. Scott Hershberger and his research team (1996) surveyed 194 gay and lesbian youth between the ages of 15 and 21 years. Of this sample, 142 were men. They found that 42 percent of the youth surveyed had attempted suicide on at least one occasion.

The feelings that lead a gay adolescent to consider suicide do not always subside as he grows older. Granted, as we age, we understand more about our sexual identity, develop a stronger support system, and find alternative methods of coping with the stress of being gay. However, we are still prone to negative feelings about ourselves, depression, and feelings of helplessness. Thus, if there were times in your younger years that you felt suicidal, it is important to gauge how you feel about yourself now.

In consideration of the high rates of suicide attempts by gay/lesbian adolescents, and because we can feel vulnerable about our sexuality throughout our life span, the following recommendations are offered:

- Do not isolate yourself from others. We need the support of others to affirm that being gay is OK.
- Stay aware of your overall self-concept. If you find yourself feeling bad about yourself for being gay, not accomplishing your goals, or for other reasons, find ways to improve your self-esteem. Focus on what you do well, not what you do poorly.
- Do not ignore depression. There are times when we all get the blues. But if you find yourself experiencing prolonged feelings of hopelessness, sadness, and crying spells, reach out. Talk with your physician or with a psychotherapist about your depression. There are effective interventions to help you through depression.
- If you are feeling depressed or suicidal, stay away from alcohol or drugs to help you cope. These only make your feelings worsen.
- If you are feeling suicidal, be careful. Remove any items that you could impulsively use to harm yourself (e.g., firearms, large amounts of medications). If your depression is not going away, consider voluntary hospitalization or staying with a friend. Your safety is the most important thing when you are feeling self-destructive.

---

of despair, we might even be less inclined to take precautions when being sexual with another person.

When our self-esteem is low, we are vulnerable to feeling bad about our attractiveness and we may even question our capacity to sustain a long-term relationship. Because sexual contact bolsters how we feel about ourselves, we can become vulnerable when someone expresses interest in us. In this state, when someone shows us attention, we may simultaneously disbelieve their sincerity while also wanting to do all we can to keep them around. Thus, we think more in terms of pleasing and satisfying them than asserting our own needs and desires. If the person we are with does not bring up the issue of safe sex, or if he tells us he does not wish to use precautions, we may not feel we have the inner strength to challenge him.

Because of the close connection between low self-esteem and unsafe sex, it is very important that we do what we can to feel good about ourselves and reduce the risk of life-threatening behaviors. Some of the things you can do to reduce your chances of practicing unsafe sex include:

- *Develop a good support system.* Loneliness increases the chances we will feel bad about ourselves. Also, when we feel lonely we are more likely to find ways of reducing these feelings by doing things that can be potentially harmful to us. When we are lonely we may feel more desperate for affection and therefore less likely to insist on having safe sex with a partner.
- *Avoid excessive use of alcohol or drugs.* These artificially increase our feelings of self-worth. In reality, they depress us and make us feel worse about ourselves. Also, try not to have sex when under the influence of substances since your judgment may be impaired.
- *Pay attention to your sexual practices.* Men who feel alienated from the gay community may feel that gay sex is their only connection to the gay life. In turn, sex becomes equated with artificial feelings of intimacy and closeness.
- *Share with your sexual partners your desire to practice safe sex.* You will communicate care and concern about him and you, while also letting him know that you still want to be sexually active with him.

## SUMMARY

The development of healthy self-esteem and a positive image of ourselves is a lifelong process. Though it helps if we got off to a good start by having good parenting, some of us have to reshape the way we look at ourselves. Sorting out negative messages about homosexuality and addressing how shame affects our life is one of our central challenges as gay men. Ultimately, we will each learn to feel that being gay is a unique and special characteristic and not something we need to apologize for—or justify—to others.

# Exercises

### *ASSESSING YOUR SELF-ESTEEM*

1 = Strongly Agree

2 = Agree

3 = Disagree

4 = Strongly Disagree

1. _____ Most of my friends find me interesting.
2. _____ I take a positive attitude toward myself.
3. _____ Most people do not think of me as foolish.
4. _____ I have respect for myself.
5. _____ I feel that I am a likable person.
6. _____ I have many positive qualities.
7. _____ I do not feel guilty much of the time.
8. _____ I feel that I have a lot to offer other people.
9. _____ I am someone other people like to be around.
10. _____ Rarely do I think of myself as a failure.
11. _____ I feel in control of my life.
12. _____ I feel that I am needed.
13. _____ I am comfortable around new people I meet.
14. _____ I am able to stand up for myself.
15. _____ I believe I am as good as most people.

Scoring:

30 points or less = Healthy self-esteem
30 - 45 points = Tendency toward low self-esteem
45 points + = Poor self-esteem

## *BEING WHO OTHERS WANT YOU TO BE*

As gay men we continually confront expectations others have of us. Some people simply do not want us to be gay, while others take the approach: Be gay, but . . .

- Do not talk about it;
- Do not pursue legal protections;
- Do not march down the street; and
- Do not act a certain way.

Think about the times in your life that you altered your personality, behavior, dress, or other features to accommodate the spoken and unspoken wishes of others. Maybe you tried to make others think you were straight, perhaps even going so far as getting married when it really did not feel right. Maybe you left your lover at home during a family gathering, not wanting to make people uncomfortable.

List examples of the above:

1. _____

2. _____

3. _____

4. _____

5. _____

What thoughts and feelings do you have on the above? Do you have any regrets or do the actions seem justifiable? How was your self-image helped or hurt by doing this? What do you wish you would have done differently, and if you had, what do you think the outcome would have been?

_____

_____

_____

_____

_____

## LIFE'S MESSAGES ABOUT HOMOSEXUALITY

Think back on the messages you recall hearing about homosexuality. Write out each one and list who (family, church, teacher, society at large) told you.

I recall hearing or being told:                    Who told me:

_____          _____

_____          _____

_____          _____

_____          _____


How have you taken steps to either change the above beliefs in yourself or to make sure you do not end up believing them? Describe:

_____

_____

_____

_____

_____

## *FEELING DIFFERENT FOR BEING GAY*

A theme in this chapter was how most gay men recall feeling different from other males at some point in life. Typically this occurred during early childhood, though some did not feel it until much later in life. Eventually, most of us came to understand this difference as our first recognition of being gay. Write down your memories of feeling different from others. When did you first attach these feeling to knowing you are gay? Did this feeling of being different feel like a secret? What do you recall about the secretive nature of this feeling? Do you remember being fearful that anyone would find out about you being different? What were your fears and feelings?

_____

_____

_____

_____

_____

_____

_____

_____

How different from or similar to other gay men do you feel? What attributes of yours make you feel different from or similar to other gay men? Describe and cite examples:

_____

_____

_____

_____

_____

_____

_____

## ARE ALL THOSE NEGATIVE BELIEFS STILL IN THERE?

The following questions address those messages many gay men received about homosexuality. After each question you will be asked (1) if you ever believed the stereotype, and (2) if you still believe it is true. Answer all questions truthfully and honestly.

| QUESTION | Once Believed | Still Believe |
|---|---|---|
| 1. Homosexuality, in the eyes of God, is a sin. | _____ | _____ |
| 2. Homosexuals are made, not born. | _____ | _____ |
| 3. Gay men cannot sustain long-term romantic relationships. | _____ | _____ |
| 4. Homosexuality is a perversion. | _____ | _____ |
| 5. I am inferior because I am gay. | _____ | _____ |
| 6. If we really try, most homosexuals can change. | _____ | _____ |
| 7. Most young boys who are molested are molested by homosexuals. | _____ | _____ |
| 8. AIDS is God's punishment on gay men. | _____ | _____ |
| 9. Gay men had overbearing mothers. | _____ | _____ |
| 10. Gay men can never truly be happy. | _____ | _____ |

It is likely that most of us heard, and believed, many of the messages above. However, the stereotypes above are fear-based beliefs that cause most gay men to maintain a low self-image when they believe them. In reality, the following are true:

- Nowhere is it written that homosexuality is a sin in the eyes of the Christian God.
- Most modern theories support an underlying biological connection to homosexuality.
- Gay men are capable of long-term, satisfying relationships with another man.
- No sexuality reversal therapy has been found effective at curing homosexuality.
- Studies show that upward of 80 percent of molestation's of young boys is done by heterosexual friends or family members.
- Not all gay men had overcontrolling mothers and distant fathers.

## EXAMINING SHAME IN YOUR LIFE

The experience of shame is one of isolation. It is the time we feel like disappearing, hiding from the world, crawling into a hole, and hoping others do not see what we have done. Often there is fear of exposure and a desire to protect ourselves from experiencing any additional harm or humiliation. Shame is very much a universal human phenomenon, and it is capitalized on by many cultures to help socialize its members. The threat of shame, in these instances, is used to prevent betrayal, disrespect, or bad manners. As mentioned, shame differs from guilt in that guilt is a feeling we have for something we have done. Shame, on the other hand, is feeling bad about who we are.

When we experience shame for prolonged periods of time, we eventually develop feelings of helplessness. Out of this, people often eventually go in one of two directions.

1. Some people feel so helpless that they develop symptoms of depression.
2. Others, in their helplessness, rebel and develop long-standing feelings of anger and rage.

Work with depressed persons, therefore, often uncovers feelings of shame, embarrassment, and helplessness that overwhelm the person's capacity to deal with such feelings. Alternately, some people become so enraged at feeling inferior to others that they throw vicious verbal jabs at people they encounter. In short, prolonged feelings of shame cause a very unhappy existence.

Our society looks at homosexuality as a condition of which we should be ashamed. We are told that we are violating the laws of God, engaging in immoral acts against society, and bringing public ridicule to our families. Even though on some level we know this is not true, we struggle to find validation outside of ourselves that we are not bad and damaged people. Still, it is difficult being gay without feeling some elements of shame during our lives.

This exercise is developed to help you identify feelings and indicators of shame in your own life. Gay men often feel shame because of our experiences of being gay in our families, because of early religious teaching, and because of how we feel about our sexuality. This exercise, therefore, encourages you to write about your experiences concerning these topic areas.

The challenge in this exercise is to confront your identity, answer such questions honestly, and to not feel humiliated for recognizing that shame is something you may carry around with you. Do not feel that you have to do the entire exercise in one sitting. You may want to share with your therapist, lover, or close friend feelings that arise as you do this exercise.

### Early Memories

How old are you now? ———

At what age did you first have vague feelings of being different from others? (For this question, remember feelings you might have had that had nothing to do with sex, but were early clues for you about being gay.) ———

Describe these feelings, memories, and/or experiences: ——————

_____

_____

At what age were you fairly confident that you were gay, even if the word gay is not one you would have used to describe your identity? ———

How did you know that you were gay? What were the indicators that your sexual feelings were not transient in nature? ——————

_____

_____

Who is the first person you ever told you are gay, or told you suspected you might be gay? Describe this encounter: ——————

_____

_____

Describe your earliest perceptions or understanding about gay people. What stereotypes did you have about gay men? ——————

_____

_____

### Religion

Were you raised in particular religion?   YES    NO

- If YES, specify the denomination:

- In a concise way, write down what official view, if any, this church or religion has about homosexuality:

At what age do you recall being aware of your religion's view of homosexuality?

Did you ever discuss your feelings of being gay with leaders or representatives of your church?    YES    NO

What do you recall telling them, and what do you recall hearing from them?

What do you recall feeling about yourself after this encounter?

Discuss the impact, if any, being gay has or had on your participation in this religion:

If applicable, discuss any "conversations" or prayers you had with your God about your sexuality. What questions did you ask? What pleas did you make? What "answers" did you get?

What steps have you taken, if any, to reconcile your sexual identity with the beliefs about homosexuality expressed by your religion? How has this changed your relationship to the religion and your God? _____

_____

_____

_____

Did you stop attending religious services of your denomination because of the fact you are gay?   YES   NO

- If YES, what has this been like for you? What aspects of your religion, if any, do you still hold on to? _____

_____

_____

If YES, do you think you would still be active in this denomination if you were not gay? _____

If YES, what is this realization like for you?

_____

_____

### Family of Origin

Have you come out to one or both of your parents?   YES   NO

If YES, think back to the time prior to coming out to your mother and/or father. How did you think they would react to learning that you are gay?

_____

_____

How did they react when you told them? Compare this with your answer to the previous question:_____

_____

_____

Were you afraid, prior to coming out to them, that you would be seen by them as damaged, inferior, bad, tainted, etc.?   YES   NO

- If YES, were these fears confirmed when you came out to them? YES   NO

- If YES to the first question, describe why you think you had these feelings. What were you taught or told early in life that indicated someone might have these feelings of you because you are gay? _____

_____

_____

_____

- If YES to the first question, do you still have these feelings prior to coming out to new people?  YES  NO

- If YES, why do you think you hold onto the fear that others will feel this way about you once they hear you are gay? Is there a part of you that believes you are damaged, inferior, bad, tainted, etc., because you are gay?

_____

_____

_____

### *Self-Disclosure*

What percentage of your immediate family members (parents, siblings, close relatives) know you are gay? _____ Of this percentage, how many know you are gay because you told them? _____

- Do you ever feel awkward or embarrassed when around any of these people because they know you are gay? If YES, describe: _____

_____

_____

- Do you have reason to believe that any of these people judge you unfavorably because you are gay? If YES, describe: _____

_____

_____

What percentage of your friends and regular acquaintances know you are gay? _____

If you have friends who do not know you are gay, describe why you have withheld this information from them: _____

_____

What percentage of your immediate co-workers/colleagues know you are gay? ———

What decision-making process do you go through before telling people you are gay?

_____

_____

_____

If applicable, why do you refrain from telling people in your life you are gay? What are your reasons for this?_____

_____

_____

_____

Do you ever feel embarrassed or vulnerable when you tell someone you are gay? If YES, describe:_____

_____

_____

Have you ever felt the need to apologize, justify, or explain in great detail to someone how or why you are gay? YES   NO

- If YES, why did you feel that an explanation was warranted? What feelings or beliefs on the part of the other were you trying to sway?_____

_____

_____

### Sexuality

At what age did you first have a same-sex sexual encounter? ———

- Describe the circumstances that preceded this encounter: _____

_____

_____

_____

• What feelings do you recall having had after this encounter?_____

_____

_____

_____

• What role did feelings of guilt or shame have in this encounter?

_____

_____

_____

Describe other sexual encounters you have had in your life when you felt guilty and/or ashamed during or after: _____

_____

_____

_____

_____

• Why do you believe that shame or guilt resulted for you from these encounters?_____

_____

_____

_____

_____

Describe your experiences with anonymous sex (sex in public places, bath houses, sex clubs, etc.):_____

_____

_____

_____

_____

• Why do you believe most of the men you have met in these places go there to have sex?_____

_____

_____

_____

- What is your motivation for going to these places? How does this compare with your answer to the previous question?

  _____

  _____

  _____

- How do you feel about yourself after having anonymous sex? _____

  _____

  Have you ever been arrested or threatened with arrest because of your sexual activity?   YES    NO

- If YES, describe: _____

  _____

  _____

- How did you feel about yourself after this encounter? _____

  _____

  _____

  In general, what is the role of guilt and shame in your views of your sexuality and sexual identity?_____

  _____

  _____

  _____

## *MALE ROLE MODELS*

List the male role models in your life. This includes those men, fictional or real, who had a very significant effect on your perception and identification with what it means to be a man.

1. _____
2. _____
3. _____
4. _____
5. _____

Circle the corresponding number if any of the above men were gay. Put a check mark at the end of each name if you feel the man listed is still a role model for you.

Who was the first man you knew who was gay? _____

In what way was this man a positive or negative role model for you? Cite examples. What other gay male role models have you had in your life? Describe how these men helped shape your self-identity and relationship to your sexuality. Do you see yourself as a role model to any gay men? Explain:

_____
_____
_____
_____
_____

## *YOUR REAL SELF VERSUS YOUR IDEAL SELF*

The ideal self is the person we would like to become. This does not include unattainable things such as being in a different body, being a different race, etc. Rather, it refers to those attributes we could potentially have, though most of us do not achieve these since we set our standards so high. The actual self is the person we really are. This includes our strengths and weaknesses, good points and bad, competencies and incompetencies. For better or worse, it is the self we see in the mirror and the self we present to the world.

List the main features that make up your real self.

1. _____

2. _____

3. _____

4. _____

5. _____

List the main features that make up your ideal self.

1. _____

2. _____

3. _____

4. _____

5. _____

What needs to happen in order for you to attain the attributes listed under ideal self? How realistic are these items? In what way does being gay help or hinder your achievement of the items listed under ideal self. Would the list be any different if you were not gay? Explain:

_____

_____

_____

_____

_____

# FEELINGS ASSOCIATED WITH COMING OUT

People report both positive and negative emotions associated with coming out to others as gay. For many, especially early in the coming out process, there is anticipation mixed with both fear and excitement. Sometimes people react favorably to us when we come out and sometimes they act in ways we did not expect. In this exercise you are asked to identify the feelings you have had at times of coming out, and to compare this list to the reactions you received from others.

## *Directions*

Identify an important person in your life to whom you came out. This could be a family member, friend, coworker, etc.
Write his or her name: _____
Relationship to you: _____
Age you came out to him/her: _____
Reason(s) or motive(s) for coming out to him/her: _____

_____

_____

_____

_____

Circle the feelings you had in anticipation of coming out to this person:

| | | | |
|---|---|---|---|
| FEAR | EXCITEMENT | GRIEF | SADNESS |
| ANGER | LOVE | HATRED | HOPE |
| NUMB | HAPPINESS | DREAD | AMBIGUITY |
| SICK | OVERWHELMED | ANTSY | SORROW |
| REGRET | RELIEF | WORRIED | IRRITABLE |
| ANXIOUS | WITHDRAWN | WORTHLESS | REBELLIOUS |
| GUILT | SHAME | INFERIOR | CHILDLIKE |
| WEAK | CONFIDENT | GRATEFUL | WHOLE |
| LIVELY | SCARED | GUTSY | HELPLESS |
| SECURE | DESPERATE | EMBARRASSED | FRANTIC |
| BOLD | POWERLESS | INDIFFERENT | AWKWARD |
| DEFIANT | ENERGIZED | _____ | _____ |

Circle those items that best describe how this person reacted to your disclosure:

| | | | |
|---|---|---|---|
| DISBELIEF | OVERWHELMED | SADNESS | ASSURED |
| FEAR | LOVE | HATRED | NUMB |
| DISGUST | ANGER | ILL | GRIEF |
| SHOCK | RELIEF | HOSTILE | DENIAL |
| AGGRESSIVE | GUILT | BLAMING | COLD |
| FOOLISH | FRIGHTENED | EMBARRASSED | HURT |
| ALARMED | FRUSTRATED | WALKED ON | EMPTY |
| DEFEATED | DISAPPOINTED | RELIEF | LEFT OUT |
| GRATEFUL | BEATEN | TRAPPED | AWKWARD |
| ABANDONED | LET DOWN | PAIN | CONCERNED |

How did your feelings and their reaction compare? Did their reaction surprise you?

_____

_____

_____

_____

How did your relationship to them change after your disclosure?

_____

_____

_____

_____

Review the different words you circled. Write about your feelings regarding some of these words. What memories do you have?

_____

_____

_____

_____

_____

# Chapter 3

# Addictive Behavior
# and Codependency in Gay Men

## *INTRODUCTION*

Do you ever find yourself wondering why you keep repeating the same behavior over and over? You may feel that you are committed to growth and change, but somehow it just seems that something is missing. You may even recognize that at times you experience sadness, depression, loss, fear, or emptiness. And sometimes it might feel that no one else has these feelings quite the way that you do. It may even be that these feelings are so overwhelming at times that you just do not want to *feel* anymore.

As gay men we are confronted with a whole range of feelings and emotions with which nongay people do not typically have to deal. Depending on our self-image, where we live, how *out* we are, etc., we may experience many of the following thoughts and feelings in a single day:

- I wonder if he is gay.
- I wonder if he/she thinks I am gay.
- I hope he/she does not think I am gay.
- If he/she finds out I am gay will they. . . .
- I wish I had a lover.
- My parents are coming to visit. What do I do about . . . ?
- Sometimes it would be easier to be straight.
- Do they think I have AIDS because I am gay?
- Do they trust me around their child?
- They probably think I am gay. Should I tell them?

- He/she is *so* homophobic.
- Maybe I should hide that book before the repairman gets here.
- No, I cannot wear *that* out in public.
- Try not to walk, sit, talk, or act that way.

The culmination of feelings that can result from constant evaluation of ourselves and of others can be enormously stressful. In turn, each of us finds our own way of coping with this stress.

A client of mine once described being gay as being in a constant state of readiness. He said he feels that he always has to be alert, on guard, and aware of his behaviors and of those around him. He said, "Sometimes I just wish there was a switch I could flick to shut it all off."

As gay men, we need to have such a "switch." Being gay in our society does require a different level of awareness and anticipation from what most nongay people experience. We know that this awareness is a skill we have, and we know that often our very survival requires the use of these skills. Being gay, we know that others perceive us in various ways. We have learned that by anticipating the words or others' perceptions of us we can avoid uncomfortable or difficult situations—if not outright prevent them.

It is no wonder, then, that many gay men feel like they are in a state of overload. Having to be alert to the thoughts and words of others takes a lot of physical and mental energy. Add to this the realities of AIDS, gay bashing, legislative attempts to deny us our rights, etc., and it is easy to see why many gay men opt to find ways of denying, neutralizing, or minimizing the feelings associated with being gay in our society.

To relieve these stresses, gay men are apt to use a variety of avenues. These are not unique to gay men, and not all gay men use them. However, my clients often seek tension reduction through the use of excessive alcohol, drugs, sex, work, or spending. Each of these behaviors can have a soothing and naturally beneficial effect in many of our lives. For some people, the over-reliance on these behaviors can have devastating effects that leave them feeling out of control of their lives. What this chapter addresses is the use of certain behaviors by gay men to ward off uncomfortable feelings.

I carry no value judgment regarding the use of these behaviors as a means of enjoyment, recreation, or release. However, as gay men, we are susceptible to relying on some or all of these behaviors to an extreme, and it is my hope that you will be able to identify the meaning these behaviors have in your own life by reading this chapter and doing some of the exercises at the end of the chapter.

## ADDICTIVE BEHAVIOR IN GAY MEN

There is no single reason why gay men have high rates of addictive behaviors. Rather, a myriad of social, cultural, environmental, and individual factors contribute to the problem. In general, however, homophobia ranks close to the top of the list.

### Homophobia

Homophobia, as a literal definition, refers to hatred of homosexuals or homosexuality. Homophobia is further broken down into two subcategories: *internalized homophobia* and *externalized homophobia*. Externalized homophobia is the term we use for others' negative perceptions of homosexuals. It is called external because it is *their* view of homosexuality. *Our* view of homosexuality may be the same or different from that of others.

Probably all or most gay men have to some extent what is termed internalized homophobia. This means that gay men are not exempt from taking in the negative messages about homosexuality that exist in our society. Thus, negative messages about homosexuality become internalized, or believed as fact. As I mentioned in previous chapters, one of the developmental tasks for gay men is to recognize that we are not as damaged as society would have us believe. Thus, we all need to reconcile our own view of ourselves and our sexuality with how others see us.

It is not uncommon for many gay men to wish, at some point in their life, that they were not gay. These feelings typically surface when gay men start to come out to themselves and others as gay. I have also seen these feelings manifest in friends and clients when they see straight couples with their children, when they attend heterosexual weddings, when they pay taxes as a single person, or at other times when they recognize the benefits afforded heterosexuals in our society. One client expressed to me his wish, after the end of a long relationship, that he were straight. He mistakenly believed that he would not have had the relationship struggles he did if he were not gay.

Most oppressed people wish, at some time, that they were not who they are. This is a natural part of the human experience. However, most people who are from different ethnic or cultural backgrounds have others like themselves to turn to for affirmation and support. Often this is provided by family. For gay men, however, by the time we find others like ourselves, we have recognized that many in society think of homosexuality and homosexuals as sinful, dirty, disgusting, immoral, and pathological (Figure 3.1). It is rare for a gay man not to be affected by some of these messages, and not feel on some level that maybe something about his gay identity is not *right*. How we clarify these messages, and particularly how we cope with the resultant feelings, is where the topic on addiction comes in.

### Are There Addictive Personalities?

There is no characteristic personality style that can be termed *the addictive personality*. Rather, there are common personality traits and symptoms that typically occur in addicted persons. This is why mental health workers rarely think of alcohol abusers and drug abusers as separate groups of people. Even though their drug of choice may differ, there are not necessarily other differences in their defense mechanisms or the reasons they use substances. In fact, most substance abusers do not rely primarily on one drug, but will use anything that changes their mood, thoughts, or pain.

An example of personality traits substance abusers share in common are:

- inability to experience the full range of feelings, and to anticipate when they are starting to feel poorly about themselves or their environment;
- low self-esteem and heightened feelings of vulnerability;

- excessive use of defense mechanisms that are used to protect themselves and blame others;
- fear of success or commitment;
- compulsive traits, whereby in addition to drugs or alcohol, the person is also addicted to food, sex, gambling, or other risky activities;
- impulsivity and an inability to tolerate frustration; and
- high need for immediate relief from physical and mental pain.

FIGURE 3.1. A look at the research: From where does internalized homophobia come?

Some gays and lesbians have lower rates of internalized homophobia than others. To find out why this might be true, psychologists Gary Hollander and Ariel Shidlo studied the perceptions gays and lesbians have about themselves (Sleek, 1996). They found three main variables that contribute to lower rates of internalized homophobia:

- People who are more open about their homosexuality with friends and acquaintances, particularly heterosexuals, have lower rates of internalized homophobia.
- People who have strong support both within and outside of the gay and lesbian communities have lower rates.
- Men who told their mothers about their sexual orientation have lower rates.

Curiously, men who said they never told their fathers about their sexual orientation showed no greater rate of internalized homophobia. The researchers suggest that this may reflect a self-protecting behavior. That is, if a gay man rationally concludes that he is better off keeping his sexual orientation from a homophobic person (such as his boss or father), his selective disclosure may not cause him psychological harm.

The researchers also offered that the internalized homophobia may be a developmental stage common to all or most gay men and lesbians. Since all gay men and lesbians are exposed to society's negative messages about homosexuality, it is a given that we will hear and be affected by some of these.

Discussing one's early experience with homophobic messages, and the ways in which each of us adapt to these, is a therapeutic challenge for all gay men.

## Substance Abusers and the Use of Denial

There are many defense and coping mechanisms that substance abusers use to avoid dealing with their reasons, motives, and feelings concerning using alcohol or drugs. We all use defense mechanisms to shield us from psychological pain or vulnerability and to help us maintain feelings of integrity and homeostasis. For the substance abuser, alcohol or drugs are often used as substitutes for defense mechanisms since most conflicts are, in essence, anesthetized from the person's awareness. When they do use defense mechanisms, substance abusers are most likely to use the defense of denial.

In order to continue using their drug of choice, substance abusers must continually deny any aspect of their environment that distorts the view they choose to have of their reliance on alcohol or drugs. Denial, in essence, helps the substance abuser distort reality. Therefore, substance abusers do not just lie about how much alcohol or drugs they consume, but they also deny the impact this has on family, friends, employment, and even themselves. They also deny how harmful their use of alcohol or drugs can be on relationships and their health. If the denial is challenged by someone, either a family member or psychotherapist, they get very angry.

The denial by substance abusers is often supported by loved ones, who either fear confronting the user or tire of not being heard or responded to. For some people, the substance-abusing personality of their loved one is the only one they know. Thus, they support the denial by avoiding any disruption to the balance of the relationship.

Part of the recovery process for substance abusers is learning how to confront their use of denial and learn how to use other, more adaptive defenses.

## Alcohol and Drug Use in the Gay Community

One of the mainstays of the gay community has been the gay bar. If you think of the Stonewall riots of 1969, it was the bar that was the centerpiece of the controversy. Bars have historically been one of the most frequently used avenues gay men have had for meeting other gay men. Most cities and towns throughout the world, if they have any services for gay men at all, will inevitably have at least one bar. Often this will be the only place exclusively for gay men to congregate in a particular locale.

Bars tend to be on the lower end of threatening places for many gay men to go to. Typically, you can stay as long as you desire, leave when you want to, and perhaps even meet someone. At the minimum, many gay men go to a bar with the idea of meeting someone to have sex with. And while you are there at the bar, there is an endless supply of alcohol for you to purchase and consume.

Alcohol is represented as a symbol of masculinity in our culture, as media images make this point clear. Media messages communicate to men that drinking alcohol increases our identification with other males, our companionship and closeness with other men, and feelings of comraderie.

Most studies estimate that there is a 28 to 35 percent incidence rate of alcohol abuse in the gay community (Beatty, 1983). Estimates for alcohol abuse in the general population is at about 10 percent. Of all minority-group alcohol-abuse estimates, gay men surpass every group except Native Americans (Trimble, 1993).

Similarly, use of other drugs aside from alcohol is quite prevalent in the gay community. Marijuana, cocaine, and amphetamines (speed) have always been popular drugs at parties and clubs, and their use continues at high rates. When the Centers for Disease Control started tracking risk groups for HIV infection in the mid-1980s it was surprising how many gay men indicated injection drug use as a risk factor in addition to their sexual behavior.

Research continues to support a genetic component for substance abuse. If you have a family history of alcohol or drug abuse, it is likely that you are at risk for abusing substances also. People from substance-abusing families should thus employ more awareness and caution in their use of alcohol, drugs, etc.

### From Casual Use to Addiction

For many of us, alcohol is the first drug we start using or experimenting with. Alcohol tends to be more readily available to adolescents, though increasingly we are seeing the use of other drugs such as marijuana, speed, cocaine, etc. As we enter adulthood, alcohol is also the most-sanctioned drug, that is, friends and others are less likely to pass judgment on us for using alcohol than for using other drugs. Since the gay bar is the institution on which many of us rely to meet other gay men, drinking alcohol in these settings is natural—even expected.

Sharon Wegscheider, in her book *Another Chance: Hope and Health for the Alcoholic Family,* points out that all drinking starts out as social drinking. Alcohol makes most of us more relaxed, and we learn through the use of alcohol that if we are feeling stressed, if we are nervous, or if we are uncomfortable, alcohol can calm some of these feelings. Since going to a gay bar or to a social gathering where you may not know many people can be stressful, most of us have learned that alcohol helps take the edge off.

Using alcohol around others who are also drinking helps us feel more accepted. Eventually, some of us come to rely on alcohol to alleviate our stress; thus, we use it whenever we are in, or whenever we anticipate, a stressful situation. My own view is that going to a gay setting, short of going with friends, is stressful for a lot of gay men, and we learn that having a drink helps calm us.

Prolonged use of alcohol, or any drug, eventually leads to abuse. In turn, abuse typically results in dependence. Indicators of dependence often include the following:

- Feeling that you cannot relax without the drug.
- Attending few or no social situations where the drug will not be available.
- Getting nervous or anxious when the drug runs out.
- Frequently thinking about the drug.
- Scheming and planning how to get the drug.
- Allowing the drug to become a major focus of your life.
- Feeling upset when those around you do not also want to drink or use drugs.

One of the key indicators of excessive use of alcohol or drugs is increased tolerance. This is where we require more and more of a drug to achieve the desired effects. For example, whereas one or two drinks used to leave us feeling relaxed and at ease, it may now take three to five drinks to feel this. Eventually, it takes more than five drinks. It is important to pay attention to whether we are drinking more, or to our friends if they tell us we are drinking more.

## The Consequences of Addiction

Prolonged use of alcohol or drugs eventually leads to blackouts, whereby the person experiences temporary amnesia, lasting minutes to hours. A client once told me that he walked out of a bar and forgot where he parked his car. He walked around the neighborhood for over two hours looking for his vehicle. What he failed to remember was that he took a cab to the bar that evening. This was the night he decided to stop drinking for good. Another client said that twice he ran into men he had previously had sex with during blackout periods. He would recognize them as looking familiar, but he never remembered having sex with them even after they reminded him of the encounter.

Most people who experience blackouts use excuses to account for things they cannot remember. As the drinking continues, it gets harder and harder to explain certain decisions and actions that seem inconsistent with whom the person is, or to find excuses for not following through on promises made.

Blackouts are just one of the many symptoms of being out of control that accompany alcoholism. Other examples include making decisions based on the availability of alcohol (i.e., "I do not want to go there. They never have any booze."), missing important appointments or obligations because of alcohol use, and continued use of alcohol despite numerous consequences.

It is the consequences from using alcohol or drugs that often lead to "bottoming out," or losing total control. This is why I often encourage others not to protect their loved ones from the consequences of using alcohol or drugs (i.e., calling the boss and making excuses for why the person who drinks is late). Only when someone has to face the realities of these consequences will they begin to fully recognize the effects of their drinking or drug use and eventually move toward sobriety. One former client of mine did not stop drinking until he had lost his job, his relationship, and most of his friends.

For most alcoholics, using alcohol provides them with a feeling of being in control. In reality, they are very much out of control. Unfortunately, the need for control does not go away after the alcoholic stops drinking. Thus, it is not uncommon for former alcoholics to try to find other ways of being in control. This can mean turning to other addictions (food, sex, gambling), trying to control others, or exercising excessive control over their environments (e.g., being overly neat and clean). Those alcoholics who rely upon the twelve-step recovery programs often find that these guidelines help them relinquish some of the need for control they feel.

In summary, a whole range of factors contribute to a high rate of alcohol use by gay men. Though not every gay man who drinks, nor every gay man who goes to a bar, is an alcoholic, we still need to be aware of our susceptibility to alcoholism. To this end, ask yourself if you come from a family where there was a lot of substance abuse. Use the genogram exercise in Chapter 1 to help you identify family patterns of alcohol or drug abuse. It is also helpful to honestly assess how much alcohol you consume, as well as to explore your motives for drinking. The exercises at the end of this chapter will help you answer these questions. You may find that alcohol is something that you enjoy, and that it does not cause problems or consequences in your life. Regardless, it is important for us all to identify the benefits and costs of using any substance that carries a high degree of risks.

## SEXUAL ADDICTION IN GAY MEN

When I was completing my master's degree in counseling, I did a paper on the incidence of alcohol use by gay men. At that time there was a wealth of published studies on the topic, and I had no difficulty finding material. What has been noteworthy as I review the current research for this book is the shift in the literature from examining alcohol addiction in gay men to examining the role of sex addiction.

Prior to AIDS, few health care professionals gave little thought to the idea of gay men having too much sex. Certainly there was concern about venereal disease, but most of these conditions responded fairly well to medication. With AIDS, however, not only have health care professionals focused more on the consequences of sex, but clients started presenting with a whole variety of mental health issues concerning the topic. What I began noticing, for example, were two major groups of men. One group was men who had a strong fear of sex, even within a committed relationship. The second group was men who recognized—or who I tried to help recognize—that they had no control over their sexual activity, which in many respects seemed to be running their lives. It was becoming very clear that sex, in the age of

AIDS, was gaining a variety of meanings that were not obvious only a few years before.

The fear of sex in some of my clients made sense. Though safe sex guidelines were published on posters, brochures, match-book covers, and through many other sources available to gay men, much controversy still existed regarding what behaviors constituted HIV transmission risk. Many gay men, increasingly seeing their friends become ill and die, had developed what appeared to be a natural fear related to sex. Some felt that gay sex was synonymous with death, and anti-homosexual forces capitalized on this to make some men afraid to even kiss another man.

The high rate of sexual activity some men engaged in, however, seemed almost contrary to what one would expect. Many clinicians, for example, would find themselves questioning how some gay male clients could have frequent sexual encounters with different partners while not using any precautions against HIV infection. Sometimes these clients would report having sex with more than three different men in a single day, canceling obligations or appointments in order to have sex, thinking constantly about ways of finding someone to have sex with, and being so grateful for having a sexual partner that concerns about safe sex practices went out the window.

It is to these types of behaviors and thoughts I refer to when I speak of sexual addiction. Sexual addiction is not about enjoying sex, wanting to have sex more frequently than others, or even having a very active sex life. Rather, in line with what I have been saying about other addictions, the core indicator of a sexual addiction is the feeling of being out of control with regard to sexual activity or fantasy.

All addictions are attempts to control pleasure and pain by inducing experiences that reduce tension and anxiety we feel due to boredom, stress, loneliness, grief, or fear. Sexually dependent persons often speak of sex as providing an outlet for aggression, a way of obtaining closeness to others, and a way of discharging energy associated with anger, anxiety, or grief. For those gay men who are dependent upon sex, they speak of sexual contact providing them with an identity for themselves, an identity that takes on more significance in this age in which popular stereotypes would have us believe that sex equals death.

The dynamics of sexual addiction is something that therapists have started to understand only recently. Similar to how AIDS grief overwhelmed our previous notions of loss, mourning, and survival, sex addiction is a phenomenon that is highly complex and not as uncommon as one might think. This section reviews a small part of what is known about sexual addiction, and I will draw from my clinical experience working with gay men who felt sexually compulsive. I encourage you to read this section and do the exercises. If you feel as though you have further concerns about your own sexual behavior then you might want to consider the recommendations offered.

### Gay Men and Sex

Sex for gay men has often been equated with a feeling of freedom and independence. For many gay men, sex with another man is often seen as the sole expression of being gay. Historically, it has not been uncommon—and there are still men who behave this way today—for men who have sex with other men to have two lives. One is the life that looks fairly ordinary to the outside observer; that is, no one would be able to look at this person and suspect anything *gay* about him. The other life involves the man going out looking for gay sex. This type of person probably does not identify as gay, may not have any gay friends, and does not desire a lasting relationship with another man. He just wants sex with men.

Even in the age of sexual liberation, many men identified as gay, but to them the only factor making them gay was their having sex with another man. Fortunately, it is easier—though by no means without its difficulties—for men to identify as gay, independent of their sexual activity. I remember a talk show once where there were priests who identified as gay, but for the most part led celibate lives. The audience could not comprehend how you can be gay if you do not have sex with another man (though clearly they felt it possible to be heterosexual and celibate).

Gay men eventually found and developed various avenues for having sex with other men. Whether they lived in large cities or in smaller communities, men found ways of having sex with other men. The discovery of AIDS provided insight into just how much sex men were having, and with how many partners. To the outsider these statistics seemed overwhelming, and were often used against us primarily by the Religious Right. For many of us, however, frequent sex and various partners just seemed a part of being gay (Figure 3.2).

Sex does have an affirming quality to it, and rare is the person who has not used sex, including masturbation, as an avenue for tension reduction. But most people are able to go about their daily lives attending to their duties and responsibilities without being consumed with thoughts and fantasies about sex.

FIGURE 3.2. A Look at the research: Gay men and public sex.

Richard Tewksbury (1995) conducted eleven in-depth interviews with men who have cruised for male sexual partners in public parks. The average age of the men was thirty-one years, with an age range from twenty-one to fifty. Ten of the men self-identified as gay, and one as bisexual. The men lived in one of three midwestern states. Tewksbury sought to discover men's reasons for having public sex, and to determine if, as Pollak (1993) suggests, cruising is a ritual of belonging for gay men.

According to the men interviewed, four main reasons draw them to public sex:

- Simply a way to find sexual partners
- Because of the challenges presented
- Because the setting is attractive in and of itself
- To find a life mate

The men indicated that public sex does offer a form of sexual release, but many said that the sex is not necessarily good. Regarding risks, most of the men interviewed said they have come to expect potentially violent encounters. Most, however, reported being more concerned about the potential of arrest rather than of gay bashing. Even when incidents of gay bashing at public parks was publicized, this did not curtail the use of the park by these men for sexual encounters. Acknowledging a thrill-seeking component to cruising, some of the men said that avoiding the possibility of arrest is a risk to be managed and overcome. Further, being discovered, either by police or park users, added to the men's sense of adventure and challenge in cruising.

The men interviewed realize that many of the men who cruise for sex in parks are either closeted gay men or heterosexual men—many of whom are married. Though some feel it an insult that these men do not formally come out, it still does not deter the men from having sex with them.

Tewksbury found that cruising becomes a game with two simultaneous objectives: one is conquest; the other is survival. For most of these men, there is satisfaction in seducing and being seduced by another man in a public setting, even though the result is, as one study participant termed it, "fast-food sex." The ultimate goal of public sex is to find an outlet for sexual expression, but the secondary gain appears to be the rewards of pursuit, danger, and the thrill of feeling that you have gotten away with something.

### Sex for the Addict

For sex addicts, however, sex becomes a major focus of their lives, and an enormous amount of energy goes into thinking about and seeking sexual contact. Such persons may spend hours hanging out in places where sex occurs or where they can meet someone for sex (e.g., parks, bathrooms, bookstores, bars). They may place advertisements for sex in various newspapers, and may not be able to be away from the phone because of their need for a potential partner to call. Finding sex thus becomes more than a desire. It becomes an obsession. And when such people cannot find sex, they may end up feeling angry, depressed, desperate, and incredibly anxious.

These feelings and behaviors are not unique to gay men, as both gay and nongay, male or female people are consumed by such obsessions—nor do they only manifest as sex. Some people have the same obsessions regarding relationships or masturbation. Some have them about love.

Clinical experience (Baum and Fishman, 1994) suggests that those persons with sexual addictions often come from backgrounds in which there were sexual secrets in their past (perhaps early sexual abuse), inappropriate closeness or distance by parents, early abandonment by parental figures, and inappropriate boundaries. By boundaries, I mean inappropriate intrusions by others into your personal space. This can be actions such as touching you, opening your bedroom or bathroom door, going through your drawers or personal belongings, reading your journal, crawling into bed with you—all without asking your permission.

Often the boundary violations or secrets are sexual in nature. Some clients report having felt seduced by their mothers, even though no sexual contact occurred. Others report that their family had a very sexualized feeling to it during their childhood. Typically, there is sexual abuse or inappropriate sex play between the child and some trusted other (usually an adult).

### Characteristics of Sex Addicts

San Francisco psychotherapists Michael Baum and Jim Fishman (1994) reported the role aggression plays in the lives of the sexually addicted. They observed that men who were victimized as children (and thus powerless and helpless) often engage in sexual relation-ships where they re-enact the aggression and victimization they experienced in childhood. This may entail having sex with minors, having unsafe sex, or purposely putting another at risk for disease.

In contrast, they found that some sexually compulsive gay men portray a picture of financial, social, and relational success to oth-ers. These men appear to have few needs of their own, and are quick to provide help and nurturance to others. They appear as "the model boyfriend, the model employee, or the model group member" (p. 267). What is unexpressed is personal needs. In essence, they feel invisible. These men typically had backgrounds that included abandonment, neglect, and exploitation. In their sexual relations, this type of man exploits others by withholding or controlling sex in a highly aggressive manner. Sex for him often presents as a sadistic expression of his aggression, for it is only during sex that he feels capable of expressing frustration and aggression.

Some sex addicts say their addiction helps them feel like some-one else. Often, I am told that it is how they feel competent, loving, attractive, or in control. One gay client of mine assumed an entirely different identity when he was in his sex-addict mode. An openly gay man, he would present himself to potential partners—most of whom were married or otherwise "straight" men—as a man who just broke up with his girlfriend. He removed anything from view in his apartment that could identify him as gay. This made the men who called him feel less threatened by him (because he is not "gay") and more likely to come over for sex.

Shame is intricately linked to the behaviors of the sex addict. Like most other addicts, decisions are often made with obtaining sex as the most important goal. Thus, they lie to friends, break engagements, and violate their core principles. Episodes of depres-sion and feelings of worthlessness are common. Yet, instead of interpreting these feelings as signs that something is wrong, the sex addict will typically seek more sex to help him feel better.

Many sex addicts admit to an increase in their sexual obsessions and behaviors when they feel stress. A run-in with the boss, a fight with a friend, or another driver cutting in front of them can elicit tremendous anger and anxiety, which they feel can only be released sexually. Stressful events, in essence, cause them to obsessively seek sex as a drug. In this state, they may avoid tending to any other obligation or responsibility until they have sex.

Why this is of particular concern for gay men is that many of us have been feeling overwhelmed because of AIDS for quite some time. Multiple losses, no cure in sight, modification to our sexual behavior, and the myriad of politics concerning AIDS all serve to make many of us feel overloaded. If sex is the only way we obtain temporary relief from these stresses, then it is easy to see how our view of sex and its meanings get clouded and obscured.

Unfortunately, the stakes are much higher now and failure to exercise more caution and awareness in our sexual lives can put us and others at risk for illness and death. Now more than ever we need to stay conscious of our sexual lives and the activities in which we engage and participate.

As you examine what role sex plays in your own life, ask yourself how much control you feel over your own sexual behavior. Does it ever seem that the opportunity to have sex clouds your judgment regarding practicing safe sex. Ultimately, the question to ask yourself is whether you feel in control of your sexuality or does it feel that your sexuality controls you?

## CODEPENDENT BEHAVIOR IN GAY MEN

- As much as I have tried, he still will not stop drinking.
- I focus more attention on him than on myself.
- I cannot stop thinking about him.
- I could do better if I tried harder.
- Sometimes I am not sure what I feel.
- If they think that about me, it must be true.
- I do not want there to be any arguing between us.
- If I tell him what I think, he will never speak to me again.
- If I do not do what he wants, he will just get mad.
- I cannot see you anymore because he does not like it.
- I try to confront him but I end up being the bad guy.
- What I do controls how he feels.
- I can do it better than others.
- Someday I would like to do what I want to do.

• If he would go to counseling, things would be better between us.
• I cannot lose control.

These are all variations on themes I have heard from clients. As you read the list, you may be struck by one or two statements, perhaps recognizing yourself or someone you know. What you will also recognize in the words is how little control the people who said them feel over their own lives. These patterns of thoughts often contribute to what is called codependency.

Codependents are people who grew up believing that their actions and words had tremendous influence over others' behavior. The thinking process of the child who grows to be codependent is as follows: "I will receive Mom or Dad's love or approval if I . . . " or "If I do/do not. . . . then. . . . " These children were keenly aware of how subtle moves on their parts could have lasting implications. The *wrong* statement could elicit Dad's fury. Doing the *wrong* thing could mean Mom or Dad might disapprove and withhold love. *Careless* statements or actions resulted in ridicule, shame, embarrassment, or the threat of abandonment.

The reality of the situation is that often the person was right. Families from which codependents come are often chaotic, dysfunctional, abusive, and frequently those in which one or both parents are addicted to alcohol or drugs. The conflicts that are frequent in such families are rarely resolved, and the tension in these families feels continuous. The balance for calm and sanity in these families is delicate, and the future codependent learns that the smallest of errors or the slightest expression of true feelings can have devastating consequences.

In adulthood, codependents have these same feelings. They are keenly aware of the feelings of others, careful not to elicit ridicule or rejection, and willing to sacrifice their own needs and desires for those of others. Typically, the main person they defer to is their primary partner. They defer to this person out of fear that to stand up to him or her will result in rejection, and rejection is the one thing the codependent cannot tolerate.

## *Are Gay Men More Likely to Be Codependent?*

Gay men are particularly susceptible to the dynamics of codependency. As you recall from my earlier discussion, it is a survival mechanism for gay men to be aware of the thoughts, actions, and motives of others. Gay men continually survey a particular person or circumstance to determine whether the threat of violence or rejection, or conversely, the potential for companionship and acceptance exists. Many gay men grow up expecting rejection for who they are; in turn, they can feel that they owe something to those who accept them.

As discussed in Chapter 2, it is common for gay men to grow up feeling little self-confidence. Gay men may take pride in certain accomplishments or skills, but on some level, many gay men feel that they are not as good as others or worthy of respect from others. Thus, in relationships it becomes difficult to assert our needs, ask for what we want, and tell another person that a certain statement or action does not feel very good. When we do not have the confidence to stand up for ourselves, it becomes easier for another person to take advantage of us.

Codependents typically feel guilt and shame related to their past. If they did not receive outright rejection and abandonment, many may have been given the message—explicitly or implicitly—that their parents would have been better off without them. These children grew up feeling that they were in the way. They interpreted the abuse, the favoritism for another sibling, and the hurtful words as indicators that they were not wanted. In turn, they grew up believing that if they were only smarter, quieter, cleaner, or more athletic, then they would gain their rightful place in the family.

Again, I see these parallels in the experience of growing up in a family knowing that you are *different*. I suspect that as many of us recognize aspects of our differences we later identify as gay, we come to know that people can be outcast for being different. Many gay men have felt rejection from their families for being different. One client of mine spoke of how, in the eyes of his parents, he was the effeminate one in the family, and thus seen as inferior. Another spoke of how his brother received all the praise from his parents—particularly his father—for being good at sports and scouting.

Another spoke of the physical abuse he experienced from his father because he was not, as his father said, "man enough to fight back."

## The Consequences of Codependency

When we grow up feeling that we can influence people by behaving as others desire, we learn that it is not OK to be us. Thus, it becomes difficult to be spontaneous and to show our true selves to the world. Instead, we withhold. We are constantly monitoring situations to see what actions or words are *required* in a particular situation. Eventually we adhere to rules and rituals that dictate how things *should* be. We make lists, take on rigid habits, and arrange things so that everything looks and turns out right. We expect perfection in ourselves and we hope for it from others. For if things appear perfect, we feel there will be little disruption and chaos in our lives.

To feel that we can influence and control the welfare of others also leaves us with an incredible sense of power. Someone who feels fragile and vulnerable will try to hold onto whatever control he feels he has. This again becomes a reason why gay men are susceptible to codependent behavior. If believing that we can influence others is what little control we feel, it makes sense that we will cherish this and use it as a survival mechanism. Unfortunately, some people take this to extreme and exert an incredible amount of control over the people in their lives. To be in this kind of person's life means to submit to his domination, for he cannot tolerate relationships in which he is not in control.

When we are constantly assessing the needs and feelings of others, we start to lose sight of where they end and we begin. In turn, boundaries get fuzzy, and it is difficult to know what we need. So much effort goes into anticipating the feelings of the other person that eventually we forget how we feel.

## Losing the Capacity to Feel

One of the first challenges for me when working with a new client who presents with features of codependency is helping them learn how to feel. Many people can only identify their feelings when they are present in an extreme state: rage, elation, despair. But it is difficult for the codependent person to be aware of any feelings on a moment-by-moment basis. This is partially because their awareness of feelings has become numbed. Thus, they will talk to me about past abuses, recent losses, and broken relationships with the casual style one usually speaks of weekend plans. When I ask, "Where is your anger?" they stare at me with blank faces. Anger is an emotion codependents cannot readily access.

Being out of touch with feelings allows some people to feel that they are engaged with life when in actuality they are emotionally numb. For some people this is highly preferable; their past experiences were so overwhelming that they feel that they cannot afford to be in touch with emotions. The numbness covers up the feelings associated with hurt, rejection, abandonment, and being treated badly for being different from others.

Children make use of fantasy in play and in imagination. Fantasy is natural for all of us, but it plays a particularly crucial part in the lives of children who feel trapped in their current environments. It is also highly common in the lives of codependents. Studies done with children who grew up in abusive or addictive families show that fantasy was the one avenue for escape these children felt they had. I have found that the use of fantasy in childhood by many of my clients was also the means they used for coping with feelings associated with feeling different from others.

Though I do not advocate that anyone stop using fantasy, it is important to note the role fantasy can have in keeping us out of touch with our feelings. If every time we feel anxiety, stress, or depression we turn to fantasy, then we are not allowing ourselves to experience the feelings that these emotions are trying to elicit in us. Sometimes it is necessary to stop fantasizing about how a situation might look different *if only,* and instead look at more realistic options for dealing with it.

## Assessing Codependency in Your Life

The following exercise will help you assess features of codependency in your own life. Circle the response that best describes your thoughts and behaviors in most situations.

0 = Never      1 = Sometimes      2 = Often      3 = Always

1.  I feel responsible for meeting other peoples' needs.     0 1 2 3
2.  I base my own view of myself on what others
    think and say.     0 1 2 3
3.  I blame myself when things go wrong in my
    relationship(s).     0 1 2 3
4.  I work hard at getting others to do things my way.     0 1 2 3
5.  I hide my feelings from those people closest to me.     0 1 2 3
6.  I feel that my self-esteem is low.     0 1 2 3
7.  I change who I am to please others.     0 1 2 3
8.  I often pretend things are fine when in reality
    they are not.     0 1 2 3
9.  I need a high degree of control.     0 1 2 3
10. Most people do not realize how easily they can
    hurt me.     0 1 2 3
11. I compromise my values and standards.     0 1 2 3
12. I am in (or I have been in) a relationship longer
    than I think I should be.     0 1 2 3
13. I have trouble with intimacy.     0 1 2 3
14. I never get what I need in relationships.     0 1 2 3
15. I do not express my feelings in my relationship(s)
    because to do so would cause conflict.     0 1 2 3
16. I let others make decisions about how we will
    spend our time.     0 1 2 3
17. I keep (or have kept) secrets from my partner.     0 1 2 3
18. I approach important topics in my relationship(s)
    indirectly.     0 1 2 3
19. If someone hurts me, I find ways of getting even.     0 1 2 3
20. I have done things my partner wanted me to
    do even though I really did not want to.     0 1 2 3
21. I feel out of control of my life.     0 1 2 3
22. I have made excuses for loved ones to prevent
    them from getting in trouble.     0 1 2 3
23. I end up looking foolish after arguments with
    important people in my life.     0 1 2 3

There is no standard checklist for diagnosing codependency. Codependency can present in a variety of ways, though the main feature is changing who you are in order to please others. Thus, there is no scoring system for the above checklist. Instead, it is important to examine how you answered the questions. If you circled more twos and threes, it is likely that you sacrifice some aspects of your individuality in order to please others or prevent conflict.

You will notice that some of the questions assess your actions specifically with regard to your primary relationship. Some people are better at setting limits with and expressing their true selves to friends than they are with their lover. If this is true of you, then it might be helpful to examine why it is difficult for you to get your needs met in your relationship. Perhaps you feel more vulnerable in your relationship than you do with friends. Maybe you feel that a bad relationship is better than no relationship at all. Sometimes people feel trapped in a relationship, feeling that there are no options for fixing things nor for getting out. These are all areas that affect the quality of your life. You do not have to sacrifice your true self for anyone.

## RECOVERY FROM ADDICTIONS

The primary goal in recovery is to avoid using substances, sex, or other behaviors for the purpose of avoiding feelings. Recovery involves a commitment to the process, and frankly it is very difficult to achieve recovery without a lot of support, guidance, and education. Even when I work together with clients toward their recovery, I cannot provide all that they need. Rather, we rely upon their use of groups, reading materials, and a support network to assist the two of us in helping the person achieve his goals.

People find their way to recovery in a variety of ways. Often an addict will experience so many consequences because of his behaviors that he literally has no choice but to surrender his addiction. Not doing so may result in the loss of a relationship, the loss of a job, or even the potential for death. Others come to realize that they are powerless over their use of substances or behaviors and subsequently seek help out of desperation or helplessness.

Recovering from an addiction requires a commitment to change, as well as being receptive to new feelings and experiences. Recovery is seldom linear in nature, and often there will be a return to old habits, patterns, and behaviors. Yet, most people who have traveled the road of recovery report great relief at having done so, and many acknowledge their belief that only in recovery can they truly enjoy and experience all that life has to offer.

Recovery does not mean being free from having to face the difficult realities of homophobia, AIDS, being gay, and all other challenges in life. It does mean feeling better able to weather these

FIGURE 3.3. A look at the research: Gay men and eating disorders.

It has been suggested that the gay male subculture imposes expectations of physical attractiveness on gay men similar to that placed on women by the larger society. One common factor between the two groups is the desire of both to attract and please men. Just as the pressure to look youthful and attractive places women at high risk for eating disorders, the same may be true for gay men. To investigate this hypothesis, psychologist, Michael Siever (1996) surveyed 250 college students, fifty-nine of whom were gay, on their attitudes and behaviors regarding body satisfaction and the importance of physical attractiveness.

The differences among the groups were highly significant and confirmed the research hypothesis. This study showed that gay men are not only more dissatisfied with their bodies than heterosexual men, but they may be even *more* unhappy with their bodies than heterosexual women. Siever suggests two possibilities for this:

1. Like heterosexual men, gay men may worry that their bodies are inadequate in terms of strength and athletic prowess.
2. Like heterosexual women, they may doubt their physical attractiveness.

The gay men in this study consistently scored high on measures of attitudes and behaviors associated with eating disorders, perhaps indicating that gay men are at risk for bulimia and anorexia nervosa.

Thus, it is important for gay men to pay attention to risk factors such as the following:

- Excessive amounts of exercise and working out
- Focusing too much on caloric intake
- Inducing vomiting after meals
- Dwelling excessively on body image
- Striving for a body ideal that may not realistically be attained

events, and to realize that a fully lived life requires experiencing all the highs and lows involved with being human.

Being reliant upon certain substances, actions, or behaviors can be a very isolating experience. People often play out their addictions in secret, and rarely does the addicted person feel truly connected with others in an intimate way. Often the people in the addict's life are there as means to sustain his addiction. That is, he spends time with others who can secure drugs for him, have sex with him, take care of his needs while he uses, etc. Thus, relationships with addicted persons are often exploitative in nature. When the addict recovers, he may find that others have no use for him if he is not addicted, and he does not need others in the way he previously required. Recovery can therefore be a very isolating experience. This is why I offer that few addicts can initiate and progress along the path of recovery without support and guidance.

My review of the recovery process is intended to only be an overview. The steps and dynamics of recovery are very complex, and you may want to read more books that focus solely upon recovery from addiction. What I hope to impart here is an understanding of some of the resources and techniques I use with clients. Those of you who would like to go further in the recovery process are encouraged to do the exercises at the end of this chapter, and to work closely with a helping professional.

## PSYCHOTHERAPY

Before you can examine why it is you are addicted to substances—food, sex, gambling, or whatever other venue—you must undergo the process of having many of your beliefs about these areas identified, and at times challenged. Beliefs of the addict often include the following:

- I cannot function without alcohol, marijuana, food, lots of sex, cigarettes.
- This is how I cope with stress.
- I cannot get angry, so instead I use, eat, have sex, smoke, etc.
- There are worse things I could do to my body.
- All my friends do it, so why not me.

- It does not really cause *that* many problems for me.
- It is how I express who I am.
- It is not like I do it all the time.
- If I did not do it, who would I be?


In psychological terms, these patterns of belief are referred to as faulty thinking. Addicts develop ways of thinking about their use that minimizes any distress, guilt, or conflict they might otherwise have about what or how much they use or do that is addictive. Most addicts recognize on some level that they are out of control of their use of a drug or behaviors, and subsequently develop ways of thinking about their use that leave them believing that they have more control than is actually true.

One of the benefits of having a psychotherapist during early recovery is that he or she can gently confront and challenge this faulty thinking. Whereas friends and family members will often go along with the addict's faulty thinking, a therapist will challenge the person on some of their beliefs, albeit in a supportive way. For example:

Client:     I only drink when I am mad at my partner.

Therapist:     You tell me that you have a drink almost every night after work. Do you find yourself mad at your partner every day?

Client:     Well, no. But sometimes he really makes me mad.

Therapist:     It sounds like you drink on days that you are not mad at him, though.

Client:     Yeah, sometimes. But I do not drink that often.

Therapist:     Again, you told me you have at least one drink a day.

Client:     Yeah, but only when I am really feeling stressed about something.

Therapist:     So you are stressed out almost every day?

Client:     Maybe a few times a week.

Therapist:     Yet you still have at least one drink a day, even if you are not mad at your partner or feeling stressed out?

Client:     Yeah, I guess.

Therapist:     It sounds to me like you are trying to make excuses for why you have something to drink every day. It is almost like you are trying to justify to me that it is okay to drink every day.

Faulty thinking also goes hand-in-hand with denial. Denial is simply choosing, consciously or unconsciously, to believe something is not true. When you come out to a family member as gay and they refuse to believe it, this is denial. When a friend of yours is in a damaging relationship and refuses to hear your perceptions about it, this is denial. Denial is what keeps us feeling secure in the face of threat. For the addict, giving up his attachment to his addiction is highly threatening, and so he uses denial to try to convince himself that his behaviors are not as self-destructive as they might truly be. Psychotherapists are trained in ways to help someone break through their denial.

A psychotherapist cannot solve all of the addict's problems, nor can he or she make the addict stop using. By building a trusting relationship, however, the psychotherapist can offer support and guidance, provide appropriate challenges and incentives, and be there for the person during the struggles involved with recovery.

## TWELVE-STEP GROUPS

Twelve-step programs are groups that offer both support and a philosophy. Whereas most support groups are led by a professional facilitator, twelve-step groups are led by peers. Though some people consistently attend a particular twelve-step group or set of groups, there is no membership. The group consists of whoever shows on that particular day or evening. Though there are more and more twelve-step groups comprised exclusively of gays and lesbians, most groups are open to all members of the community.

Popular examples of twelve-step groups that apply to the topics covered in this chapter include Alcoholics Anonymous, Narcotics Anonymous, Sex and Love Addicts Anonymous, Codependents Anonymous, Gamblers Anonymous, Overeaters Anonymous, and Al-Anon. You will notice that most contain the word "anonymous." This reflects the emphasis placed in these groups on your anonymity, to whatever extent you desire. Though the use of first names is often encouraged, you are under no obligation to disclose any more about your life than you feel comfortable doing. In fact, you do not even have to speak. This is not to say that friendships and after-meeting dinners do not occur in these groups. The emphasis, however, is on bringing a group of people with similar patterns of behavior together to share whatever it is they need to at a particular meeting.

Twelve-step meetings vary in size. It depends on how many similar meetings are being held in the community, and how specific the group's structure is. Some groups are just for men, women, gay men, lesbians, or people who have been in recovery for a certain period of time. Most, however, are open to anyone who wants to attend. Meetings might begin with a few announcements, and maybe a special talk by one of the members, but usually members are offered the chance to speak for about of two to three minutes.

The idea behind the twelve-step meeting is that by listening to others share their stories and experiences you will recognize that you are not alone in your own struggles with addictive behavior. Though every story is unique, it is likely that you will hear themes reflected in the lives of others that closely approximate your own. Inevitably, you will also hear from those with situations and challenges much worse than your own, and you will hopefully realize that if they can venture into recovery in light of their circumstances, so can you.

An example of what you will hear at twelve-step meetings include the following:

> Hi, my name is Tim. I stopped drinking six months ago. But last week my ex-lover phoned. He just wanted to say hello. Though I did okay during the phone call, I immediately wanted a drink afterward. I called my friend, Lisa, though, and it helped. I am here tonight just to be with others who are also trying to stay sober.

> Hi, my name is Richard. I have been feeling out of control of my sex life. My therapist suggested that I come here tonight. Being gay, I have sex with men. I spend hours each day trying to get sex. I will hang out at a local bookstore, I have a sex ad running in a local newspaper, and I have some guys who contact me regularly for sex. Yesterday I missed an important business meeting because some guy called wanting to have

sex. In the past I have stood up friends, not shown [up for] appointments, and done some pretty awful things just to have sex. I wanted this one guy so bad I let him have unsafe sex with me. So I am just here to see what this meeting is all about.

Unlike with therapy groups, there are very few rules that apply to twelve-step groups. The most common rule in twelve-step groups is that you do not engage in cross-talk. This means that if someone else is speaking you do not interrupt, ask questions, or interfere with what they are saying in any way. This helps the person who is speaking feel safe to say whatever it is he needs to without concern about being challenged or having to offer more than he feels like sharing on that day.

## TWELVE-STEP SPONSORS

Most twelve-step groups offer the opportunity to have a sponsor. A sponsor is another group member who will mentor you through your own recovery process. Persons eligible to be sponsors have typically been in recovery for a year or longer. They are generally available to talk with you over coffee, speak with you on the phone, or be there for you during particularly troublesome periods. Having gone through the process of recovery themselves, they know the challenges and pitfalls. Some will even give you homework exercises to do.

The sponsor is an unpaid group member, and he may be a sponsor to more than one person. Having a sponsor helps you feel less alone as you begin recovery, and it provides you with a different level of support than can be offered by a psychotherapist. You can ask at the meetings about obtaining a sponsor for yourself.

## THE TWELVE STEPS

Most twelve-step programs are guided by what are called the Twelve Steps. These were developed out of Alcoholics Anonymous, but are applicable to all addictions. Some programs replace the word "God" with "Higher Power" in order to minimize the reaction some people have to religious overtones.

The twelve steps are a tool you use in recovery to acknowledge that there are some behaviors over which you have little or no control. This may be use of alcohol or drugs, your sexual behavior, compulsions, attachments you form to others, excessive behaviors, etc. Since most people who recognize being out of control often identify themselves as feeling "crazy" regarding their addiction(s), the twelve-steps speak in terms of believing that a higher power can restore "sanity."

By applying the twelve steps to your own life you are accepting a principle, in part or full, that in your addiction you have at times jeopardized or compromised the well-being of yourself or someone close to you. This may mean saying hurtful things to others, acting irresponsible because of your addictive behaviors, using others for personal gain (financial, sexual, etc.), putting others in harm's way, etc. The twelve steps encourage that you examine these actions on your part, and where appropriate, attempt to make amends to yourself and others.

The twelve steps acknowledge that surrendering our reliance on addictive behaviors is difficult and challenging, and that we need reminding that at times we require the comfort and guidance that can come from prayer or meditation.

1. We admitted we were powerless over addiction—that our lives had become unmanageable.
2. We came to believe that a Power greater than ourselves could restore us to sanity.
3. We made a decision to turn our will and our lives over to the care of God *as we understood Him.*
4. We made a searching and fearless moral inventory of ourselves.
5. We admitted to God, ourselves, and to another human being the exact nature of our wrongs.
6. We were entirely ready to have God remove all these defects of character.
7. We humbly asked Him to remove our shortcomings.

8. We made a list of all persons we had harmed, and became willing to make amends to them all.
9. We made direct amends to such people wherever possible, except when to do so would injure them or others.
10. We continued to take personal inventory and when we were wrong, promptly admitted it.
11. We sought through prayer and meditation to improve our conscious contact with God as *we understood Him*, praying only for knowledge of His will for us and the power to carry that out.
12. Having had a spiritual awakening as the result of these steps, we tried to carry this message to addicts and to practice these principles in all our affairs.

## TWELVE-STEP GROUPS AND GAY MEN

One of the realities of twelve-step groups is that they reflect the composition of the community in which they are. Thus, if the community as a whole tends to be homophobic, these attitudes may very well be reflected in the twelve-step meetings. You do not have to tell anyone that you are gay at these meetings, but to withhold this information may limit the group's effectiveness for you. Imagine having a sex addiction but not being able to tell the group that it is with men that you are engaging with sexually. It also compounds for you one of the key principles of twelve-step program, which is that you are "only as sick as your secrets."

One tenet of many recovery programs is that you limit your social contact with people who engage in the same addictive behaviors as you. The idea behind this is that you are more likely to act on your addiction if you are with friends who do the same. Some addicts speak of having drug or drinking buddies, but they will also have friends who do not use. Gay men, on the other hand, may have more limited social networks. That is, we may choose to be around those who are also gay or who accept us for being gay. If we end these relationships for the sake of recovery, we may find ourselves feeling little support since we have stopped socializing with those we feel comfortable being ourselves around. Gay men who frequent bars for social contact may also find the prospect of limiting this activity threatening.

Gay men who are HIV positive might also find it uncomfortable sharing this information at a twelve-step program for fear of peoples' reactions. Thus, they can sometimes feel that it is easier not to go to a twelve-step group than to assess the responses of the group to this information.

Some gay men report that it is difficult for them asking someone to be a sponsor. The person may not be gay themselves, and some gay men fear rejection if the sponsor finds out they are gay. Other gay men—and this is particularly noteworthy in sex addiction groups—report feeling sexually attracted to their sponsor. For them, they have to question whether their motive is supportive or sexual in nature, and they must also ascertain whether or not to share their sexual attraction with the sponsor.

The ultimate solution to this is to find twelve-step groups that are gay or gay-friendly. If you live in a large city, chances are good that there will be at least one gay twelve-step group. You can also phone the local Alcoholics Anonymous hotline since they keep lists of all twelve-step groups in the area. You can ask the operator if he or she knows of any gay or gay-friendly groups. Phoning a local gay-identified psychotherapist might also help you find this information.

## *BOOKS ON RECOVERY*

If this chapter has enticed you to learn more about addictions and recovery, you may want to read other books that examine these issues in more depth. Just as this is a workbook that can be used in conjunction with psychotherapy, there are many books on recovery that can be used in the same way. Most bookstores have sections for books on addictions and recovery. If they do not, look in the psychology section.

# Exercises

## *ASSESSING YOUR COPING STYLE*

List three to five events or circumstances in your life that felt overwhelming to you. For each, circle the coping mechanism(s) you used during that time:

1. Event or Circumstance: _____

   _____

   Coping Strategies:   • Talking with friends • Psychotherapy
   • Support group • Drinking more frequently
   • Drug use • Avoided thinking or talking about it

2. Event or Circumstance: _____

   _____

   • Talking with friends • Psychotherapy
   • Support group • Drinking more frequently
   • Drug use • Avoided thinking or talking about it

3. Event or Circumstance: _____

   _____

   • Talking with friend • Psychotherapy
   • Support group • Drinking more frequently
   • Drug use • Avoided thinking or talking about it

4. Event or Circumstance: _____

   _____

   • Talking with friends • Psychotherapy
   • Support group • Drinking more frequently
   • Drug use • Avoided thinking or talking about it

5. Event or Circumstance: _____

   _____

   • Talking with friends • Psychotherapy
   • Support group • Drinking more frequently
   • Drug use • Avoided thinking or talking about it

What were some of the healthy ways you dealt with these circumstances?

_____

_____

_____

_____

_____

_____

_____

_____

What were some unhealthy ways you dealt with these circumstances?

_____

_____

_____

_____

_____

_____

What, in general is the main method you use for coping with stressful circumstances? Cite examples:

_____

_____

_____

_____

_____

_____

_____

## *ASSESSING INTERNALIZED HOMOPHOBIA*

Think of descriptions or stereotypes of gay men that you recall from your life. A popular example is: Gay men molest children. List as many stereotypes as you can think of:

1. _____

2. _____

3. _____

4. _____

5. _____

6. _____

7. _____

Circle the item number for each stereotype listed above (1) if you ever believed the statement, or (2) if you wondered on some level if the stereotype was not really true. Are there any stereotypes written above that you still fully or partially believe?  YES  NO

• If YES, describe and explain: _____

_____

_____

• For each of the stereotypes written above, describe the ways in which you learned to disbelieve the stereotype: _____

_____

_____

_____

• Describe the major consequences to your life in once believing the above stereotypes:_____

_____

_____

_____

• Which stereotypes are difficult for you to disbelieve? Explain: _____

_____

_____

_____

_____

_____

_____

• In what way(s) do you view yourself as a *stereotypical* gay man?

_____

_____

_____

_____

_____

_____

• What attitude(s) or belief(s) about homosexuality do you most wish you could change in yourself? _____

_____

_____

_____

_____

_____

• What attitude(s) or belief(s) about homosexuality do you most wish you could change in other people, particularly people you know? _____

_____

_____

_____

_____

_____

_____

## *ASSESSING DEPENDENCY IN YOUR LIFE*

Respond to each of the questions/statements below. These questions will help you identify current or potential addictive behavior in your own life.

### *Alcohol and/or Drugs*

1. When you drink or use drugs, does it take more than it used to to obtain the desired effect?          YES   NO

2. Do you ever wake up to discover that you cannot remember all or part of the previous day or evening?          YES   NO

3. Do you drink or use drugs in response to work and/or relationship stress?          YES   NO

4. When drinking or using drugs with other people, do you try to sneak a few extra drinks or drugs so that others will not notice?          YES   NO

5. Do you ever feel guilty or ashamed about your alcohol or drug use?          YES   NO

6. Has anyone close to you expressed an opinion that you drink or use drugs too much?          YES   NO

7. Do you ever say or do things when drinking or using drugs that you end up regretting when sober?          YES   NO

8. Do you try to avoid family or friends when you are drinking or using drugs?          YES   NO

9. Do you ever drink or use drugs to eliminate morning anxiety or "shakes"?          YES   NO

10. Do you eat less when you drink or use drugs?          YES   NO

### *Sex*

1. I think about sex several times a day.          YES   NO

2. I strategize and scheme ways to have sex.          YES   NO

3. I have gotten into trouble because of my sexual behavior (e.g., been arrested, experienced violence).          YES   NO

4. I have stayed out looking for sex longer than I should have.          YES   NO

5. I have had unsafe sex with someone other than my lover at least once in the last three years.          YES   NO

6. I get bored having sex with only one partner.                          YES     NO

7. I was sexually abused as a child.                                      YES     NO

8. I spend more on phone sex than I can afford.                           YES     NO

9. I use sex to feel loved, accepted, attractive, etc.                    YES     NO

10. I use sex as a way of dominating others.                             YES     NO

11. I get very angry and/or depressed if I am not able
    to have sex when I want it.                                          YES     NO

12. I seek out sex in risky places (bookstores, parks,
    restrooms).                                                          YES     NO

13. I have experienced threats to my job, relationship,
    friendships because of my sexual behavior.                          YES     NO

14. I feel out of control of my sexual behavior
    (including masturbation).                                           YES     NO

15. My sexual behavior has (causes or) caused me to feel
    ashamed and/or embarrassed.                                         YES     NO

There is no formal scoring system for the above exercises. Rather, if you answered YES to any of the above questions, you may have some problems with your drinking, drug use, and/or sexual behavior. The more times you answered YES indicates more problems in these areas.

## AM I AN ADDICT?

Perhaps you admit you have a problem with drugs, but you do not consider yourself an addict. All of us have preconceived ideas about what an addict is. There is nothing shameful about being an addict once you begin to take positive action. The following questions were written by recovering addicts in Narcotics Anonymous. If you have doubts about whether or not you are an addict, read the questions below and answer them as honestly as you can.

1. Do you ever use drugs alone?    YES   NO

2. Have you ever substituted one drug for another, thinking that one particular drug was the problem?    YES   NO

3. Have you ever manipulated or lied to a doctor to obtain prescription drugs?    YES   NO

4. Have you ever stolen drugs or stolen to obtain drugs?    YES   NO

5. Do you regularly use a drug when you wake up or go to bed?    YES   NO

6. Have you ever taken one drug to overcome the effects of another?    YES   NO

7. Do you know people or go to places that do not approve of your using drugs?    YES   NO

8. Have you ever used a drug without knowing what it was or what it would do to you?    YES   NO

9. Has your job or school performance ever suffered from the effects of drug use?    YES   NO

10. Have you ever been arrested as a result of using drugs?    YES   NO

11. Have you ever lied about what or how much you use?    YES   NO

12. Do you put the purchase of drugs ahead of your financial responsibilities?    YES   NO

13. Have you ever tried to stop or control your using?    YES   NO

14. Have you ever been in jail, hospital, or drug rehabilitation center because of your using?    YES   NO

15. Does the thought of running out of drugs terrify you?    YES   NO

16. Does using interfere with your sleeping or eating?    YES    NO
17. Do you feel it is impossible for you to live without drugs?    YES    NO
18. Do you ever question your own sanity?    YES    NO
19. Is your drug use making life at home unhappy?    YES    NO
20. Have you ever thought you could not fit in or have a good time without drugs?    YES    NO
21. Have you ever felt defensive, guilty, or ashamed about your using?    YES    NO
22. Do you think a lot about drugs?    YES    NO
23. Have you had irrational or indefinable fears?    YES    NO
24. Has using affected your sexual relationships?    YES    NO
25. Have you ever taken drugs you did not prefer?    YES    NO
26. Have you ever used drugs because of emotional pain or stress?    YES    NO
27. Have you ever overdosed on any drugs?    YES    NO
28. Do you continue to use despite negative consequences?    YES    NO
29. Do you think you might have a drug problem?    YES    NO

Are you an addict? This is a question only you can answer. The actual number of YES responses is not as important as how you feel inside and how addiction has affected your life. These questions, when honestly approached, may help to show you how using drugs has made your life unmanageable.

---

## *MY OWN THOUGHTS ON THE TWELVE STEPS*

Read the Twelve Steps from the text. Write your thoughts or reactions to each step. In addition, write how each step may apply to your own life.

1. _____

_____

2. _____

_____

3. _____

_____

4. _____

_____

5. _____

_____

6. _____

_____

7. _____

_____

8. _____

_____

9. _____

_____

10. _____

_____

11. _____

_____

12. _____

_____

## IF SOMEONE YOU LOVE IS ADDICTED

Addiction is about control. The addict feels on some level that he has no control and his addiction leaves him with a false sense of control. People who are intimately involved with addicts also get caught up in the cycle of control. They try hard to control the addict, and if they cannot, they try to control the chaos that often exists in the relationship system of the addict.

Answer the following questions to determine whether or not you need some support for being involved with an addicted person. As you answer the question think about a specific person: a lover, friend, or family member. The questions are phrased in terms of alcohol or drug use, but you can substitute other addictive behavior if you wish. The more times you check YES, the more severe the matter may be, and the more out of control you may feel.

1. I worry about how much someone close to me drinks or uses drugs. YES NO

2. I often try to cover up someone else's drinking or drug use. YES NO

3. I feel that if the person I am thinking of really loved me he or she would stop drinking or using drugs. YES NO

4. I secretly try to find out if my loved one has been drinking or using drugs. YES NO

5. My loved one would not drink or use so much if he did not hang around the people he or she does. YES NO

6. Sometimes I threaten my loved one by saying, "If you do not stop using, I will. . . ." YES NO

7. I am afraid others will find out how much my loved one drinks or uses drugs. YES NO

8. My loved one's drinking or drug use is a big embarrassment to me. YES NO

9. My relationship with my loved one gets violent (or I fear violence) when he or she has been drinking or using drugs. YES NO

10. When I cannot control how much my loved one drinks or uses, I feel like a failure. YES NO

11. I have threatened to hurt myself if he or she does not stop drinking or using drugs. YES NO

12. Most of our problems would be solved if he or she stopped using alcohol or drugs. YES NO

13. I find myself getting depressed when my loved one drinks or uses drugs.     YES    NO

14. I stopped inviting people over because of how my loved one acts when drinking or using drugs.     YES    NO

15. I have made bargains with my loved one concerning his or her alcohol or drug use (e.g., If you don't drink so much I will stop seeing my friend Richard).     YES    NO

## SECRETS, SHAME, AND ADDICTION

People who feel out of control of their use of alcohol, drugs, sex, food, etc., inevitably feel a great deal of shame about their behaviors. Often there is embarrassment about being reliant upon these behaviors. In turn, those who depend upon these substances or behaviors to feel better about themselves will try to obtain gratification in private. Thus, they will drink or use drugs when alone, eat large amounts of food when no one is around, and/or have a secret sex life that no one else knows about. The behavior becomes a secret that the person tries not to let others know about.

Think about your own use of substances, sex, food, etc. Take some time to reflect on your own use of substances or behaviors that have a secretive or shameful quality to them for you. Write about why you keep this behavior secret from others. What do you think or fear would happen if others found out? If you could, with whom would you like to share your secret? What do you feel it would take for you to give up this behavior?

_____

_____

_____

_____

_____

_____

_____

_____

_____

_____

_____

_____

_____

_____

# Chapter 4

# Developing and Maintaining Gay Relationships

## *INTRODUCTION*

As I write this chapter, a growing national debate on the issue of gay marriages is occurring. In anticipation of a decision by the State of Hawaii Supreme Court on the matter, state and national politicians are lining up to voice their opposition. The irony in much of this is the subtle way in which gay relationships are being acknowledged. Whereas antigay forces once stereotyped gay men as being uninterested in and unable to sustain long-term relationships, there very clearly is the acknowledgement of gay relationships in this debate. However, some people do not want gay couples to have the recognition and benefits afforded heterosexual couples in our society.

Gay relationships remain a mystery not only to members of broader society, but often to those of us who identify as gay. It is not uncommon for many men who have been openly gay for most of their adult lives to never have had an ongoing romantic relationship with another man. Similarly, I am struck by the number of gay men who do not know any gay couples. To compound the issue, gay and nongay persons alike look upon themselves and are frequently looked upon by others as having problems if they are not involved in a primary relationship (McWhirter and Mattison, 1984).

Something I feel many of us can learn from the gay marriage controversy is the ways in which gay couples are both similar to and different from heterosexual couples. Many gay couples have no interest in establishing a traditional marriage; thus, they have no intention of becoming legally married if given the opportunity. Others, however, see their relationship as a replica of that of their heterosexual friends, with their same-sex gender being one of the few differences.

This chapter will examine common issues and patterns involving gay men who seek to develop a long-term committed relationship with another man. Challenges and dynamics faced by gay male couples will also be discussed. The exercises at the end of the chapter are designed to help you identify aspects of your own relationship needs. Unlike many of the other exercises in this book, some of the exercises in this chapter can be done with your lover if you are in a relationship.

## GETTING STARTED

### How Gay Men Meet

Just as there is no universal way heterosexual couples meet, the same is true for gay male couples. McWhirter and Mattison (1984), for example, in their survey of 156 male couples, found that the men they interviewed met in a variety of ways. This included at bars, at steam baths, at gay beaches, in the military, at parties, on planes, and through professional contacts. Bryant and Demian (1994), in their study of 506 gay couples, found that only 39 percent met through anonymous or sexually charged arenas.

The stereotype that many gay men hold is that the only way to meet other gay men is through the gay bar. Though this has worked for some, the above studies indicate that the gay bar is not the only place to meet other gay men. In fact, as other options for meeting gay men increase, fewer men are relying on the gay bar as the sole source for finding a prospective partner. Meeting someone through a group or activity you enjoy ensures the possibility of having something in common with him. This is not always the case when you meet someone at a gay bar. Also, the man you meet at the bar may be a heavy drinker, and this may not be the partner you want.

Other options for meeting other gay men include the following:

- Volunteering for a local AIDS organization.
- Getting active in community politics and public policy.
- Attending a gay athletic or sporting activity (running, hiking, bike riding, etc.).

- Becoming active in the performing arts of your area (choruses, plays, etc.).
- Joining a gay support group.
- Placing a personal ad for friendship.
- Accepting your friends' offers to go to parties or dinners.
- Attending a gay religious or spiritual group meeting.

Also, do not fall into the trap of believing that you will only met gay men at gay events. Instead, become active in things that are of interest to you. This could include attending community education classes, taking lessons to learn how to swim or ride a horse, or becoming active in groups in your community. Even if the people you meet are not gay, you may develop some enriching friendships, and perhaps these people can introduce you to friends they have who are gay.

### Does Age Matter?

Many older gay men report difficulty finding permanent male partners. Though some attribute this to the youth-oriented aspects of gay subculture, there may be other explanations.

For example, as we age we become less accommodating of change than when we are younger. In our twenties we expect change. Our jobs change, our place of residence may change, and we often lose and gain friends in response to the changes in our lives. We are also more flexible in young adulthood because we are generally less committed overall than when we grow older. By the time men reach their forties and fifties, a significant number have attained financial security, a permanent residence, and many personal possessions. Additionally, few men of this age can move somewhere else at the spur of the moment.

When a gay man in his forties or fifties meets a potential partner, each must assess how much change they can accommodate and tolerate as they think of joining their lives. Who, for example, will move in with whom? The chances are good that the more settled man will not want to leave his current residence. If a man moves in with his partner who is more settled, he may have questions about how he fits into the already well-established patterns and traditions of his new partner. One man I know said that a man he was dating walked into his house and saw all the art, furniture, and belongings he had collected through the years. He said, "There is no room for me here," and subsequently pulled away from the developing relationship. Though he was responding to the material belongings of the man he was dating, metaphorically he was also acknowledging the ways in which the other man seemed entrenched in a particular way of life. It is easier for two people to build their lives together than it is for one to adjust to being with someone whose lifestyle is fairly well established.

Thus, the question "Does age matter?" sometimes has less to do with chronological years, and more to do with how flexible we are with bringing a new partner, new traditions, and new experiences to the life we currently lead (Figure 4.1).

## Differences in Dating Patterns for Gay Men

Clients and friends often tell me that, as gay men, they do not know how to date. Attempts on their part to replicate a heterosexual style of dating fail, and many report falling into dating patterns that feel awkward. In fact, the whole concept of dating is foreign to many gay men. For example, it is not uncommon to see books and articles on gay relationships that do not include any reference to dating. Part of this is

FIGURE 4.1. A look at the research: Age preferences of homosexuals and heterosexuals.

Researchers at Arizona State University examined the age preferences expressed by homosexuals and heterosexuals looking for relationships. To do this, they examined 753 personal ads from magazines and newspapers around the country, looking for references to age preference from those persons placing the ads.

The researchers found that heterosexual women of all ages tend to prefer men from their own age to several years older. Heterosexual men, on the other hand, change with age in that younger men show an interest in both older and younger women, but older men express progressively stronger interest in women younger than themselves. Homosexual men, the researchers found, prefer increasingly younger partners as they age. They found that homosexual men generally do not express a desire for older men.

The researchers concluded that biological forces may dictate an interest in younger women by heterosexual men (since younger women would theoretically be better able to produce offspring). However, this would not explain why homosexual men desire younger men. Regardless of sexual preference, however, data clearly suggest that older men prefer younger partners.

in response to how gay male relationships have traditionally developed. It may also stem from the desire by some in the gay community to avoid replicating heterosexual relationship dynamics.

Whenever I meet with a couple, or an individual client who is in a relationship, I want to know how they met. Further, I want to know how the early stages of their relationship progressed, and how it came to be that they identified as a couple. Often, what I am told is that the two men just found themselves in a relationship. Sometimes there is no clear boundary between when they were getting to know one another and when it was that they identified as a couple. Take the following example, said to me by a client who came to therapy shortly after his five-year relationship ended:

> It just happened. I am not really sure when we knew we were a couple. I guess after we met. He came over, we had sex, and two weeks later we were living together. We certainly never dated. We just fell into this relationship, and now, five years later, it is over.

Regardless of whether you feel that gay relationships differ from those of heterosexual relationships, there clearly are unique challenges faced by gay men who seek to develop a committed relationship. Perhaps the biggest challenge is meeting other gay men who might also want a relationship. Though larger cities are seeing the development of gay dating service and matchmaking services, avenues for meeting other gay men have traditionally been limited. I have also heard from clients that once they do meet someone, it can be difficult finding places other than a gay bar to go to where they feel they can comfortably be themselves.

Whereas single heterosexual men and women are likely to be introduced to the single friends of their co-workers, neighbors, friends, and family members, rarely does this happen for gay men. More common is the well-meaning friend, unaware of the gay friend's sexuality, who tries to introduce him to the *right woman*. If people do know that their friend is gay, oftentimes they will assume that he is already meeting people through gay bars and might not offer to introduce him to others.

A lot of gay men also think more in terms of the goal rather than the process when looking to develop a romantic relationship. In our socialization in the gay community, we have not been taught that sometimes it is better to see a potential partner a few times, each time in a different setting, before making up our minds about relationship potential. It is not uncommon for some people to make up their mind on the spot that the person they just met is the right one for them. For them, the only criteria they seem to hold is that the other person be an eligible gay man. This becomes a risk in that the focus can be more on being with someone—anyone—rather than on having a quality relationship.

### Sex and Dating

Many gay men are also likely to have a sexual relationship with someone they just met. In fact, many couples report that their first contacts were sexual. Unfortunately, some men in the gay community do not feel they have the option to postpone sex with someone they have just met. Rather, they report that sexual feelings between them and a new partner have a hurried or rushed quality to them.

This feeling of needing to rush to have sex occurs for various reasons. Certainly mutual attraction makes sex desirable, but often gay men will have sex early in a relationship because they fear that the other person will lose interest in them if they do not. Many gay men also feel that it is expected of them to have sex shortly after meeting someone—that it is "just the way we do things."

Gay men have told me they fear, by postponing sex, communicating disinterest to someone they recently met. Thus, they give in to the pressure to have sex even though they would rather wait. One client told me a man he went on a date with said that my client's desire to wait before having sex diminished spontaneity and thus he did not want to see my client anymore. Also, some gay men approach new partners with the primary goal of having sex. If something more develops, it is seen as more of an accident.

One of the problems with having sex with someone shortly after meeting them is that it clouds the boundaries between the two people. Ultimately, we need to have some space or autonomy from another person in the early stages of dating. This gives us the distance we need to have perspective on how we really feel about the person, whether we want something long-term with them, and whether we feel there is room for mutual respect. Because of the nature of sexual relationships it is easy for someone to feel that they can take certain liberties with our bodies or relationship because of the sexual activity experienced. My view is that this creates the potential for an artificial feeling of closeness between both persons before it has had time to develop.

Ultimately, there is no right time to have sex with someone for the first time. What is more important is feeling that you have the right to say when and how you want to have sex. If these wishes and desires can be respected by another person, chances are good that he can respect you in other ways as your relationship develops. Taking your time with someone you recently met is one way to test more of your expectations from a potential partner.

## Personal Ads

This chapter cannot discuss in depth all the avenues available to gay men for meeting other gay men. However, I want to address the role of personal or relationship advertisements, which have recently become quite popular. Increasingly, mainstream newspapers regularly carry personal ad listings. Though men looking to meet other men have sometimes been grouped under "Alternative Lifestyles," more and more newspapers are including a subcategory titled "Men Seeking Men." This reflects the growing use of personal ads by gay men looking to meet other gay men, as well as the understanding by media sources of gay relationships.

Gay men I have known, both personally and professionally, who have used personal ads for meeting others report varying degrees of satisfaction. Collectively, what I have been told is that the ads placed in mainstream newspapers (rather than in the gay press) yield more responses and by a more diverse group of men. Contrary to the perception some people hold about men who place such ads, few of these men are desperate, lonely, antisocial, or without relationship potential. Rather, many people who place ads have limited options for meeting other gay men. Others appreciate the opportunity to talk with potential dating partners without the awkwardness of going to a bar.

Many couples report great happiness and success having met through a personal ad. One couple I know who met through a personal ad just celebrated their tenth anniversary; another will be acknowledging their fifth anniversary soon. Some people report that they have developed close friendships with men they met through personal ads, even though nothing romantic developed between them.

Personal ads are not a poor choice for meeting someone, but often the information provided in the ad is sparse. In turn, the person answering the ad anticipates meeting the person who placed the ad with unrealistic expectations. Ads that work, like most other forms of advertising, provide the reader with enough information to warrant a reply. This helps eliminate responses from people who answer every ad hoping to get lucky.

Consider the following two personal ads:

Sincere, gay white male, 34. 5' 10". Slender. Fun. Cute. Likes good conversation. Average build. Race unimportant. Must be between 21 and 40. Picture guarantees response. Call anytime.

37-year-old white male. Professional, homeowner, runner. Interested in cooking, old movies, outdoor sports, European travel. Looking for someone committed to personal and relationship growth, spirituality. Wanting to create life with man who is adventurous, sensitive, dog lover, health conscious.

Which ad would you consider answering? The first ad gives very little information about the person. Being 34, cute, and enjoying conversation is not enough to sustain a relationship. It is also not enough information to know whether talking to or spending time with him is worth your time.

The second ad gives more information, and in so doing limits who might respond. In the first ad you know that the only criteria for responding is your age; in the second ad you get an impression about the person and what he is looking for. He has given his age, but he has not ruled out someone older or younger than he. Someone is also more apt to respond to this ad based on similar interests, rather than on how he looks, how tall he is, what he is into sexually, etc. The implicit message in the second ad is that he is more interested in a committed relationship with someone of similar background, and that age and looks are not the only determining factors. With the first ad, all we know is that he is looking to meet someone within a particular age range (Figure 4.2).

FIGURE 4.2. A look at the research: How gay men present themselves in personal ads.

A 1993 study by Gonzales and Meyers examined personal ads placed by gay men, lesbians, and heterosexual men and women. A total of 300 advertisements were sampled, with twenty-five of these placed by gay men. The researchers found that compared to gay men, heterosexual advertisers were more likely to pursue long-term relationships, and to make reference to sincerity and financial security through the use of personal ads. Gay men were more likely than the other three groups to mention sexual topics in their ads, emphasize physical characteristics, and specify their HIV status more than members in the other categories did. Heterosexual women, perhaps because they earn less than men, were more likely than other advertisers to seek a partner who is financially secure. The researchers conclude that personal ads provide us a window into the lives and relationship needs of others.

I am very much in support of people who use personal ads for meeting others. However, it does entail risks: you need to be up-front with someone if you are not interested and you must be able to handle that form of rejection yourself. If you answer ads, try to limit your responses to people who define their personality, hobbies, interests, etc. It is too stressful trying to figure out who someone is and what they want without much data. Also, if you share some characteristic that is expressed in the ad (e.g., love of opera) this gives the two of you something to talk about during your initial call or contact. In essence, it affords the opportunity to discuss mutual interests rather than superficial topics such as age, body type, sexual preferences, etc.

If you place an ad, try to be as honest and descriptive as possible. It is worth the extra twenty-five cents a word to give the reader more information about yourself. Some people fear that to be descriptive limits the number of responses they will receive. Though this may be true, you are more assured of hearing from other men who share your interests and passions in life and there will be less weeding out to do.

## Dating Men with Children

Many gay men have children from previous marriages. Thus, getting involved with them usually means having to eventually forge your role as a stepfather. This can be quite frustrating for some men as they realize they have entered an already-entrenched system. The gay father may be obligated to spend time with his children and/or ex-wife on certain holidays or birthdays, for example. The new partner, thus, feels bitter and left out. Complicating this is the fact that his lover's children may feel resentful of this new man who has joined the family.

Depending upon the age(s) of the children, the new lover may also have ideas about what role he wants to play in parenting the children. For example, if the children are quite young, he may want to have more of a say in key decisions that affect the children. If the children are adolescents, he may want to be active in setting limits with them. The father/lover then needs to decide how much involvement he truly wants his new lover to have in raising his children.

A common dynamic is that the childless lover perceives his partner to be too lenient or overindulgent with the children, often in response to guilt over being gay and breaking up the family. The new lover, witnessing how the children take advantage of their father's vulnerability, gets frustrated and angry and tries to find ways of exerting control. What often happens is that the father/lover is then put in the middle between his lover and his children, and the potential for conflict between them increases.

These types of relationships can work, but they require a great deal of mutual—and frequent—conversations between the two men, as well as the capacity for compromise and flexibility on the part of the new lover.

### Is He Mr. Right?

I usually discuss with clients the concept of *testing*. Testing is a term borrowed from Control Mastery theory. According to the theory, we all have conscious and unconscious beliefs about ourselves, ideas about our values and standards, and expectations of how we feel and fear others will treat us. In our interaction with others, we pose a series of tests by which we assess whether our beliefs and expectations are real, and if others treat us in certain ways that are consistent with our beliefs, fears, and expectations. We then make decisions about what kind of relationship we will have with that person based on whether they pass or fail our test.

For example, my pet peeve is that I need the person I am talking with to listen to what I am saying. There were many times in my life when I did not feel as though others took me seriously or bothered to listen to what I had to say. Thus, on some level, I grew up believing that what I had to say was not worth anyone else's time. However, I also grew to learn that there are times when what I am saying is important—at least to me—and that common respect dictates that the person to whom I am talking not tune me out when I am speaking.

My test, therefore, when I develop new relationships with people is whether or not they are capable of and willing to listen to me. On the one hand, I am challenging my earlier belief that what I have to say is not worth someone listening to. On the other, I am testing the person to see if they meet my values—that is, willing to respectfully listen. In turn, I base decisions on what kind of relationship I will have with that person on whether they pass or fail my test. I am not willing to open up and share intimate details of my life with someone who is not paying attention.

This is what we do in most major relationships of our lives, and it gets played out with particular sensitivity with potential romantic partners. One client of mine was severely abused as a child. To him, love was equated with getting physically hurt. Thus, in adult relationships he expected to be hurt, and if he was not it meant that the other person did not love him. So in a relationship he would engage in a series of behaviors to test whether the other person really loved him. This meant provoking his partners to be mean to him. His test, therefore, was (1) I am not worthy unless I am being abused, and (2) if you really love me, you will hurt me too. By failing to abuse him, the person fails the test. By abusing him, he passes.

We all have our idea of what kind of relationship we would like to have, and perhaps an idea of what kind of man with whom we would like to be involved. As we meet prospective partners we engage them in this testing process. We may pose a variety of tests to determine the following:

- Is he trustworthy?
- Will he try to dominate or control me?
- Can he be sensitive to my needs?
- Is he committed to having a long-term relationship?

I usually encourage friends and clients to go slow when entering a relationship. I suggest this out of my belief and experience that we need to take time to see who it is we are potentially getting involved with—to see if the person passes our tests. Unfortunately, many people—and this is not just gay men—desire a relationship so strongly that they enter one with little idea of whom it is they are involved with. As gay men, one of our challenges is to break the expectation and assumption that we will know if the other is Mr. Right after one evening, one phone call, or one sexual encounter.

## GAY MEN AND TRUST

Trust means believing someone will not harm you or exploit you. As gay men we have been raised to be cautious about other people, especially men. Because we have spent so much of our lives protecting our identities from others, and carefully assessing whether or not someone is threatening to our well-being, we can be very sensitive to any attempts by others to manipulate or control us. I have had men tell me, for example, that they refuse to ever trust another man after going through a difficult relationship or experience with another man. For them, not trusting others is a very deliberate effort.

Ultimately, it is in our best interest to allow ourselves to trust other men. By not trusting others we prevent them from getting to know us in genuine ways, and in our defensiveness, we find that we do not ever know who they really are. Trusting someone does not mean making yourself totally vulnerable all at once. Rather, take your time. Disclose only what you feel comfortable telling another person until you are sure they will respect what you tell them. Do not hesitate to set limits and boundaries with someone. Get to know someone before making yourself vulnerable, but do not hold back on ever sharing with another who you are.

## MAKING RELATIONSHIPS WORK

### Relationship Stage Theory

In the late 1970s David McWhirter and Andrew Mattison interviewed 156 male couples living in Southern California. The relationships of the couples lasted between one and thirty-seven years. McWhirter and Mattison interviewed the couples, asking how they met, how they handled matters such as monogamy and finances, how they allocated household chores, how they dealt with family members, etc. The findings of their study were published in their 1984 book, *The Male Couple.*

One of the most pronounced findings from their interviews was that, regardless of the differences among the men, the relationships themselves formed separate entities and passed through a series of six developmental stages. The couple, in turn, moved through these stages as the relationship grew. Rather than going through the stages in a strictly linear fashion, however, couples typically went in and out of the stages, and not necessarily at the same time.

McWhirter and Mattison note that as we age, maintaining flexibility is one of the secrets of continuing vitality. The same is required in our relationships. They stated the following:

> Couples start out together by losing themselves in the blending of their individual personalities in Stage One. The continuation of their partnership over time depended upon their ability to separate and to find themselves individually without abandoning the relationship. The balancing act of togetherness needed complementarity and independence, conflict and resolution, constriction and restoration. (p. 125)

Thus, the stage theory gives us an overview of common dynamics and themes that male couples experience. Knowing the stages helps other couples know what to expect in their relationships, and how to recognize certain feelings or behaviors as characteristic of gay relationships.

The stages and major features of McWhirter and Mattison's group of couples include:

*Stage One:*   Year One of the Relationship
  • Merging: The two men becoming like one.
  • High Sexual Activity.

*Stage Two:*   Years Two and Three
  • Finding Compatibility: Learning to live in harmony.

- Ambivalence: The mixture of positive and negative feelings about the relationship and each other.
- Homemaking: Setting up the mutual home.

*Stage Three:* Years Four and Five
- Reappearance of the Individual: The men learn they can move away from the relationship and gain confidence that each will be present and available to the other upon his return.
- Taking Risks: Telling each other more about themselves; a higher level of trust develops.
- Handling Conflict: The men learn how to compromise.

*Stage Four:* Years Six through Ten
- Establishing Independence: Partners confer less on decisions that do not affect both of them.
- Dependability: Reassurance that each can rely upon the other, and that the relationship can survive the differences between the men.

*Stage Five:* Years Eleven through Twenty
- Trusting: Though not new to the relationship, the quality of trust between the men is more tangible.
- Taking Each Other for Granted: Expressions of love and praise, frequent in earlier stages, are greatly reduced. Even though the relationship is secure, each may feel neglected by the other.

*Stage Six:* Beyond Twenty Years
- Achieving Security: Faith in their shared history with one another. Feelings of financial, personal, and relationship well-being.
- Restoring the Partnership: The couple utilizes their capacity to breathe new life into the relationship.

McWhirter and Mattison believe that couples are most at risk for breaking up at the end of the first year together. This, they found, is based on two misleading beliefs: (1) That the quieting of high romantic intensity means the end of love, and (2) the belief by one or both men that male couples do not last long anyway. The challenge for gay men, therefore, is to expect variations in how intense their emotions and sexuality feel during a relationship, and to know that two men can make a relationship work.

## CHALLENGES MALE COUPLES FACE

The Partners Task Force for Gay and Lesbian Couples in Seattle, Washington, surveyed 560 gay male and 706 lesbian couples in 1988 and 1989. Respondents, representing all but two states, had been in a relationship an average of six years. The survey asked the respondents to categorize the two greatest challenges to their relationship. The breakdown is as follows:

| Category of Challenge | Men |
| --- | --- |
| Communication | 49 percent |
| Career | 30 percent |
| Money | 28 percent |
| Sex | 22 percent |
| Relatives | 18 percent |
| Health | 12 percent |

### *Communication*

It is not surprising that close to 50 percent of the men surveyed in the Seattle study indicated that communication is a significant challenge in their relationships. Of the male couples I see in psychotherapy, most come because their attempts to discuss and resolve important matters have been ineffective. Some have tried to discuss important issues in the relationship, while others report that one partner takes a passive role when communication is warranted. The effects of poor communication become very frustrating; for some couples this calls into question the stability of the relationship.

Communication difficulties between two gay men occur less because they are gay, and more because they were raised as males in our society. Typical male conditioning engenders feelings of self-reliance, dominance, competition, power, control, and high needs for achievement. Men are raised to avoid thinking about—let alone talking about—feelings, especially with another man. Further, acknowledging problems leaves many men feeling inadequate.

As Betty Berzon points out in her 1988 book on gay and lesbian relationships, *Permanent Partners: Building Gay and Lesbian Relationships That Last,* people in relationships sometimes use communication, or the withholding of it, to control their partners.

A common example is the person who refuses to talk about significant issues, give input on his lover's comments, or express any willingness to discuss important issues in the relationship. Often he will say to his lover, "I *am* listening," or "*You* are the one with the problem." The message, however, is "I do not want to talk about it." This withholding of communication is usually indicative of a power struggle between the two men, with the silent one using his silence as a way of maintaining some image of control.

Communication in relationship is not just about conflict and discussing strong feelings. Rather, communication is about all that is said between the two partners. When a couple comes to see me for psychotherapy, I initially try to get them away from telling me about the problems they are having. Rather, I will say: "Tell me about how you met," or "Tell me about the good things between the two of you," or "What was something highly personal that each of you shared with one another?" What I am attempting to do is get them talking to each other about seemingly neutral matters so I can hear how they communicate in general—not just how they handle conflict.

How your partner listens to, and communicates with you, during calm times is a good indicator of how he will be when the topic might be more heated or uncomfortable. If the two of you are able to share personal stories, feelings, or life events, and do so in a way that feels like mutual dialogue, there is good potential for discussing more sensitive topics.

I basically see communication in a relationship as a shaping process by which we teach the other person how we want to be talked to. I mentioned earlier that my pet peeve is people who will not listen to me. If I am talking with someone important to me and I sense that they are preoccupied, I will stop talking. I might then say, "This is important to me, and it is easier to express it if I feel that you're paying attention." When people know that something is important to us, they will often try to keep this in mind during future encounters. By expressing our needs directly and particularly early on in the relationship, we are more likely to feel good about the communication between ourselves and our partner. We also teach the other how to communicate with us, and in turn learn from them how they want us to communicate with them (Figure 4.3).

### Pick Your Battles

Even if you have a relationship in which communication is good, it is important to sort out what you want to bring up as an issue for discussion and when to do so. There are times in a relationship when inevitably the other person will be in a bad mood, say things that might sound hurtful or unkind, or just generally get on your nerves. Members of a couple find various ways of dealing with this

FIGURE 4.3. A look at the research: Where do gay couples turn when they need help?

Modrcin and Wyers (1990) surveyed fifty gay men and seventy-eight lesbians who were currently in coupled relationships regarding where they turn when they needed help resolving problems. The researchers were interested in knowing if gays and lesbians are likely to turn to mental health professionals when they have relationship problems, and if so, what specifications they have concerning the gender or sexual orientation of the therapist.

The researchers identified categories of problems for which gays and lesbians would seek professional services. Some of these were as follows:

| Problem Area | Percent of Sample |
|---|---|
| Communication | 26% |
| Sexual | 19% |
| Impending Separation | 10% |
| Alcohol or Drug Use | 6% |

The researchers found that lesbian couples are more likely to seek the help of a psychotherapist than are male couples. They surmised that gay males may find it difficult to ask for help and admit that they are unable to solve all of their problems on their own. For those gay males willing to seek the services of a mental health professional, the sample was divided on the issue of gender, with most indicating that skill or expertise of the professional was more important. Lesbians, on the other hand, generally preferred working with female psychotherapists. Sexual orientation of the therapist was not a significant factor for either gay men or lesbians, suggesting that gays and lesbians may feel that heterosexual therapists are just as competent as gay or lesbian therapists at conducting couples therapy.

including ignoring it, snapping back, raising the behavior as a topic for discussion, or walking away. The challenge is knowing when to express your feelings or concerns about things your partner does and when to ignore it. Thus, I often say to clients in relationship, "pick your battles carefully."

If you call your partner on every comment or behavior he does that is annoying, you risk being seen as overly critical and judgmental. You are then seen less as a lover and more as a critical parent. No one likes to be treated poorly or to be in the presence of someone who is in a bad mood. Yet, if you ignore hurtful comments, you risk being victim to them in the future. The delicate balance is knowing when something your partner says or does warrants mentioning it.

One helpful response to a hurtful comment is, "Ouch." This communicates that you did not like what was said, that it was somewhat hurtful, and that you would appreciate not hearing it again. Saying this helps avoid a confrontation over a simple comment while potentially helping you feel better. In turn, you feel less resentful and the person usually gets the message that his comment was hurtful. It also comes across in a fairly gentle way which prevents the other person from getting defensive and saying, "You are too sensitive."

Timing is one of the key components of dealing with issues or feelings you want to discuss with your partner. Though the impulse may be to respond as soon as a hurtful word is said or the offensive action happens, it may be more helpful to waiting until your partner is in a different frame of mind before saying something may be more helpful.

The following is an example:

> Your lover tells you over dinner, "You overcooked this dish. I do not think the dog could chew through this."

If you ignore the comment you are likely to feel hurt and resentful, and chances are good that you will find a way of getting back at him for the comment at a later time. One option in this situation is to snap back, "Look, I have been working all day, too. If you do not like my cooking, I will never make another meal again!" Though you might feel better for saying this, it is probably a more extreme response than his comment called for. A more workable option is to postpone your reaction and raise it after the two of you have had time to relax.

You:        "Did you get enough to eat?"
Partner:    "Yeah. I am feeling pretty full. Dessert was good."
You:        "I am sorry about the meat. With the phone ringing all night it was hard watching the oven."
Partner:    "Don't worry about it. It's okay."
You:        "I did feel bad when you said your comment, however."
Partner:    "What comment?"
You:        "When you said that even the dog could not chew through it."
Partner:    "I was just kidding."
You:        "You probably were. But it still stung. I was not really in the mood to cook tonight anyhow, and your comment made me wish I hadn't."

As difficult as it can be to wait until you or your partner has calmed down before raising an issue for discussion, my experience is that you usually get better results. Your partner will feel less accused, you will both be less defensive and reactive, and you will help each other better understand your feelings.

### Compromising

My uncle and his male lover have been together for over thirty-five years. When I asked them about the factors that helped maintain their relationship for so long they said that compromise was at the top of the list. Compromise means letting go of the power struggles that can happen with two men. It means that sometimes you get your way and your needs met, and other times you need to defer your interests and desires to those of your partner.

Two people, no matter how compatible, will never have the same needs at the same time. One may want to go see a romantic movie while the other wants comedy. One may want to go to India for vacation while the other wants to go to Disneyland. One may want to have more of a separate life while his partner desires mutuality. The examples are endless, and they surface continually in relationships. Unless each man refuses to relinquish the power struggle, compromise can usually be achieved.

McWhirter and Mattison (1954) found that in the second and third years of being together, male couples work toward finding ways of living together in harmony. As they note, this comes easy for some men while others find it is more difficult:

> The blending of Stage One capitalizes on the attractions and minimizes the distractions. The nesting of Stage Two highlights differences and minimizes similarities. Compatibility depends on how the differences are balanced. Once couples recognize their differences they search for harmony by resolving, ignoring, or denying them. (p. 47)

In order to achieve compatibility in a relationship, each person must give in to the needs of the other person at times. Sometimes the decisions are as simple as where to go for dinner on a particular evening, but often the decision at hand requires more accommodation. With one couple I saw in counseling, one member desperately wanted to vacation in Japan, a country he spent some time in during his adolescence. His partner, on the other hand, had zero interest in vacationing anywhere but in the United States. For their own reasons, each had strong feelings about their ideas for vacation. It took a lot of discussion, working through individual resentments, and having to compromise on other areas of their relationship. Eventually, however, they did work through their struggles and both had a great vacation in Japan.

We cannot control our partners, and there will be time when we do not get all that we want in our relationship. But by compromising with one another we can hopefully feel better about meeting each other's needs in the relationship.

## THERE IS YOUR FATHER, AGAIN

Just as we are socialized by society how to handle feelings, communication, and self-disclosure, we also learn about communication in our families. When one member of a couple says to the other, "You sound just like your mother," he is probably not far from speaking the truth. When working with couples, therefore, I always take an extensive family history that includes information about how communication was or was not handled. Specifically, I assess the following:

- When your mother spoke to your father was she direct ("Please do not do that in front of the children") or indirect ("One of these days you will be on time and I will drop over dead")?
- When your parents spoke to you were they direct ("You cannot go out to play until you do your chores") or indirect ("You are going to wear that in public?")?
- Were you treated less like a child by one parent and more like an equal (e.g., Your mother tells you when you are twelve, "Your father and I just do not have as much fun as we used to," or "I am worried that your father drinks too much")?
- Were people spoken about ("I sure wish your sister would not go out with that boy") or spoken to ("Janet, I do not approve of the young man you are seeing")?

Inevitably, family styles of communication influence our adult relationships. Parents often tell us, and we dislike hearing it, "You are more like your father every day." My own mother can be highly opinionated at times. As fair as I try to be in my own assessments of the world, occasionally a thought passes through my mind or a statement comes out of my mouth that sounds less like me and more like her. These always catch me off guard, and I doubt that I will ever be able to stop it from happening. Thus, all I do is laugh at it and say, "Whoops, there is my mom."

I find this intervention helpful for couples, also. It helps defuse a tense situation, pokes fun at what is really happening, and gives mutual acknowledgment to behaviors or comments that might otherwise create tension in the relationship. For example, a couple I was seeing in therapy talked about how one of them would periodically have moments when he would get grouchy, angry, and condescending toward everything. This drove his lover crazy, and in turn his lover would snap at him. Inevitably a fight would occur. I was able to help them recognize that the grouchy lover was acting just as his father did. Just as with his father the outbursts were infrequent and short in duration, and inevitably created tension in the household. I also helped the grouchy lover recognize that these outbursts were very bothersome to his lover. Eventually, whenever the outburst occurred, they were able to say, "There is Rich, again," and laugh about it.

By sharing with our partners the dynamics in our family of origin, we help them understand more about the environment in which we were raised. In turn, they get to know the values held in our families, the expectations we have of others, and the petty or irrational habits that were commonplace as we were growing up. Aspects of our personality or behavior can then be seen as extensions of patterns learned in our family. When such characteristics bother your partner, you can both step back and see that these are features you learned that may or may not change. Recognizing these features does not mean that your partner will not be bothered by them, but perhaps he will feel that you are not deliberately trying to be mean, hurtful, or annoying.

## THE ROLLER COASTER OF ROMANCE

A client of mine came for psychotherapy because of his concern that his relationship was having problems. He and his lover had been together for twelve years, and both had developed a comfortable relationship, complete with friends, frequent trips, and a nice home. His lover, ten years older than he and recently retired, had just befriended a much younger man. The two of them had dinners together, shared their interest in a particular hobby, went shopping together, and even talked of weekend trips that sometimes would or would not include my client. Though the younger man had significant identifications with my client's lover, he had no intention of having sex with him. My client eventually came to recognize that what was going on between his lover and this younger man was an emotional, not a sexual affair.

My client felt excluded from a major life event that was happening with his lover. To his credit, his lover told him that he felt he had something with this younger man that he did not have with my client, but that he still felt very good about their relationship. He also made it clear that he had no intention of ending his friendship with the other man. As he put it, it is what he needed to do at that time of his life, and said he would understand if my client similarly pulled away from him.

This presented my client with a tremendous dilemma. Most aspects of his relationship were very good. He felt quite happy with his life and he enjoyed being in relationship with his lover. He knew that his lover had no intention of leaving the relationship, and the two of them still shared good times, though certainly less frequent than before the third person entered the picture.

My client considered having an affair of his own, but on one level recognized that this is not what he wanted. His lover was who he wanted. He struggled with how insistent to be that his lover stop seeing this other man, but knew that even if his lover gave in to these demands, it would cause further resentment and problems between them. He tried befriending his lover's friend but realized he was jealous of him, did not particularly care for the man's personality, and would typically end up feeling like the "fifth wheel" when the three of them were together.

The motivations for the lover's behavior were complex. Much of it was related to his retirement, his feelings about aging, and his need to be admired by someone other than my client. My client, on the other hand, was unexpectedly forced to confront many aspects of his own life, including his dependency in his relationship, his own life satisfaction, and how much individuation on his lover's part he could realistically tolerate.

Though the circumstances of this example are specific to one couple, the themes that permeate throughout are not. Inevitably, there comes a point in most relationships when things change. Each person then decides to adapt to these changes or not. Couples at all stages of relationships are at risk for having to deal with circumstances that upset the familiar balance to which each has grown accustomed.

Two people in a relationship rarely live static lives; therefore, most relationships do not stay the same over time. As the members of a couple grow or change, so does the relationship. In turn, each person is affected by the developmental and circumstantial changes the other faces. Some relationships manage to adapt to these changes and survive while others end as a result of the new challenges.

Here are a few examples of life events or feelings that affect one member of a couple, and in turn can affect the balance of the relationship:

- One person changes jobs or his career; maybe he even goes back to school.
- The couple moves to a new location, leaving the familiarity of friends, usual activities, jobs, etc.
- One person retires while the other does not.
- One person is dealing with midlife issues.
- One person wants to open the relationship to outside sex.
- One person becomes involved with a person, group, or activity the other has no interest in.
- One person expresses needs he feels cannot be met in the relationship.
- One person experiences depression or substance abuse.
- One person desires more autonomy from the relationship.
- One person is HIV positive (See Figure 4.4).

There is no *right* way to deal with these circumstances when they arise in a relationship. It is neither best to break up or stay together when the stressful effects of these changes take their toll. Each person must ultimately decide what is best for him.

What is important to keep in mind is that relationships must grow and change in order to meet and accommodate the needs of each member. You and your partner can sometimes anticipate the effects of change on your relationship, while at other times it sneaks up on you. Talking about the changes each of you experience is a good way to stay aware of any potential effects of the change on your relationship. Questions you can ask one another include the following:

- How can we best adapt to the change in our financial position as a result of going back to school, changing jobs, retirement, etc?
- If you need to take more time for yourself, what can we do to handle my feelings of loss and abandonment?
- If you retire, you will have more time on your hands. What do you feel you will need from me during this time?
- How can I help assure you of my love and commitment during this vulnerable time?
- What clues can we look for to tell us it may not be possible to stay together during this time of change?
- How will we know if the change we are going to experience (or are experiencing) is causing problems in the relationship?

- There is a change in the amount of sex we have in our relationship. Can we talk about how we feel about this?
- You have needs I cannot fulfill, and I do not want to prevent you from getting them met. But can we talk about how this could affect our relationship?

## WHO IS IN CHARGE HERE?

Think about the stereotype of the traditional marriage. Each spouse fulfilled a role and responsibility that the other did not. For example, the husband typically worked outside of the home and provided the family with income. The wife cooked and cleaned and managed the day-to-day needs of the children. In essence, each had a skill that the

FIGURE 4.4. A look at the research: How couples cope when one partner is HIV positive.

AIDS has introduced a tragic element into the lives of male couples. When one or both members of a male couple tests positive for HIV, the couple must deal with a variety of life and death issues that are likely new to them.

Robert Remien of the HIV Center for Clinical and Behavioral Studies at Columbia University has conducted research on the effects of HIV on male couples. In 1992, Remien and his research team interviewed 75 gay men who were in mixed-status relationships. This means that one member of the couple was HIV positive, while the other was HIV negative.

The researchers found that HIV had an equally detrimental effect on each member of the couple. Thus, the distress of one member of the couple led to distress in the other. In 45 percent of these couples, at least one member scored high on measures of anxiety, depression, and hostility. Generally, only 15 percent of gay men score high on these measures.

Mixed-status couples, Remien found, tend to deny or suppress problems in the relationship. The couples also avoided discussions of whether the infected member would infect the other. Lovemaking, relationship satisfaction, and mutual support were low in these relationships, and the HIV-infected member generally worried about being able to satisfy his partner sexually.

Finally, Remien found that these couples experienced disapproval by friends of mixed-status couples. This caused additional stress and conflict in the relationship. These couples also reported having higher levels of hopelessness than do single men who are HIV infected.

Remien concluded that efforts need to be directed toward working with both members of mixed-status couples instead of just the HIV-infected member. When mixed-status couples receive support, isolation decreases, communication improves, and the couple experiences more hope for the future.

other did not have, and each was reliant upon the other to provide this skill. In turn, few women were able to secure high-paying jobs, and few men were able to master housework and basic childrearing.

Inevitably, gay couples get asked the naive question, "Who is the man in the relationship?" or "Who is the dominant one?" Such questions stem from the stereotype that relationships must have a dominant and submissive member. Rarely, however, do male couples function in these roles. McWhirter and Mattison (1984) found that daily chores, for example, got divided up based on work schedules or the particular skill of one of the members. Thus, cooking and cleaning was not handled by a *passive* member and finances by an *active* member.

Ultimately, a male couple works best when each member has his own strengths and competencies. For example, one member may be very skilled socially and thus facilitate friendships for the couple. Another might be more organized, so he handles the paying of bills. These types of strengths help neutralize the power struggles that can occur between two men. Also, since gay men often meet in situations that are specific to being gay and neutral to social class or income status, it is not uncommon to find a couple with large income discrepancies. Since power in our society is often allocated to the one with more education or income, having other strengths and resources in the relationship can help even out this imbalance.

Some couples, however, play out a scenario where one member assumes and takes most or all the power in the relationship while the other feels helpless. The dominant one is quite content being in this role, whereas the less dominant member feels victimized at times. The less dominant member can actually feel exploited in that the couple does what the other wants, the dominant one makes all the decisions, and the exploited member gets no say and is typically blamed when things go wrong. I have seen this dynamic played out with several male couples, and often the relationship degenerates into pure chaos.

One client, for example, reported to me how his lover threatened to kill the dog if he came to see me for psychotherapy. Another client said his lover would "punish" him by going out and having anonymous sex whenever he did something "wrong." Another would grab the remote control and turn down the volume every time his partner put on music he liked. These are all examples of being controlled in a relationship, and the characteristics closely parallel that of battering relationships. If these are the dynamics in your relationship, I strongly encourage you to speak with a professional, gay-sensitive counselor.

## *VIOLENCE IN GAY RELATIONSHIPS*

The physical, verbal, and sexual abuse experienced by children and women in our society has been well documented, and fortunately there is more awareness of this phenomena. If the highly publicized trial of O.J. Simpson did nothing else, it brought tremendous awareness and attention to the incidence of domestic violence. Violence between gay male lovers, however, is seldom talked about, and only recently have mental health providers recognized the magnitude of gay domestic violence.

Clinical work and advocacy with victims of same-sex domestic violence show that the types of abuse that gay men endure are the same types of abuse that heterosexual women suffer.

Pam Elliott, president of The Gay and Lesbian Antiviolence Project in Minneapolis defines same-sex domestic violence as follows:

> Sexual abuse in same-sex couples includes any non-consensual sexual act or demeaning language, such as minimizing a partner's feelings about sex, withholding sex, jealousy and anger about the partner's friendships, or making humiliating remarks about the partner's body. . . . Emotional or psychological abuse can often be more intimidating than a direct slap. The abuser's goal in this type of abuse is to put the partner down through the use of insults or shaming language. Threats to harm pets or children of the partner, threats to kill oneself, manipulative lies, and control of finances and friends are common means of emotional abuse. A unique type of psychological abuse for gays and lesbians is the threat of "outing" to family, landlords, employers, or others. (p. 4)

The Gay and Lesbian Community Action Council found in 1987 that of 1,000 gay men surveyed, 17 percent reported having been in a physically violent relationship. Patrick Letellier (1996) writes that current estimates are that approximately 500,000 gay men are victims of partner violence each year, or about one in five couples.

Violence in gay male relationships closely parallels that of heterosexual couples in some respects but not in others. As is true with violence in heterosexual relationships, there is often a calm, honeymoon period following a violent episode. Whereas battered heterosexual women feel isolated in their abusive relationships, the isolation for the battered gay man is much more extreme. Gay men who are battered also report an unwillingness on the part of others—including domestic violence treatment centers—to take their abuse seriously. Patrick Letellier, case manager of the Family Violence Project in the San Francisco District Attorney's Office, writes that many gay victims are criticized for not "standing up for themselves, fighting back, or learning to take it like a man" (p. 74).

Disclosing the abuse may mean having to come out as gay to strangers, and there is no civil rights protection for gay victims as there is for heterosexual victims of abuse. Letellier writes how police often misdocument gay domestic violence as mutual combat. In essence, most victims of gay domestic violence find themselves in the role of having to convince others they are traumatized and victimized. Also, many gay victims tell advocates that they do not complain about the abuse because being victimized by their lover is less frightening than being victimized by the system (Elliott, 1996).

Studies of gay batterers (Farley, 1996) suggest that they come from all segments of the population, including all ethnic, racial, economic, and occupational backgrounds. Most, if not all, experienced childhood abuse themselves, particularly sexual abuse, and many hold a perception of themselves as victims. A high number of batterers are also addicted to alcohol, drugs, or other substances, with many reporting other compulsive behaviors such as sex and food addictions. Batterers are also more likely to describe themselves as "dependent" rather than as a "rescuer" or "helper."

Sinclair (1990) reports that perpetrators of domestic violence say they use physical violence against their partners because it is a highly effective means of control. Dan Byrne, founder of a Washington, DC, clinic for lesbian and gay survivors and perpetrators of violence and abuse, notes the prevalence of self-hate and fear due to one's homosexuality in the lives of perpetrators:

In the initial stages of treatment, it is not uncommon that abusive gay males experience marked difficulty identifying positive personal characteristics or attributes. Most, however, have no difficulty identifying negative personal characteristics. They tend to perceive themselves as bad persons rather than persons with intrinsic worth who have learned or exhibited inappropriate behaviors. (Byrne, 1996, p. 110)

Men who are on the receiving end of abuse feel controlled in all facets of life. They feel that their every move is being watched or monitored, and often they are correct. Deviation from what is expected is constantly feared, as the verbal or physical wrath of their lover will be the punishment. Hope Aldrich, in a 1996 story on gay domestic violence, quotes one man she interviewed:

I always had to keep a salad ready for him in the refrigerator. I had to keep both our cars at least one-quarter full. It could never be less or he would fly into a rage. I wasn't supposed to smoke cigarettes. One time I smoked one out in my office. He came in and smelled it. He picked up a flower pot and hurled it at me. I still have the scar. In the middle of the night, he'd grab me and shake me awake. He'd make me sit up. "What did you do for me today?" he'd demand. "Turn around. Talk to me. What have you done for me?" I knew whatever I answered would only make him mad. "I made lunch," I'd say. "You call that doing something?" he'd scoff.

In a very candid way, the man interviewed by Hope Aldrich continued:

Then we'd be eating dinner. A plate would come flying at me. Then a chair. He'd tell me, "If you make me leave, I'll kill you." I felt like an abused animal. After these outbursts, he'd sit passively in a chair for the rest of the evening, as though he was at peace. I wished for death every day. Life was such hell. I'd think that things had gone as low as they possibly could go. That was my big mistake. Not only *can* it get worse, it will.

## ENDING THE CYCLE OF VIOLENCE

As you can surmise from the Aldrich interview, violence in gay relationships is highly complex and a very serious matter. Rarely will a batterer stop the abuse without intervention, and the abused partner is often limited in what he can do to stop the abuse. Your best bet, if you are the abused partner, is self-protection. Remember, *you cannot control your partner's behavior*, but you can control whether you stay in the relationship.

Rik Isensee, in his 1990 book on male relationships, *Love Between Men: Enhancing Intimacy and Keeping Your Relationship Alive*, offers the following guidelines for gay men in abusive relationships:

1. You cannot keep your partner from being violent by trying to "do better."
2. You cannot predict when your partner will be violent.
3. You're *not* responsible for getting hit.
4. You do not deserve to be humiliated, threatened, or hit when your partner is disappointed in you (even if you are disappointed in yourself).
5. You are not responsible for how your partner feels about himself.
6. You can recognize and acknowledge the severity of the abuse.
7. You can set limits, with consequences, to your partner's behavior.
8. You deserve to have a relationship in which you have no fear of being assaulted.
9. You can learn where to go if you need a safe place.
10. You can learn how to get a temporary restraining order, and how to deal with the criminal justice system if you decide to press charges. (pp. 190-191)

## IF THE RELATIONSHIP HAS TO END

### Sometimes It Just Does Not Work Out

The reality is that sometimes we find ourselves in a relationship that is not meeting our needs, and we eventually realize that staying in the relationship is not in our best interest. Though I encourage all couples to work with the inevitable conflicts, changes, and differences, I do not advocate that someone stay in a relationship that compromises physical or mental well-being. Ultimately, the decision to end a relationship is a difficult one, and rarely are there firm guidelines for knowing when to leave. My hope is that each person asks himself if there are not workable solutions available before taking efforts to end the relationship.

In a study I conducted on gay male relationships, I asked a sample of men why their previous long-term relationship with another man ended. What became apparent is that, just as there is no single reason couples stay together, rarely is there a single reason why the relationships end. Examples included the following:

- Relocation of one partner for occupation or education
- Growing apart
- Violence
- Substance abuse
- Lack of communication

Even though you may experience relief or gratitude that the relationship is over, it is still a significant loss in your life. Depending on who ends the relationship, you can expect that you will experience varying degrees of sadness, anger, regret, helplessness, and fear. Regardless of what you may have felt in previous situations of a similar nature, or what your friends tell you of their own similar circumstances, your situation will be unique.

Whenever someone I am working with experiences a significant death, such as the loss of a lover, I encourage them to refrain from making any significant life changes for at least a year. Though a similar time line may not apply when a relationship ends under less severe circumstances, it is still best to take the time and space you need after the end of relationship to best determine what is in your best interest.

Other areas of focus after the loss of a long-term relationship include the following:

- *Expect to have normal grief reactions.* This will include feelings of anger, denial, depression, acceptance. You may feel that you accept the new reality one day only to find yourself incredibly sad or angry the next.

- *Know that other areas of your life will be affected.* You may have difficulty concentrating at work. You may have less energy than you normally do. You may find that your friends are not as supportive as you thought they were. You may not know with whom who you can be friends, especially if you and your partner had mutual friends.
- *Loss always changes us to some extent.* You will experience changes in your personality, perspective on life, interactions with others, etc.
- *Whereas you were once a we, you are now an I.* You may have new roles, expectations, and values. Your goals and fantasies about the future may change. You will probably need to assess your dependency and independence on self and others.
- *Even if you do not keep in contact with your ex-lover, you will be required to develop a new relationship to him.* This person had an impact on your life, and you have changed by being with him. Do not attempt to erase all memories of him. It is important to acknowledge that there were many aspects of the relationship that were good, perhaps healthy and important to you.
- *Do not give up hope that relationships can be good, even if you choose to refrain from being in one for a while.* All relationships are not doomed and destined to end. Many people do have good relationships, and perhaps someday you will find another relationship that feels good for you.
- *Find rewarding new things, and perhaps new people, in which to invest your time.* Take a class, join a group, explore new activities. Go to the places you did not go to before because your partner did not want to. Find people who can be supportive and fun.
- *Ritualize the loss.* Symbolic gestures can be very powerful. Find a way of symbolically representing the end of your relationship. Options include burying some reminder of your lover; planting a tree to represent life after experiencing so much grief; burning a picture of your ex-lover; going to and saying good-bye to places the two of you once visited; having jewelry he gave you made into a piece that looks different; or

donating to charity things he gave you that you no longer want.

- *Find a way of forgiving him and forgiving yourself.* I have heard many stories of chaos and horror regarding relationships. Ultimately, each person does his best with whatever resources he feels are available. Do not be hard on yourself. Remember, you have grown because of the relationship, and you have learned much about love, life, and being part of a couple.

# Exercises

## *NOTES TO MYSELF: RULES FOR DATING*

Though your style of dating is a very individual matter, there are a few basic rules of dating to keep in mind. Below is a list of these rules to remember as you date. Review this list and add your own ideas below. Then, prior to your next date, review these rules and your notes.

- Do not talk only about yourself.
- Create romance, not seduction.
- Do not mentally walk him down the aisle.
- Contain your nervousness.
- Do not come across as desperate.
- Try to be the kind of person you are looking for: If you want someone who is compassionate, be compassionate.
- Do not try too hard to impress your date.
- Ask your friends how you come across to new people.

Write your own ideas and rules below:

- _____
- _____
- _____
- _____
- _____
- _____
- _____
- _____
- _____
- _____
- _____

## *IDENTIFYING YOUR CRITERIA FOR DATING*

By defining your rules and standards about dating in advance, you can maximize the possibility of setting and clarifying limits and boundaries with those you date. Answer the following questions about dating with your own needs and desires in mind.

How do you typically meet the men you date?_____

_____

How much do you know about the men you date before you get together with them for the first time?_____

_____

Where do you like to go on a date, and where would you not like to go?

_____

_____

How do you feel about payment of movies, dinners, etc., on a date?

- I want us to split the expenses.          _____
- I typically want to pay.                  _____
- I prefer that he pay.                      _____

How do you feel about where you meet for the first date?

- It is OK if he comes to my house.         _____
- I do not want him at my house.            _____
- I do not want to meet at his house.       _____
- I am fine with going to his house.        _____

What are your standards with regard to sex and dating? When is it OK for you and someone you are dating to have sex for the first time? _____

_____

_____

What information do you need before consenting to sex? _____

_____

Is it OK with you to go "all the way" the first time? Why or why not. ___

_____

What decisions do you make about a person based on your first sexual encounter?_____

_____

_____

How would you feel about a man who brought a condom on the first date?

_____

What criteria do you use to know if a man you date is someone with whom you want to have a relationship? _____

_____

Do you feel it is OK for the man you are dating to simultaneously see other men?  YES    NO

• If YES, do you want him to tell you he is seeing others?  YES    NO
What topics of discussion are off-limits on the first few dates?_____

_____

_____

What information do you feel you need to have about someone after the first few dates?_____

_____

_____

What are the clues you look for that a permanent relationship with some-one might be possible?_____

_____

_____

## WRITING A PERSONAL AD

If placing a personal ad is something you would consider, this exercise will help you identify those features about yourself and a potential partner that are important to you. Personal ads, by nature of cost and space limitations, need to be brief. Yet, there are ways of communicating who you are in four to six lines.

Circle the words that best describe your personality and features.

| | | |
|---|---|---|
| OUTGOING | SHY | LIKES SPORTS |
| ANIMAL LOVER | IN RECOVERY | RELIGIOUS |
| MONOGAMOUS | CAUTIOUS | LIKES READING |
| LIKES MOVIES | SPIRITUAL | FINE DINING |
| TRAVELING | LIKES COOKING | HUMOROUS |
| DEVOTED | ACTIVIST | LIKES GARDENING |
| HIV NEGATIVE | HIV POSITIVE | CREATIVE |
| ADVENTUROUS | SCHOLARLY | IMPULSIVE |

Add below other words that describe who you are. Think of including your occupation, where you live, your hobbies, specific things you like to do for fun, etc.

_____

_____

_____

_____

### Practice Writing an Ad

Include as many of the words from above that really capture who you are. Turn some of these words into short sentences. For example:

LIKES READING . . . . Science fiction stories
LIKES SPORTS . . . . . Especially baseball
SHY . . . . . . . . . . . . . . Except when around close friends
LIKES COOKING . . . Especially Asian foods
SPIRITUAL . . . . . . . . Practicing Buddhist

Write four to six brief sentences that include the words you circled or wrote, and the sentences made from these words. If it is important to you, include your age, race, special preferences or characteristics, and other information that would be useful for someone reading your ad.

Consider showing what you have written to a friend for feedback. If you place the ad, ask some of the people who respond what they liked about the ad. Make a note of this.

## QUALITY OF RELATIONSHIP ASSESSMENT

It is not uncommon to feel differently about your relationship at various periods of time. This scale is designed to assess how you currently feel about your relationship. My recommendation is that you complete it and include the date at the top. At a later time, you might want to fill it out again to see how your feelings do or do not change over time.

This is an exercise that both you and your partner can do. Each of you should fill out your own survey. If you have a relationship in which you can talk openly with one another, you may choose to share and discuss your answers. How you both answer each question is more important than the score you each derive. Consider talking with your partner about how current feelings might have changed over time and why. If your discussion indicates boredom or restlessness in the relationship, perhaps the two of you can discuss ways of revitalizing it. This is also an exercise that you can discuss in individual or couple's therapy.

Please indicate approximately how often the following occurs between you and your partner:

1 = Almost always
2 = Frequently
3 = Occasionally
4 = Rarely
5 = Never

1. _____ My partner and I fight or quarrel.
2. _____ My partner and I discuss or consider breaking up or separating.
3. _____ I rarely share secrets and intimate details with my partner.
4. _____ After an argument my partner and I do not make up very quickly.
5. _____ I feel that things are not going well in my relationship.
6. _____ I seldom find myself feeling good about being in this relationship.
7. _____ I do not see my partner as a friend.
8. _____ Sometimes I think things could be different between us.
9. _____ I feel that I no longer care about what my partner says.

10.   ————      I wonder if this is the right relationship for me.

Total: ————

    Scoring:

    9 points or below    =  Low relationship quality
    10 to 20 points      =  Average relationship quality
    25 points or more    =  High relationship quality

## RELATIONSHIP EXPECTATIONS

We all have expectations of how our relationship should be. This is based on our previous relationship experiences, our fantasies about relations, and observation of the quality of relationships our friends and family members have. This checklist is designed to assess your own relationship satisfaction based on your expectations.

This is an exercise you can do on your own or with your partner. If your partner participates have him fill out his answers on a separate sheet. If the two of you can talk openly with one another, consider sharing and discussing your answers. How have your answers changed over time?

Circle the number that best approximates your current feelings about your relationship.

| -3 | -2 | -1 | 0 | +1 | +2 | +3 |
|----|----|----|---|----|----|----|

| Does not meet my expectations | Meets my expectations | Exceeds my expectations |
|---|---|---|

1. The degree of compatibility between my partner and I.          -3 -2 -1 0 +1 +2 +3
2. The overall quality of my relationship.          -3 -2 -1 0 +1 +2 +3
3. The amount of sex in my relationship.          -3 -2 -1 0 +1 +2 +3
4. The quality of sex in my relationship.          -3 -2 -1 0 +1 +2 +3
5. The amount of time we spend together.          -3 -2 -1 0 +1 +2 +3
6. The quality of time we spend together.          -3 -2 -1 0 +1 +2 +3
7. The amount of trust my partner and I share with one another.          -3 -2 -1 0 +1 +2 +3
8. The amount of conflict between my partner and I.          -3 -2 -1 0 +1 +2 +3
9. The quality of communication in my relationship.          -3 -2 -1 0 +1 +2 +3
10. How committed my partner is to me.          -3 -2 -1 0 +1 +2 +3
11. My partner's jealousy.          -3 -2 -1 0 +1 +2 +3
12. How attracted I am to my partner.          -3 -2 -1 0 +1 +2 +3
13. Feeling good about the future with my partner.          -3 -2 -1 0 +1 +2 +3
14. The amount of love I experience in my relationship.          -3 -2 -1 0 +1 +2 +3
15. My overall happiness in my relationship.          -3 -2 -1 0 +1 +2 +3

Totals: _____

Total all scores: _____

Scoring:
   +20 or Above  =  Overall expectations about relationship met
   -15 or Below   =  Overall expectations about relationship not met

## *Ask Yourself After Completing This Survey*

- Does your score surprise you any way?
- What do you feel your relationship expectations are based on?
- What would have to happen for your relationship expectations to be met?
- How do you think your answers compare with how your lover would answer?

_____

_____

_____

_____

_____

_____

_____

_____

_____

## RELATIONSHIP COMMUNICATION

As mentioned in this chapter, most gay couples report that the greatest challenge in their relationship is communication. Communication in relationships involves anything that is talked about between two partners. It does not just refer to talking about problem areas. This survey assesses the degree to which you and your partner are able to talk about a variety of topics.

Place the corresponding number to the left of each question or statement using the following guidelines:

1 = Never
2 = Rarely
3 = Sometimes
4 = Frequently
5 = Almost always

_____  1.  I talk with my partner about how my day went.
_____  2.  In most instances, my partner knows what it is I am trying to say.
_____  3.  My partner and I talk regularly about current events.
_____  4.  My partner shares with me the good things that happen during his day.
_____  5.  My partner shares with me the unpleasant things that happen during his day.
_____  6.  I accommodate what I need to say based on my partner's mood.
_____  7.  I can tell what my partner is feeling based on his facial expressions.
_____  8.  My partner can tell what I am feeling based on my facial expressions.
_____  9.  My partner talks to someone other than me about our problems before discussing them with me.
_____  10.  I talk with someone other than my partner about our problems before I discuss them with him.
_____  11.  We can go days or weeks without discussing a problem in our relationship that we need to talk about.
_____  12.  It is difficult for us to talk about things the other does that we do not like.

———— 13. We openly discuss matters pertaining to our sex life.

———— 14. When we fight or argue we do so in a fair and respectful manner.

———— 15. My partner and I talk to one another about our personal problems.

Total: ————

Scoring:
| | | |
|---|---|---|
| 50+ | = | Good relationship communication |
| 30-50 | = | Relationship communication could use improvement |
| 15-30 | = | Poor relationship communication |

## Ask Yourself

- Is it easier to talk about some topics but not others? If so, why? Do you feel that you each assume mutual responsibility for this?
- If there are topic areas that are difficult for you and your partner to discuss, what could be done to help make this easier?
- Do you withhold things from your lover? What are you protecting or hiding? What do you think would happen if you stopped doing this?

_____

_____

_____

_____

_____

_____

_____

_____

_____

_____

_____

## A COUPLES EXERCISE

As pointed out earlier in the chapter, communication is one of the most problematic areas male couples deal with. This exercise is designed for couples, to provide you with an avenue for expressing your feelings while finding out about those of your partner. It is best not to do this exercise without the support of a psychotherapist when tension between you and your partner is high. Rather, since this exercise has been developed to help the two of you communicate more with one another, it is best done when both of you are not feeling defensive or angry.

There are a few different ways you can approach this exercise. Choose whatever way is best for you and your partner:

- You can read the questions aloud in therapy and then take turns answering them.
- You can each do the exercises on your own, and then share your answers with one another.
- You can sit at a table or lay in bed together and take turns answering the questions.
- You can each write your answers in a journal and selectively share your answers with one another.

It is important to recognize that you and your partner may have answers that differ from one another. Rather than having an argument over this, or blaming each other, try discussing with each other how these differences in experiences or perceptions developed.

### Questions

How did you and your partner meet? _____

_____

_____

Who pursued whom?_____

_____

How soon after meeting one another did the two of you first have sex? ___

_____

- Who initiated this?_____

How long was it after meeting one another that each of you knew you wanted to be in relationship with the other?_____

_____

_____

How and when did you decide that you were in relationship with one another? _____

_____

_____

_____

Who was the first person each of you told about the other? What did you say?_____

_____

_____

_____

Regardless of how long you and your lover have been together, what is the glue that has held your relationship together? _____

_____

_____

_____

What is your understanding of the agreement you and your lover have regarding monogamy?_____

_____

_____

_____

How was the agreement regarding outside sex in your relationship reached with your partner? Write or talk about the conversations the two of you have had on this topic:_____

_____

_____

_____

How has sex with other partners during the course of your relationship affected issues of trust, sexuality, and communication between you and your partner?_____

_____

_____

_____

_____

What, for you, is the best part of your relationship?_____

_____

What, for you, is the most challenging part of your relationship?_____

_____

What has been the single greatest challenge to your relationship, in your opinion?_____

_____

- Do you think other couples deal with similar issues? YES NO
- If YES, how do you think most couples resolve these issues? _____

_____

If you could change three things about your lover, they would be:

1. _____

2. _____

3. _____

What three things do you think your lover wishes he could change in you?

1. _____

2. _____

3. _____

How well do you feel you and your lover communicate with one another?

　　　EXCELLENT　　　GOOD　　　FAIR　　　POOR

- If communication between you and your lover is not very good, what do you do that contributes to this?＿＿＿＿＿＿＿＿＿＿＿＿＿＿

＿＿＿＿＿＿＿＿＿＿＿＿＿＿＿＿＿＿＿＿＿＿＿＿＿＿＿

＿＿＿＿＿＿＿＿＿＿＿＿＿＿＿＿＿＿＿＿＿＿＿＿＿＿＿

＿＿＿＿＿＿＿＿＿＿＿＿＿＿＿＿＿＿＿＿＿＿＿＿＿＿＿

- What topic is most difficult for you to talk with your lover about?＿＿＿＿＿

＿＿＿＿＿＿＿＿＿＿＿＿＿＿＿＿＿＿＿＿＿＿＿＿＿＿＿

＿＿＿＿＿＿＿＿＿＿＿＿＿＿＿＿＿＿＿＿＿＿＿＿＿＿＿

＿＿＿＿＿＿＿＿＿＿＿＿＿＿＿＿＿＿＿＿＿＿＿＿＿＿＿

- What could make it easier for you to be able to share this with him?＿＿＿＿

＿＿＿＿＿＿＿＿＿＿＿＿＿＿＿＿＿＿＿＿＿＿＿＿＿＿＿

＿＿＿＿＿＿＿＿＿＿＿＿＿＿＿＿＿＿＿＿＿＿＿＿＿＿＿

＿＿＿＿＿＿＿＿＿＿＿＿＿＿＿＿＿＿＿＿＿＿＿＿＿＿＿

What is the most private, sensitive, or difficult thing you ever told your lover?＿＿＿＿＿＿＿＿＿＿＿＿＿＿＿＿＿＿＿＿＿＿＿＿＿

＿＿＿＿＿＿＿＿＿＿＿＿＿＿＿＿＿＿＿＿＿＿＿＿＿＿＿

＿＿＿＿＿＿＿＿＿＿＿＿＿＿＿＿＿＿＿＿＿＿＿＿＿＿＿

- How do you feel about how your lover dealt with or responded to what you told him?＿＿＿＿＿＿＿＿＿＿＿＿＿＿＿＿＿＿＿＿＿

＿＿＿＿＿＿＿＿＿＿＿＿＿＿＿＿＿＿＿＿＿＿＿＿＿＿＿

＿＿＿＿＿＿＿＿＿＿＿＿＿＿＿＿＿＿＿＿＿＿＿＿＿＿＿

＿＿＿＿＿＿＿＿＿＿＿＿＿＿＿＿＿＿＿＿＿＿＿＿＿＿＿

- How did your lover's response to what you told him influence or affect what details about your life you chase to share with him?＿＿＿＿＿＿

＿＿＿＿＿＿＿＿＿＿＿＿＿＿＿＿＿＿＿＿＿＿＿＿＿＿＿

＿＿＿＿＿＿＿＿＿＿＿＿＿＿＿＿＿＿＿＿＿＿＿＿＿＿＿

＿＿＿＿＿＿＿＿＿＿＿＿＿＿＿＿＿＿＿＿＿＿＿＿＿＿＿

If you share more of your life experience and feelings with someone other than your lover, who is this person? _____

_____

_____

_____

- What makes it easier for you to talk with this person than with your lover?

_____

_____

_____

- What would have to happen for you to be able to talk with your lover the way you talk with this person? _____

_____

_____

_____

- Do you feel that your lover judges you in harsh or negative ways? YES NO

- If YES, describe and cite examples: _____

_____

_____

In what ways do you feel you judge your lover in harsh or negative ways? Cite examples._____

_____

_____

What do you want the future to look like for you and your partner? _____

_____

_____

_____

- What steps are you taking to make this happen?_____

_____

_____

_____

## DOING POSITIVE THINGS FOR EACH OTHER

Particularly when couples experience conflict there is a tendency for each to think of all the things the other person does not do. Thus, by the time they come to therapy, each has a list of items reflecting all the errors, mistakes and oversights they see in their partner. In couples therapy some clients would like for me to have them read the list, express the hurt and anger they feel, and thereby have me see what a mean and selfish person the man they are involved with is. Rather than exploring their list, however, I feel it can be more helpful for couples to reverse the process and look at the good things they do for one another.

Ultimately, positive change in relationships has to be done by each person on a day-to-day basis. Thus, one exercise I give to couples is the following. The goal is to help them focus less on what the other person is doing wrong, and more on what *they* are doing right. This takes the focus away from what you want your partner to do for you, and places it on what you do that strengthens the relationship.

This is an exercise for you and your partner to do together. Though you will both be participating, however, do not share your lists with one another.

### Directions

On a piece of paper I want each of you to develop a list of things you do that you feel are pleasing to your partner. Draw from experiences where you have done something and your partner has expressed his appreciation or desire for more of the same. Examples might include: Taking him out to dinner, ironing a shirt for him, buying him chocolate, giving him compliments, getting in bed first to get it warmed up, rubbing his feet, keeping the kitchen clean, phoning him at work, initiating sex, making his breakfast, playing his favorite music in the car.

At the beginning of each week I want you to make a commitment to yourself that you will do one or more of items on your list. As you do it, however, you are not going to tell him that you are doing something from the list. Just do it.

### After One Month, Ask Each Other the Following:

- When I did the things I thought would be pleasing to you, did I feel you were happy or appreciative? If not, do I need to refine my list or do I feel you were purposely withholding your appreciation?
- Do I feel you correctly identified behaviors that would be pleasing to me? What are some examples? Do I feel you need to refine your list? Do I feel I expressed appreciation? Do you feel I expressed appreciation?

## IF IT HAS TO END

Sometimes relationships need to end. You may need to leave your relationship for your own well-being, or maybe you find that your lover has ended the relationship on his own. Regardless, you can expect to feel varying degrees of sadness, anger, relief, acceptance, fear, and ambivalence.

This exercise is to help you identify feelings associated with the loss of a relationship.

Write down the name of the person you were involved with: _____

_____

How long were the two of you together? _____
Who initiated the break up? He did/I did/We both did
How long ago did the two of you break up? _____
Do the two of you:   Talk to each other/Write to each other
Did you live together?   YES     NO

- If YES, who moved out:   He did /I did

- How was this decision reached? _____

_____

Were either of you in relationships before this one?  YES  NO

- If YES, how did your prior relationship(s) end?_____

_____

_____

- How did the prior relationship(s) of your lover end? _____

_____

_____

Are there similarities in how either you or your lover's prior relationship(s) ended and how the relationship between the two of you ended? __

_____

List what you consider to be the top three contributing factors to why your relationship ended:

1. _____
2. _____
3. _____

Circle the top five feelings you still have about the relationship and its termination.

| | | |
|---|---|---|
| ANGER | DEPRESSION | HELPLESSNESS |
| RELIEF | SHOCK | JOY |
| REVENGE | REGRET | DOUBT |
| DENIAL | CONFUSION | JEALOUSY |
| FEAR | REMORSE | GUILT |
| SHAME | EMBARRASSMENT | SELF-RESPECT |
| VINDICATED | REJECTED | WORTHLESS |
| DISBELIEF | STUNNED | |

What do you miss the most about the relationship?_____

_____

_____

What are you glad to be rid of now that the relationship is over? _____

_____

What is your greatest regret about your role in the relationship?_____

_____

What is your greatest hurt about the relationship?_____

_____

_____

What do you feel you cannot let go of about the relationship, even though it may be in your best interest to do so?_____

_____

_____

What keeps you holding onto this? _____

_____

_____

What would happen if you let it go? _____

_____

What are your fears about a future relationship?_____

_____

What will you do differently in a future relationship?_____

_____

What items, events, or features best characterized your relationship?_____

_____

How can you integrate one or more of these into a ritual that will symbol-
ize the end of the relationship?_____

_____

What can you do in order to forgive yourself and forgive your ex-lover? ____

_____

If you are in a new relationship, what are you doing now to prevent similar
problems from occurring?_____

_____

_____

# Chapter 5

# Friendship in the Lives
# of Gay Men

Moving into the world, we try to distinguish fiction from fact, our fantasies and dreams from what actually happens. Moving into the world, we try to accept the compromises of childhood's end. Moving into the world beyond the ties of flesh and blood, we try to form untainted ties of friendship. But these voluntary relationships, like all of our relationships, will have their disappointments as well as their joys.

Judith Viorst
*Necessary Losses*

## *INTRODUCTION*

Friendships are important to all persons because of the many needs they satisfy. For gay men, however, friendships often mean a lot more to us than just companionship. It is through our friendships that we find acceptance, camaraderie, and others who love and accept us without the fact we are gay posing conflict or difficulties. For many gay men, the friendships we develop become substitutes for family ties and provide us with the kind of support others may look to their families of origin to provide. Our friends, in essence, become vital to us as we negotiate the many challenges associated with being gay in this society.

Those who have studied and written about friendship (Nardi and Sherrod, 1994; Viorst, 1986) categorize or differentiate different subtypes of friendships. Though these are typically classified as casual, close, and best friendships, writer Judith Viorst has broken this down further. She lists six different categories of friendship:

1. *Convenience Friends.* Though an emotional distance is maintained with these friends, we still interact and exchange favors with them as neighbors or office mates. As Viorst writes, "I'll talk about being overweight but not about being depressed" (p. 179) with these friends.

2. *Special-Interest Friends.* These are friends with whom we share a mutual interest and therefore often engage with one another for a certain activity. These might be friends we socialize with only at political rally's, sporting events, the local club, or at an office lunch. However, we rarely interact with these friends outside of these venues.

3. *Historical Friends.* This refers to those friendships we had at an earlier time of our lives, but whom we seldom see or talk to. These are friends who knew us in a previous era of our life.

4. *Crossroad Friends.* These are also friends we had at an earlier time of our lives. Perhaps we were roommates, were in the military together, or shared another significant life event with. Though we do not keep in contact with these friends on a regular basis, there is a bond that does not necessarily exist with *historical friends.*

5. *Cross-Generational Friends.* These are the friendships that develop between two persons of significant differences in age. As Viorst writes, "Across the generations the younger enlivens the older, the older instructs the younger" (p. 180).

6. *Close Friends.* These are the friends to whom we let our true selves be known. The emotional connection we have with these friends fosters our personal growth, and the intimacy we share is unlike that currently had with the other categories of friends.

Perhaps we as gay men can add another classification. This would include those friends who are much more than close friends, for without their presence in our lives we would feel truly alone. They are the friends who provide us not only with a strong emotional connection with another, but who know we are gay and help us manage the many conflicting experiences and emotions that can come with being a sexual minority.

## ARE WE FRIENDS OR LOVERS?

A unique aspect of being gay is that many of us live in small cities or towns where there may not be many gay men. As we look to the potential pool of men that we want to have as friends, sex partners, or lovers, the boundaries can get blurry. Whereas in large cities you may be able to avoid someone you dated or had sex with, this is more challenging in smaller communities. Thus, it is not uncommon that a group of gay men in one town or city are friends with men they may have been sexual with at one time.

There is also a developmental quality to the notion of having sex with your friends. When many of us were coming out, we did not go to bars or places where gay men meet. This may have been because we were not old enough or brave enough, or for some people, these places just were not around where they lived. Thus, sexual exploration often took place with the safety of a friend, who himself may have been dealing with sexuality issues. Many gay men report having had sexual relationships with good friends in high school, a college roommate, or with another male they spent a lot of time with. Even though the friendship continued through the years, the sexual component did not.

Some gay men also feel at liberty to be sexual with a friend, knowing that it is nothing more than sex between friends. I am not implying that this does not happen with people who are not gay, but there appears to be more acceptance of this in gay circles. Even when there has been a sexual encounter between two men, both may find it easy and natural to remain close friends. Part of this may stem from our conditioning as males, where we are groomed to equate sex with intimacy.

Peter Nardi and Dury Sherrod at Pitzer College in California surveyed 283 gay men and lesbians about their same-sex friendships. In their 1994 article, they reported finding that gay males were more likely to have had sex with casual and close friends, but not best friends. It might be useful to ask yourself if this has been your experience.

## FRIENDSHIPS OF GAY MEN

A friend of mine was telling me recently about attending his thirtieth high school reunion. Prior to this event he decided that he was tired of concealing his sexuality from others. To this end, whenever someone at the gathering asked if he is married, he informed them that he is gay and involved in a twenty-year relationship with another man. The responses he received from his classmates were generally positive. Though he felt good about the ways in which others handled his disclosure, it made him think about friendships in his life that he had let go out of fear of how the other person might react to his being gay. Thus began a lengthy process of evaluating what impact coming out to friends at earlier times in life would have had on the relationship. Unfortunately, all he is left with now is, "What if . . . ?"

How many friendships have you let end because of concerns about how disclosure of your sexuality might affect it? It is actually quite common for many gay men to be confronted with dilemmas over maintaining certain friendships and being gay. Sometimes the friendship ends because the one who is gay had a crush on his friend and was afraid the other would find out. Some men report getting involved with gay friends or the gay community only to experience their friendship with other nongay men drifting away.

When we come out as gay to another person, we are taking a bold step. Though acknowledging our sexuality to another is a way of affirming our identity, it is also an invitation to the other person. In essence, we are sharing a very personal and significant piece of information about ourselves, and in so doing we are testing the other person to see if there is room in the relationship for the true us. Sometimes we get the affirmation and acceptance we desire. At other times we get subtle or blatant rejection. Certainly it is more difficult when rejection comes from someone with whom we felt we had a close friendship, and it is for this reason that many gay men choose not to come out to some of their friends. This is especially true in the earlier stages of recognizing one is gay.

One result of this is that many gay men choose to have other gay men as their main source of support. Out of fear, distrust, or simply by limiting with whom they socialize, some gay men opt for an exclusively gay support network. Thus, friendships of the past are seen as incongruent with the newfound life of being gay.

Other gay men, however, are able to strike a balance between having friendships with gay men and with those who are not gay. Many people assume that we only socialize with others like us, and therefore believe that we do not maintain closeness with women or nongay men. Part of this makes sense in that we are likely to meet other gay men through mutual friendships and gay-related activities. Thus, we may actually have more gay male friends than not. But ask yourself the following: How many of your friends are heterosexual women? Heterosexual men? Lesbian?

In answering these questions, it is likely that you are able to identify one or more close heterosexual women in your life. Many gay men find it easy to talk to straight women about intimate matters of their life, and many of these women enjoy the closeness with a man that does not include pressure to have sex. Some heterosexual women also feel that they gain more of an understanding of men in general by nature of the candid discussions they share with gay men.

But what about the other two categories? Were you able to identify any heterosexual males or lesbians that you consider close friends? If you were not, it could be helpful to examine any feelings or fears you have about socializing with non-gay men. If you do have friendships with other people besides gay men, it is likely that you are able to identify unique ways in which they enrich your life.

## FRIENDSHIPS WITH HETEROSEXUAL MALES

The traditional definition of male sex roles suggests that a male internalized his masculinity by becoming aware of his membership in the group, adopting the characteristics of that group, and acting according to the widely shared and accepted beliefs about how that group should act (Lazur, 1987). For many men, an unattainable vision of what it means to be a man in this society has dictated their interactions with women and with other men. Thus, many men grow up feeling that to be successful at being a man means doing well in sports, conquering women sexually, suppressing emotions and any indicators of vulnerability, and maintaining a facade of control at all times.

Gay men, too, internalize many of these messages. Yet, rather than strive to attain this hypermasculine image, many gay men retreat from the task and channel their energies into safer, more comfortable areas. For some this meant engaging in activities that were seen by others as not very "manly." For example, instead of playing football or baseball in school, some young gay men opted for drama club or an art class to find a way to express themselves. Regardless of how well they did in these other areas, many gay men grew up feeling inadequate and inferior in their role as men. For some, a mind-set developed that included those men who succeeded at being a man (usually seen as a heterosexual, sports-minded man), and those who fell short of the task (usually seen as themselves and other gay men). Ironically, many heterosexual males grew up believing the same thing.

Early on, therefore, a division was made in the minds of many males that there were activities and interests that straight men had that differed from that of gay men. A consequence of this stereotyping is that it makes it difficult for gay and straight men to believe that they can understand and interact with one another. Fear is often a significant factor for both. The gay man often envies, yet fears, the physical prowess and confidence that many straight men present with, and the straight man fears the sensitivity and vulnerability he perceives in the gay man.

Fortunately, not all gay and straight males buy into this view of what it means to be a man. Men of both persuasions have shown the capacity to be friends with the other without this posing a threat to identity, masculinity, or sexuality. Many straight men have close friendships with gay men in which there is not the veiled concern, "Does he find me attractive?"

One of the central challenges for both gay and straight men is the recognition that friendships between the two groups do not have to feel strained, sexualized, or uncomfortable. Just as some straight men believe that gay men are focused solely on sex, many gay men similarly believe that straight men focus exclusively on sports or women. By opening up and sharing more of who we are, we learn that there can be mutual interests or experiences that can help bridge what we perceive as differences.

Because males are conditioned in our society to believe that relationships between men must be competitive, I hear many gay men express the view that they feel disadvantaged compared to straight males. These men have internalized the negative views of homosexuals so intensely that they feel incapable of having a friendship with a straight man. Thus, they report, straight men take on a mystique that has both a fearful and sexualized quality to it. One client of mine felt so inadequate compared to straight men that he purposely sought these men out as sexual partners. For him, having sex with a straight-identified man neutralized his feelings of inadequacy by bringing the straight man "down to his level."

Fortunately, there are many straight and gay men who consider members of each group among their closest friends. It is a testament to our changing society and our understanding of the broader definitions of manhood that gay and straight men can find intimacy and closeness with one another. I remember my own challenges in this area when I entered my college dormitory my first year of college. As one of only two openly gay men in the dormitory, I witnessed the conflict of men who were forced to confront their prior views about gay men. My roommate, who did not know I was gay for the first five weeks we roomed together, confessed that he would have requested a room transfer had he known in advance I was gay. Yet, we became close friends, and my sexuality was just one other feature of me, just as his interest in racing cars was just one feature of him.

## FRIENDSHIPS WITH HETEROSEXUAL FEMALES

It is not easy being gay or being a woman in our culture. Both groups are subject to being demeaned or ridiculed by the broader heterosexual male community, and both feel the need to prove to others they are more capable, resilient, and intelligent than others might choose to believe. It is quite common for a gay man to first disclose his sexual identity to a woman. It feels safer, there is less of a threat of rejection, and many women are comfortable with this level of disclosure. Alternately, many heterosexual women feel safe around gay men. A complaint from many women is that straight men sexualize many of their mutually intimate encounters. Thus, a simple foot rub or a deep talk about one another's life leads to a sexual encounter. As gay men we are also prone to sexualizing our encounters with other men. By neutralizing the sexual component, gay men and straight women are free to deal with one another in other ways.

As gay men, we are raised feeling more comfortable with women. We learned very early that women are better able to hold and contain our feelings and emotions than we believe men to be. As I alluded to, we often grow up fearing other men. But with women we feel we can share more of our intimate thoughts and feelings, and that we will be accepted for who we are. Thus, we expect nurturance and support from women, and oftentimes this is exactly what we receive from our heterosexual female friends.

Just as many of us feel safe with our female friend, she too feels safe with us. Some women have experienced a great deal of rejection or hurt from nongay men. Their friendship with a gay man helps affirm their womanhood, offer feelings of safety and protection, and provide them with the male companionship they desire. In some instances, straight women actually fall in love with their close gay male friends. Some experience great pain at hearing their gay male friend talk of his romantic adventures, his dating patterns, or the man with whom he has recently fallen in love. I have had many women tell me of the love they have for their gay male friend. Typically these feelings go unexpressed, and the woman silently grieves the loss of the kind of relationship she desires but knows she cannot have with her friend.

Most gay men I know have one or more close straight female friends in their lives. Often this woman has been with them through many years, many loves, and many experiences. It is not uncommon to hear the men and women in these friendships acknowledge the closeness by saying, "If you were not gay/female, I would marry you." Though in a somewhat joking manner, this statement often has an element of truth to the statement, for do not we all desire a love relationship with someone with whom we can be open, loving, and supportive, and who we feel will be with us through all of life's trials?

A dynamic I have often witnessed with several gay male clients is one in which a gay man and straight woman, by all external appearances, are in relationship with one another. They go to the same parties or clubs together, they spend weekend nights together, they travel together, and in some cases, even work or live together. One client of mine had long-term plans with his female roommate to move to a particular island when they retire. It is almost as if the unspoken agreement between them was that neither would end up in relationship with someone else. An uncomfortable reality in these relationships, however, is that sometimes one of the persons does find a romantic partner. When one or the other develops an intimate relationship with someone else, the friend with whom they have spent so much time feels abandoned.

What we teach one another as gay men and straight women is valuable for both. Straight women learn that they can have intimacy and closeness with another man, and that not all men are bad. Similarly, we learn that intimacy does not have to be sexualized, and that tenderness and love can be had outside of the intensity of sexuality.

## FRIENDSHIPS WITH LESBIANS

A curious shift has happened between gay men and lesbians in recent years. It would be overly simplistic to say that gay men and lesbians have historically never befriended one another. Yet, in the broadest terms, post-Stonewall life for lesbians and for gay men differed with regard to where the energy was placed for each. Whereas many lesbians were politically active in both the women's and lesbian movements, gay men were taking advantage of the social and sexual opportunities of the times.

With the onset of AIDS, the attention of many gay men turned toward survival and political activism. Lesbians, who were highly experienced in the areas of political and social change, were instrumental in instructing gay men in the art of protest, advocacy, and working with various systems. Thus, we began to learn that we each had something in common besides our sexual minority status: an investment in being taken more seriously by the larger society.

Beginning in the early 1980s, gay men were fighting for their lives, and many were taking care of friends and lovers who were dying in large numbers. As most major cities developed social service and mental health agencies to cope with the need for support and guidance, gay men were simultaneously finding their energy and resiliency depleted. Many gay men did do the work required to keep these agencies operable, but the lesbian community was instrumental in providing money, resources, and people power to the numerous needs prompted by AIDS.

This union of gay men and lesbians, each fighting for and working toward a common goal, brought the two communities together in ways not seen prior to the AIDS epidemic. Naturally, close friendships between gay men and lesbians developed, and each learned that it is possible for gay men and lesbians to be friends.

Another current cultural shift is in the number of lesbians choosing to bear children. Though many seek the services of sperm banks where the donor is totally anonymous, many lesbians are contracting with gay male friends and associates either to donate sperm or in some cases, to coparent together. Lesbians are also recognizing the value of having male friends they trust who can model opposite-gender behavior for their children. In turn, many gay men now find themselves serving in the role of godfather and/or mentor for the children of their lesbian friends.

## SUMMARY

In conclusion, friends mean a great deal to us as gay men. The support we receive from our friends may be unlike any kind we have ever felt before. Ultimately, a good support system will help us through many of the challenges we have to face as sexual minorities. Further, it is beneficial for us to have friends from all kinds of backgrounds. Just as we, as gay men, add a special and unique quality to their lives, so do they for us.

When we have the support of others, we are better able to handle many of the stresses and difficulties that being gay can entail. Friends, therefore, provide us with a buffer from the harsh treatment or attitudes many of us encounter in our lives.

# Exercises

## *REVIEWING YOUR SUPPORT SYSTEM*

Write down the names of the people you consider to be closest to you. Do not include family members. Though it can be difficult ranking friends in order of closeness, try to include your closest friend(s) first.

_____      _____

_____      _____

_____      _____

_____      _____

### *Questions to Consider*

- What makes each of the above friendships unique from the others? Write down two or more features of each friendship that you consider unique and special about that relationship.

Name: _____

What I consider special and unique about this friendship: _____

_____

_____

_____

Name: _____

What I consider unique and special about this friendship: _____

_____

_____

_____

- What role does your sexual identity play in these friendships? Do you feel that you are closer to or less close to someone because you are gay?

Would the nature or quality of the friendships be different if you were not gay? Does anyone on your list not know you are gay? If so, how do you think your disclosure would affect the friendship?_____

_____

_____

_____

_____

_____

_____

- Even though the list of names includes those friends you consider to be the closest nonfamily members to you, are there needs you desire from a friendship that you do not have with any of the people listed above? If so, what are these needs?

_____

_____

_____

_____

_____

_____

_____

## ALL MY FRIENDS ARE GAY

### Part I

It is not uncommon for some gay men to only have gay male friends. Sometimes this is by choice, while at other times it is just the way things developed. Though there is nothing wrong with having a support network made up exclusively of gay men, it can be helpful to explore if this occurs because of attitudes, stereotypes, or fears you have of nongay people. Thus, this exercise is designed to help you identify the beliefs you have about heterosexual men or women and lesbians.

Please circle the following statements you believe to be true:

- Most lesbians hate men.
- Most women who have gay friends are secretly in love with them.
- Most heterosexual men who have gay friends secretly want to have sex with another man.
- Most lesbians had horrible experiences with men and therefore distrust them.
- Most heterosexual men do not want me as a friend.
- Even if a heterosexual man is a friend to a gay man, he would never admit this to his friends.
- Only a gay man can truly be a friend to another gay man.
- Most lesbians actively compete with men.
- I could never trust a nongay friend the way I do my gay friends.

Each of the statements listed above are comments or beliefs I have heard expressed by clients of mine. If you indicated that you share any of these beliefs I think it is important to examine from where the belief comes. Sometimes our opinions are shaped by experience. At other times our opinions are shaped by stereotypes. Describe below how it is you came to believe that the statements you circled above are true. Afterward you might want to share your thoughts with another friend to see if he or she feels the same as you.

Statement: _____

Why I believe it may be true: _____

_____

_____

_____

_____

_____

Statement: _____

Why I believe it may be true:_____

_____

_____

_____

_____

Statement: _____

Why I believe it may be true:_____

_____

_____

_____

_____

## Part II

Even if the statements do not apply to your belief system, you may have other feelings or beliefs about friendships between you and nongay men. Some of these feelings may be based on personal experience, while others may be based on stereotypes you have, things friends have told you, etc.

In this exercise you are asked to write out your feelings and opinions about heterosexual men and women and lesbians. The goal is to help you identify beliefs you have that prevent you from having close relationships with nongay men. Even if you do not desire such friendships, it can be helpful to identify your belief system, acknowledge how it developed, and discuss this with friends or a therapist. Many people have their own opinions about gay men, and we are just as vulnerable to holding onto our beliefs about others.

How do you feel about friendships with (1) heterosexual men, (2) heterosexual women, and (3) lesbians? If you do not currently have close friendships with people in these categories, could you see yourself having a close friendship with one?

_____

_____

_____

_____

What do you believe would interfere with your having a friendship with a (1) heterosexual man, (2) heterosexual woman, and (3) lesbian? What would you need to discuss with this person before you felt that a friendship is possible?

_____

_____

_____

_____

What are your fears about being friends with a (1) heterosexual man, (2) heterosexual woman, and (3) lesbian? Where do these fears come from? Cite examples.

_____

_____

_____

_____

Name three positive and three negative experiences you have had with (1) heterosexual males, (2) heterosexual females, and (3) lesbians in your life. How were these events influenced by your sexuality?

_____

_____

_____

_____

# Chapter 6

# Gay Male Survivors
# of Childhood Abuse

## *INTRODUCTION*

It is difficult to know exactly how many children are physically or sexually abused in our society. Current estimates are that one in four girls under the age of eighteen, and one in five boys under the age of ten will be sexually abused. Estimates of the physical abuse of children are higher.

What we do have a better understanding of are the effects of childhood abuse and trauma on adult functioning. The experience of sexual abuse, physical abuse, and trauma each have lasting effects on our capacity to trust others, develop satisfying relationships, maintain appropriate boundaries with other people, and feel safe in the world.

All abuse, regardless of how it occurs, is defined by its misuse of power. It is also about violating boundaries. No one has the right to hit a child, subject a child to sexual activity, or place a child in a situation in which he may not be able to voice his opposition to what is happening. Yet, countless numbers of children are victims of violence, sexual exploitation, and emotional torment by one or more family members. Sometimes the abuse happens only once. For others, it is a chronic experience that continues throughout childhood.

## *THE EXPERIENCE OF ABUSE*

A question that arises for me as I write this chapter is whether gay men, in childhood, are at greater risk of being physically, sexually, or emotionally abused. Many of the clients I have seen in my psychotherapy practice indicate such experiences, but clearly there are other gay men who have not been victimized in these ways. Children who grow up to be gay may not necessarily experience more abuse than others, but there are factors that potentially place young gays at greater risk for abuse. These include the following:

- *Greater risk for physical abuse* because they may be seen as timid and unable to defend for themselves. Parents, particularly fathers, may be angry about not having a masculine child who can mirror these attributes back for him. Thus, these fathers may be more likely to take their aggression out on their child.
- *Greater risk for emotional abuse* because he may be seen as different. By not understanding what this difference is about, parents may withdraw, leaving the child vulnerable to feelings of abandonment and depression. Alternately, the sense that their child is different may stir up feelings of vulnerability or inadequacy in the parents. In response, they may punish or harass the child in order to feel more competent or in control.
- *Greater risk for sexual abuse* because of the recognition of attractions toward members of the same sex. These attractions may get sexualized in ways a child does not fully understand. Some adults (or adolescents), sensing the sexual attraction, may engage the young person in inappropriate sexual activity. In response to this, the young person, having his sexual preference validated, may not perceive the experience as abusive. Rather, he reframes it for himself as an initiation.

Regardless of issues of sexual preference, there are common effects or symptoms of childhood sexual or physical abuse. These often include the following:

- Depression
- Withdrawal
- Oppositional behavior
- Difficulties in school
- Anger and hostility
- Running away
- Delinquency

- Low impulse control
- Difficulty making friends
- Fear and distrust of others
- Low self-esteem

In adulthood, the lasting effects from sexual or physical abuse can result in:

- Aggression
- Passivity or overcompliance
- Withdrawal from others
- Poor choice of romantic partners
- Difficulty maintaining relationships
- Sleep disturbance
- Eating disorders
- Inappropriate or compulsive sexual behavior
- Distrust of others
- Hypervigilance
- Substance abuse
- Poor work performance

Eliana Gil (1988) in her study of ninety-nine adult survivors of childhood abuse, found the following symptoms to be common:

- Depression, particularly lethargy, sadness, and sleep disorders.
- Dissatisfaction, or the feeling that nothing is ever working in their lives.
- Low self-esteem, manifested by an inability to identify positive aspects of the self in realistic terms.
- Lack of motivation, defined as an inability to get the energy to go after what they wanted in life.
- Control issues, whereby they described feeling out of control.
- Physical complaints, including frequent headaches, stomach aches, skin problems, and sore throats.
- Relationship difficulties, including fear of commitment, poor choice of partners, and violence.
- Sexual problems, including orgasmic disorders, sado-masochistic practices, and promiscuity.

## HOW DO I KNOW IF IT WAS ABUSE?

The abuse and exploitation that some children experience is so blatant that there is little doubt in their minds that they were sexually, physically, or emotionally abused. For others, violence, heightened sexual tensions, and/or inconsistent parenting just seemed a natural part of growing up in their families (Figure 6.1). Thus, when asked if they ever experienced abuse, they will typically say no.

For some people, it is important for them to believe that they did not experience abuse in childhood. For example, I have had some clients who felt that to acknowledge abuse in their history meant having to face up to some of the deficiencies in their upbringing. Others feel that they only "got what was coming," and that defining certain experiences as abusive would mean having to assume additional blame or responsibility. As Engel and Ferguson (1990) write, "It is just too terrifying for them to think that their parents might be vindictive, unjust, or psychologically troubled" (p. 98).

Granted, it can be a fine line determining whether certain events in your life constitute abuse or not. To help clarify this confusion, I often ask clients to reflect on the following questions:

FIGURE 6.1. A look at the research: Are children at risk for sexual abuse by gay men?

A research team, led by Carole Jenny at The Children's Hospital in Denver, Colorado, wanted to find out if gay men are more likely than nongay men to sexually abuse young children. From July 1, 1991 through June 30, 1992, they reviewed the medical charts of children who were evaluated for suspected child sexual abuse at their hospital. The charts of 269 children, with an average age of 6.1 years, all of whom were sexually abused by adults were reviewed.

Of the male children, 74 percent were allegedly molested by a man who was, or had been, in a heterosexual relationship with the child's mother, foster mother, grandmother, or other female relative. One male perpetrator had been living with the molested child's father, and therefore it was possible that he was gay. However, no other information suggested that the other perpetrators were homosexual or bisexual.

The researchers concluded: "In this sample, a child's risk of being molested by his or her relative's heterosexual partner is over 100 times greater than by someone who might be identifiable as being homosexual, lesbian, or bisexual" (p. 44).

- How was discipline handled in your family? How were you punished, and for what reasons? What was the method of punishment (being grounded, getting talked to or yelled at, spanking under or over clothing and to what part(s) of the body, being hit with a belt, stick, shoe, book, etc.)? In your estimation, did the "punishment fit the crime"? Did the punishment received leave visible scars or bruises?

- **Discussion:** Physical punishment can be an effective, though controversial, way of communicating to a child the parent's anger, dissatisfaction, or disappointment with his behavior. Yet, this is only OK when the child is not placed at risk for physical harm because of the punishment. The likelihood that you were physically abused depends on how the punishment was given. For example, if you were spanked with an open hand over your clothing, it is less likely you were abused. But if your parent(s) used a closed fist, an object such as a coat hanger, belt, stick, etc., the probability of abuse increases. Also, if you were hit on your bottom, this is less severe punishment than being hit in the head, the back, or in your stomach. Though it can be difficult determining this, ask yourself how much control you had, and how out of control you perceived your parent to be, as you were punished. The less control you felt, and the more out of control they seemed can help you determine if the punishment you received was excessive.

- Think back on your earliest experiences with sexual contact with another person. Who was the person or persons? How old were they compared to you? What action(s) took place? Did anything sexually happen with this person on more than one occasion? Who initiated the action? Were you ever asked not to tell anyone what you and this person did? Did the action seem like mutual exploration or did it feel to you that he or she knew more than you did about sex? Did you feel you could have stopped the action(s) without fearing what the other person would do, say, or think? Were you ever told by this person to keep what happened between the two of you a secret?

- **Discussion:** Sexual abuse does not just refer to genital contact between a child and another person. Rather, sexual abuse can take many forms. This can include being touched in a sexual way by another person, being talked to in sexual ways, being looked at in a seductive or provocative manner, having to see others having sex, masturbating, showering, or being naked (if the intent is to stimulate or arouse you), or having someone ask you to take off some or all of your clothing against your wishes.

- Sexual abuse is best viewed as a power imbalance between you and another—usually older—person. If two boys of the same general age are playing "doctor," masturbating, urinating together, or comparing body parts, it is doubtful that this is an abusive situation. Each boy, in this example, is likely a willing participant, and rarely are there threats or coercion in these types of encounters. However, if you are six years of age and a person who is ten, fifteen, or older engages in the same behavior with you, you are at a disadvantage. You may be fearful of what this person might say or do if you choose not to participate. Also, it is probable that he is not just experimenting, but rather engaging you in activities that he previously experienced, perhaps with someone older than he. Technically, it is sexual abuse if the other person does not have the same basic age, knowledge, and experience as you do.

- Sexual abuse has little to do with whether or not you experienced pleasure during the encounter. Most perpetrators of sexual abuse do what they can to minimize having you feel that you are being attacked, brutalized, or harmed in any way. Rather, most of their efforts at engaging a child sexually are skillfully planned so that it appears to you as if "it just happened." Contrary to the stereotype of the *dirty old man* who hangs around playgrounds, most sexual perpetrators are likable, respected, hardworking members of their community. Also, sexual contact, unless forced upon us, is usually enjoyable. This can be true for children, too. I have had clients tell me that they never felt the sexual activity that occurred between an older person and themselves was abusive since they enjoyed it. You may have felt pleasure in what happened between you and an older person, but it can still be considered abusive.

- Many people report growing up in families that had an atmosphere of sexuality to them. Perhaps their mothers dressed provocatively around them, someone hugged them a little too long each time, someone had a pattern of peering into the bathroom while a parent, child, or sibling was in there, etc. Though no overt sexual contact occurred, these types of situations can still leave a child feeling exposed, vulnerable, ashamed, dirty, or seduced. These types of actions are also classified as boundary violations, and they can instill in the observing child feelings that are similar to those felt by the sexually abused.

- Finally, if anyone ever told you to keep the sexual act that occurred between you and they a secret, the chances of the encounter being exploitative are high.

- How were you communicated with by your parents? Did they speak to you in age-appropriate ways? Do you feel you had respect in your family? Were you ever belittled, ridiculed, shamed, or laughed at by your parents? If so, did this ever happen in the presence of others? Were you neglected, left to provide for yourself, left at home alone, etc., at a very young age? Were you ever made to feel bad for being alive, being born, being male, or for being different from other boys?

- **Discussion:** As John Bradshaw (1988) points out, our emotions are part of our basic power. The emotions we have—sadness, fear, guilt, shame, joy, anger—help us monitor our basic needs and provide us with the fuel to act. Without emotion we are psychologically deadened, never knowing who we are or what we need.

- Emotional abuse refers to the ways in which parents neglect or deny us the recognition and affirmation that we are a significant part of their lives, that we are autonomous beings with futures ahead of us, and that we are worthy of love, respect, and the protection we require from them. Some parents, because of their own inability or unwillingness, have a passive indifference to the needs of their children. Unless the child's need is extremely obvious (e.g., hunger), these parents often do not notice or pay attention to them. Therefore, these children either strive to find ways of communicating that they need praise, physical contact, time together, for the parent to come to school events, etc., to their parents, or they learn to do without.

- Children who are emotionally abused are often characterized by behaviors that include hoarding things, acting socially inappropriate, or acting as loners. Emotional abuse can also refer to the deliberate and hurtful things parents say or do that leave the child feeling inferior, stupid, ashamed, and worthless. For gay men, having feelings of vulnerability in childhood because of our difference from others makes any additional rejection or hurt much more severe (Figure 6.2).

FIGURE 6.2. Male perpetrators of childhood sexual abuse: Who are they?

William Prendergast wrote a 1991 book on male sex offenders. In it he describes his experience in working with men who commit sex crimes against others, often younger males. After thirty years experience treating sex offenders, he has identified some common traits and characteristics of male sex offenders. Though there are many, here are a few typical examples:

*Obsessive-Compulsive Disorder:* A significant number of the men Prendergast writes about experience compulsive and repetitive acts and obsessive thoughts prior to actually committing a sex crime. For example, many develop a fantasy of what they would like to do, sexually, to another. Even though they try to eradicate these ideas, they persist, eventually becoming an obsession. The obsession results in a masturbation fantasy that becomes habitual. Over time, masturbation no longer satisfies the obsession and the fantasy gets acted out in some other way. This can be through voyeurism or exhibitionism, but will eventually result in the victimization of someone if the opportunity arises.

*Inadequate Personalities:* Sex offenders typically measure themselves against others. Regardless of how well they do, they constantly feel they "should have done better." Perfectionism thus becomes a part of their lives, but they never feel they reach it. This stems from being raised in families where there was a never-satisfied parent. Prendergast writes, "In my experience, sex offenders handle criticism and insults far better than compliments or praise, although the need for acceptance and approval simply gets stronger and stronger" (p. 13).

*Exaggerated Need for Control:* Control is a central and constant factor in the lives of sex offenders. Not only do they utilize control by sexually abusing their victim, but they use it in other aspects of the victim's life, including making the victim dependent on the offender for love, affection, support, etc.

## *YOU CANNOT JUST FORGET THE ABUSE*

Regardless of the extent of abuse you may have experienced in childhood, you cannot just ignore it and pretend it has no effect on your life. Because of the violations of trust and boundaries to which we have been subjected when someone abuses us, it is difficult not having these experiences affect our adult relationships.

One of the ways we try to regain a sense of control in our lives when we have been abused is to find ways of controlling other people. This can be sexual, emotional, or physical. As mentioned in other chapters, for example, people who were physically abused often grow up and abuse others. Also, people who were sexually abused often grow up with mixed feeling about sexuality and try to control others in sadomasochistic ways.

Since abuse is about taking our control away and violating our personal boundaries, we need to find ways of feeling in control of our bodies and minds without exploiting other people. You can do this by doing the following:

- *Refusing to keep the secret.* If an individual abused you, and afterward told you not to tell anyone, you can regain some control by refusing to give in to this request. Even if it is too late to tell someone who can talk to the abuser, by sharing the secret with another person you take back your power by refusing to obey the command of secrecy.
- *Confront the abuser.* When you were younger, it may not have been possible to stand up to the person who was abusing you and tell them that what they were doing was hurtful, shameful, or against your wishes. In adulthood, no one should have so much power over us so that we cannot tell them how we feel. Even if your abuser is not in your life anymore you can still write him or her a letter or role-play a scenario of you telling this person how you feel, etc.
- *Tell others you were abused.* When people know you were abused, they can be more aware of how certain actions on their part might feel hurtful or intrusive to you. Particularly in relationships, it is important to let our partners know we were abused since issues of intimacy are intricately interwoven with abuse.

- *Recognize that you are not to blame.* It is never your fault that you were abused. It does not matter how bad you were, how provocative you could be, or how much your behavior might have bothered others. If you were abused, the person(s) who did this should have known better. You, on the other hand, have no responsibility for them stepping over the line of appropriate and acceptable behavior.

# Exercises

## *ABUSE IN YOUR CHILDHOOD:*
## *ASSESSING THE IMPACT*

You may feel quite confident that you were abused in childhood. On the other hand, you may be unsure. It is not uncommon to feel certain you were abused one day, only to feel entirely different the next. It is natural for survivors of abuse to wish the abuse never happened. Survivors also do not want to confront all the feelings associated with being a survivor of abuse. Thus, it is easy to feel confused and to wonder if you ever will have all the answers to the questions you have about abuse in your life.

Survivors of abuse inevitably have difficulty with trust. They have a hard time trusting others, and they can have a difficult time trusting their own feelings, reactions, or memories. Issues concerning trust can also result from having been manipulated psychologically and/or sexually at a time of life when you were quite vulnerable.

This exercise is designed to help you identify behaviors and incidents in your childhood that may have been of an abusive nature. You may find that there are questions for which you do not have answers. This is OK. Take your time, do the best you can, and consider making this exercise part of your work with a therapist.

In what way(s) do you feel you might have been abused (circle one or more)?

Sexually     Physically     Emotionally     Other

At what age do you feel the abuse first began? _____

At what age did the abuse stop? _____

Was the abuse chronic or just one time? _____

How frequent were the abusive encounters? _____

List examples of what actually happened to you during the abusive encounters:

_____

_____

_____

_____

_____

Who was/were the perpetrator(s) of this abuse?_____
_____

- If this was a nonfamily member, what was his or her relationship to your family?_____
- What is your current relationship like with this person(s)? _____
_____
_____

- If you still have contact with this person(s), how does this generally feel to you?_____
_____
_____

- Do you know if this person(s) has abused others?   YES   NO
- How do you know this?_____
_____

Was your abuse ever reported to the authorities?   YES   NO
- If YES, describe: _____
_____

Did the abuse leave you with any physical scars that are still present?
YES    NO
- If YES, where are they?_____
- If YES, how do you feel when you see these scars? _____
_____

- Has anyone else seen these scars? If YES, how did you explain the scars and how did they react?_____
_____
_____

Was the abuse sexual in nature?   YES   NO
- If YES, briefly describe: _____
_____
_____

If YES, circle the words below that pertain to the abusive encounter(s):

| | | | |
|---|---|---|---|
| COERCION | ALCOHOL | DARK | COACH |
| DRUGS | RAPE | PARENT | PENETRATION |
| FORCE | LAUGHING | SURPRISE | EJACULATION |
| SHAME | FEAR | WEAPON | TRAUMA |
| PAIN | CAMERA | OTHERS | ARREST |
| ORAL | NIGHT | DAY | SCHOOL |
| SAFETY | SECRECY | PEER | BROTHER |
| SISTER | CHURCH | SHOWER | GENTLE |
| ROUGH | TORTURE | RESCUED | ESCAPE |
| BRIBE | CHOKING | IMPOTENT | ERECTION |
| BREAST | VAGINA | CLOTHING | YELLING |
| ANGER | DISSOCIATION | KISSING | MASTURBATION |
| EROTIC | THREATS | TEACHER | TESTIMONY |
| RESISTED | _____ | _____ | _____ |

• What feelings do you have now as you circle the items?_____

_____

_____

• What associations/memories do you want to write down regarding the words you circled?_____

_____

At the time of the abuse, did you know you might be gay? If YES, in what way(s) did the abuse affect or impact this awareness? _____

_____

How does the sexual abuse affect your current sex life?_____

_____

_____

Does the abuse hold any positive memories for you?   YES   NO
• If YES, describe: _____

_____

• What are the negative consequences for you because of having been sexually abused? _____

_____

_____

- What efforts toward healing have and are you taking in your life? _____

_____

_____

Regardless of the nature or circumstances of the abuse, what coping mechanisms did you use to help you get through (e.g., dissociation, thinking of something else, pretending to be asleep, fighting back, fantasy?)_____

_____

_____

As a survivor of abuse which of the following apply for you when you think of the abuse?

| | | | |
|---|---|---|---|
| GUILT | SHAME | ANGER | DISBELIEF |
| DENIAL | FLASHBACKS | NIGHTMARES | FEAR |
| DISTRUST | IMPOTENCE | PROMISCUITY | RAGE |
| STRENGTH | DEDICATION | FANTASIES | PICTURES |
| REVENGE | ILLNESS | UNCERTAIN | COURAGE |
| VULNERABILITY | SAFETY | PHOBIA(S) | PAIN |
| SCARS | DISTRUST | HOPE | GRIEF |
| SUICIDAL | DISBELIEF | PANIC | MASOCHIST |
| SADIST | LOSS | CONFUSION | AROUSAL |

- Are there one or more others who you feel need to know about the abuse, but you have not been able to tell them? YES  NO

If YES, explain. _____

_____

_____

- Why have you not told this person(s)? _____

_____

_____

- What do you fear will happen if you tell this person?_____

_____

_____

Can you agree that you are not to blame in any way for the abuse you received? YES NO

If NO, why not? Explain in detail:_____

_____

_____

## TALKING ABOUT THE ABUSE YOU EXPERIENCED

For most people who were abused, secrecy, silence, and isolation are part of the experience. Many perpetrators of abuse will threaten their victims by saying:

- Do not tell anyone. This is our secret.
- If you tell, you or I will get into trouble.
- This is something special between you and me. Do not tell so and so.
- If you tell anyone I will say that you made me do it.
- If you tell anyone you will get yours.
- You do not want me to get into trouble, do you?

In addition, most people who were abused grew up feeling that no one was there to protect them. The abuse was something they felt they had to endure, and most did so without telling another person what was going on. Some gay men report not wanting to tell their family members that they were sexually abused out of concern that their family will use this as explanation for why they are gay.

For many adults who were abused as children, they believe it is easier to forget about their abusive past and just move on. They mistakenly believe that to keep the abuse to themselves will help them feel better. I am surprised at the number of clients I know who were abused as children, yet no one in their life—not even long-term lovers—knows of their abusive past.

When you share with another person that you were abused as a child you begin to break the cycle of secrecy that surrounds abuse. You also learn that you no longer need to be afraid of the perpetrator of your abuse. By disclosing the abuse, you begin the process of grieving that was never done. Inside of you is the child you once were who is longing for protection from the physical or emotional pain he experienced. By talking with another person about the abuse, you help heal a painful part of your childhood so that you can have more satisfying adult relationships and experiences.

When you tell another person you were abused in childhood, you can have many positive feelings and experiences. These include the following:

- Feeling relief
- Exposing the offender
- Being honest with those to whom you are close
- Getting in touch with your feelings concerning the abuse
- Stop falling into the trap of obeying the offender
- Finding out you are not the only one
- Recognizing how you might be acting like the offender
- Confronting your denial

The following questions are designed to help you examine your experiences and feelings with disclosing the fact you were abused in childhood to others. Take your time and think about the important people in your life and what you have or have not told them about this sensitive topic.

What was the nature of abuse you experienced as a child?
Sexual   Physical   Emotional

What is the earliest age you remember this happening?_____
Who have you since told about the abuse? _____
Have you told anyone in your family?     YES   NO

_____

• If YES, who?_____

• How was this disclosure of yours received by them?_____

_____

_____

• If NO, why have you not told anyone in your family? _____

_____

_____

_____

What friends of yours have you told? _____

_____

• Describe one or more positive experiences or feelings that resulted from your telling this person(s): _____

_____

_____

_____

• Describe one or more negative experiences or feelings that resulted from your telling this person(s):_____

_____

_____

_____

Of the people you have told, what information have you *withheld* about the abuse you experienced? What are your reasons for having done this?

_____

_____

_____

Who is in your life now that you are close to—perhaps a lover—who does not know you were abused as a child?

_____

_____

_____

- What are your reasons for not telling, or not wanting this/these person/people to know you were abused?_____

_____

_____

- What is your greatest fear or concern about him/her/them knowing you were abused?_____

_____

_____

- What would have to happen for you to disclose this information to the person(s) listed above?_____

_____

_____

Did you ever confront your abuser?   YES   NO

If NO, what has prevented you from doing so? _____

_____

_____

If YES, describe this encounter and bow you feel now about having confronted him or her: _____

_____

_____

# Chapter 7

# AIDS in Our Lives:
# Assessing the Impact

One of the ways in which AIDS has purified so many of us is in how much it tells us that this is not a dress rehearsal. You are being tested, even if there is no headmaster in the sky marking the grades or giving you board scores on those tests. We are being tested by something as deep in ourselves as we could ever be. If you needed any further proof that the material world is not enough to nourish you, that success and money and career are not enough, that the only real nourishment that you can count on is love and that love is possible for all of us, that we can generate it and find it, this is it. What's going to matter to people when they come to the end of their lives is how much they've loved.

Paul Monette
"On Becoming"

## *INTRODUCTION*

Unless you are a relatively young reader, most of you have experienced the full range of the AIDS epidemic, including its discovery, its progression in our lives, and its effects on our community. Increasingly though, younger gay men are aware of the history of AIDS and its impact on the lives of all gay men. I doubt that there are any gay men whose lives have been untouched by AIDS. Even if you are not infected yourself, or have never been involved with someone who is or was, it is likely that one or more of the following have affected your life:

- Modifying your sexual behaviors to prevent HIV infection.
- Having others view you as a gay man in light of their beliefs about AIDS.
- Needing to integrate AIDS into your identity as a gay man.
- Being a member of a community overwhelmed with grief.
- Knowing how many men your own age—or younger—have died from AIDS.
- Becoming friends or lovers with people who have lost loved ones to AIDS.
- Caring for someone who has AIDS.
- Hearing and reading about AIDS monthly, if not more.
- Having people ask you if you have AIDS because you are gay.
- Dealing with the experience and grief of losing someone close to you to AIDS.

Regardless of the ways in which AIDS has affected your own life, ours is a community that is defined and shaped by what has happened over the past decade and a half. Our community is divided into those who have died and those who are living—those who somehow made it through, and those who did not. In essence, we have all been part of a prolonged war—a war that still continues. As is true with all wars, there are those who survive and those who do not.

One of the most difficult things for many of us is assessing what impact this disease has had on our lives, our sexuality, our psychological health, and our overall identity as gay men. Few have wanted to examine this, and unfortunately, some have not had the luxury of time to explore these issues. Sometimes it just seems easier to try to forget all that we have gone through concerning AIDS.

This chapter is for gay men who want to examine the impact of the AIDS epidemic on their lives. This chapter is not designed to be an overview of AIDS nor to educate the reader about AIDS transmission or prevention. Rather, it is a guide to help you take stock of what AIDS has and does mean to you. Regardless of your current health status, we are all survivors of the AIDS epidemic. Because of this, we have witnessed and experienced a great deal. The exercises in this chapter will assist you in the fragile and painful process of taking stock of the role and meaning of AIDS in your life.

## *OUR COLLECTIVE EXPERIENCE OF LOSS*

No two gay men have had identical experiences dealing with the AIDS epidemic. In fact, the only unifying aspect of AIDS for most of us has been the component of loss. I have had clients who have lost their entire support network—forty friends or more—to AIDS. Others have only known people with AIDS in minimal ways. Personally, I have been with men as they were diagnosed, and with others as they lay dying. I sometimes believe that if I were to carefully assess the amount of loss and grief that has affected my life because of AIDS, I would become immobilized. Yet, for whatever reason—if there is one—I have made it this far in life and my challenge is to stay conscious of the effects of AIDS in my life without getting too overwhelmed.

Because AIDS has been with us for so long—almost two decades—we are accustomed to the highs and lows associated with the disease. We hear hopeful medical news, but still our friends get sick and die. We think we cannot experience any more grief, and we unexpectedly find out someone close to us is ill. By necessity, many of us have neutralized our grief, choosing to believe instead that we have already experienced the worst. Yet, we all know that what the doctors and researchers tell us is true; AIDS will probably not go away as we once hoped it would. Rather, in absence of a cure, it will likely become a chronic, manageable condition.

Most of us, however, would be remiss if we did not also acknowledge the benefits to our lives because of AIDS. Many of us can identify influential people in our lives who may not have taught us what they did were it not for them having AIDS. Others can identify profound spiritual experiences and changes in their understanding of our purpose in this world because of AIDS. We have also had our sexual identity challenged in ways we would have never thought possible because of AIDS. Subsequently, we have been provided with the chance to examine what it really means to be a gay man.

Through it all we have seen our individual and collective resiliency as we helplessly stood by and watched a virus that seemingly appeared out of nowhere take our friends, lovers, and members of our community away from us.

## THE CONCEPT OF GRIEF

Grief is the natural response to loss. Even though different individuals and cultures express and approach grief somewhat differently from others, the bereavement we all share when a loved one dies is universal. For those people unaccustomed to the feelings associated with grief, it can be an overwhelming and sometimes terrifying process. However, this is a natural reaction. As psychologist Therese Rando writes: "Grief is the process that allows us to let go of that which was and be ready for that which is to come." Judith Viorst writes: "Mourning is the process of adapting to the losses of our life."

What is sometimes difficult for me is my awareness of two very strong feelings. The first one is intellectual in nature. It is the message inside of me that says:

> *Life is not fair. We will all die eventually. It is to be expected that we will lose loved ones in life. Grief, therefore, is a natural response to this and therefore what you and many of your friends and clients feel is to be expected.*

The other feeling is more reactive and fueled by anger and frustration. It is the struggle within that says:

> *None of us asked for this . . . this thing called AIDS. Don't we have enough struggles as gay men without having to have this added one? It does not make sense that so many people should have their lives taken away because of this disease. Who or what can I get angry at and blame for this? I am tired of the loss, tired of the pain, tired of being worn so thin by it all.*

But whether I or we like or understand any of the realities associated with AIDS, the truth is it is here. It has been here, and it very well may remain part of our world for quite some time. The researchers and physicians can try to address the management and cure of the disease, and the mental health community can examine issues of prevention and coping. Yet, we sit here as gay men watching as the disease takes its toll, and for many gay men, the task is how to keep on going day after day, loss after loss.

This is all part of the grieving process. No one wants to experience the death of their loved ones. Thus, whenever someone dies, it is expected that we will try to deny the reality of it and ask *Why them?* Whether we lose one person or many, the adjustments or tasks we each face are the same. Grief takes energy and it takes work. We may feel that we do not have this energy, or that we want to do the work, but to forestall grief means making our lives even more painful.

## The Basic Task of Grief

Grief is not a passive process. It is much more than just acknowledging the death of a loved one, feeling sad for a period of time, and then moving on with life. Rather, grief is about our identity with ourselves and with the person who has died, and how we reconcile this relationship once they are gone. We typically invest a lot of energy into our friendships and our family and love relationships. When someone close to us dies, we need to adjust—to pull back—on the energy we invest since that person is no longer physically in our lives.

Because of this, the most significant task in the grieving process is to adapt to—and work with—the change that has occurred in one's relationship with the deceased. This does not mean forgetting about the person or ignoring what you and the other had. Rather, it means looking closely at how you invest your energy into this other person. As Rando writes:

> What is changed is the griever's ongoing investment in and attachment to the deceased as a living person who could return the investment. The energy that previously went into keeping the relationship with the deceased alive must be channeled elsewhere, where it can be returned.

This means that we have to view and interact with the world as a place that no longer has our loved one(s) in it. We may have to adopt or learn new skills, take over duties or roles the other once fulfilled, form new relationships, and often learn to function as an *I* instead of as a *we*. Dreams, goals, or fantasies that we once held about our future may all be changed after a loved one dies. Thus, when someone close to us dies, we not only lose our present but our future.

## Physiological Symptoms Associated with Grief

Grief is not just a mental process and experience. Rather, when someone we love dies, it is natural that our bodies will react to the loss. This can be very scary for many gay men who start to worry that they too might have AIDS. These symptoms do not happen all at once, and some can manifest long after the deceased has passed away. Particularly if one fights or prolongs the grieving process, these symptoms can continue and eventually lead to chronic physical or psychological problems.

The following are the more common physical symptoms associated with grief. It is helpful to understand that many of these symptoms should be expected and anticipated during the grieving process.

- Sleep difficulties
- Crying spells
- Physical exhaustion or fatigue
- Difficulty concentrating
- Gastrointestinal disturbances
- Heart palpitations or shortness of breath
- Restlessness

When we fail to adequately grieve the death of someone close to us, these symptoms can remain. Thus, instead of being natural reactions to loss, they become permanent conditions that can cause us further problems and complications with our physical and mental health.

## Psychological Symptoms Associated with Grief

In addition to physiological symptoms that occur during the grief process, it is common to have many psychological symptoms as well. Some of these can feel very overwhelming and can cause great distress. For example, after someone dies—particularly a lover—it is common to experience guilt. You may feel guilty for things you said to your partner during the relationship, or you may feel guilt for things you did of which he was not aware. When you recognize that guilt is a common feeling after losing someone, you can hopefully find ways of not being so hard on yourself.

The following psychological symptoms can manifest during the grieving process. It is important to know that they are natural responses to grief and therefore should be anticipated.

- Guilt
- Depression
- Anger
- Feeling disorganized
- Yearning and searching for the deceased
- Mental numbing
- Hostility
- Loss of capacity to love
- Disbelief
- Withdrawal from others
- Panic and despair
- Fear

### Three Stages of Grief

Therese Rando (1984) identifies three broad categories associated with grief. Viewing grief in stages helps us see that grief is a progressive, rather than an isolated, event. The stages Rando identifies are:

- *Avoidance.* Just as the body goes into shock after a large insult, so does the human psyche. As recognition of the loss sets in, so does denial. Denial has a therapeutic quality to it during the early stages of grief by preventing us from becoming totally overwhelmed.
- *Confrontation.* This is the stage that grief is experienced most intensely. Rando terms the stage *angry sadness.* Emotions are extreme in this stage, and the recognition that we are behaving

and feeling differently than normal makes the experience more painful and frightening. Common reactions include anger, guilt, and depression. Rando writes: "In an effort to attempt to gain some control and understanding over what appears to be a meaningless, unmanageable event, the bereaved often engage in an obsessional review of the circumstances of the death."

• *Re-establishment.* In this phase, the loss is not forgotten, but merely put in a special place which, while allowing it to be remembered, also frees us to go on with life. Guilt can be expected in this stage, however, as we may erroneously feel we are betraying the deceased by enjoying and resuming our life.

## GRIEF AND AIDS

Although there are exceptions, grief is often an isolated event. When a lover dies, for example, many people are affected. However, no one experiences the loss in the way that the surviving partner does. Family and friends may rally around this person for the immediate days following the death, but it is common that people start to pull back and the surviving partner is left to deal with his feelings and loss mostly on his own.

AIDS has not necessarily changed this, but the other people who experience the loss to AIDS have their own unique feelings and circumstances. Surviving multiple AIDS deaths has become the norm for many gay men. This affects not only the individual survivor, but also the entire gay community. Thus, our community is now defined by the amount of loss we have experienced. Therefore, when any of us lose someone to AIDS, it reminds us of all the previous losses we have experienced. This is not necessarily the case when a loved one dies of cancer or in an automobile accident.

As David Nord writes:

Loss from AIDS includes much more than death. While deaths certainly compose a significant part of the loss experience resulting from AIDS, and the other losses arise mainly because of the reality and risk of death, other types of losses are important to the analysis of effects. Particularly in the gay community, multiple AIDS-related loss includes death, loss of social support, loss of community leaders, loss of role models, loss of sexual spontaneity, loss of potential and loss of future plans. (1990, p. 2)

Also, if you look at death resulting from cancer, auto accidents, plane crashes, shootings, etc., these often have a feeling of being removed from us. We know that we are all potentially at risk for such occurrences, but it always seems unlikely that it will happen to us. As gay men, however, we come to expect that gay men die of AIDS. We cannot help, therefore, feeling on one level that our own fate is death from AIDS. Each AIDS death reminds us of these feelings.

I remember one client I worked with for three years when I had my private practice in California. Five months into his therapy, he and his lover of fourteen years decided to get tested for HIV for the first time. His lover tested positive and he tested negative. This turned out to be one of the most devastating events of his life. Having already lost most of his gay male support system to AIDS, there was now the possibility of losing his lover. The grief he felt—and anticipated—was just too overwhelming, for he not only had to grieve past losses, but the future ones as well.

## SURVIVAL GUILT

A former client of mine came out as gay while attending college in San Francisco. At college he met six other gay men and they all developed strong friendships. On weekends, the seven of them would go to the bars and clubs, dancing until dawn. They also went to concerts together, met one another's boyfriends, did drugs together, and went to the baths together. This was in 1978.

After graduating from college, each of them continued to live in the same general area. Even though their lives were busier than in college, they still got together on weekends, and continued to share with one another the most intimate details of their lives.

By the time my client came to see me in 1990, all but he and one of these other men had died. The friend that was living was very ill, and my client knew it was just a matter of time before this friend would also die. One year after my client started therapy with me, his friend died. My client had been with him up until his death, telling him stories of their college days, and offering support during his final hours.

Two days later my client was placed in a psychiatric hospital on suicide watch. The death of his sixth friend had been too much for him to handle, and he did not feel he could go on living.

Some may read the above scenario and see my client's desperation as a natural response to losing the last of his group of friends. Though this was very much a part of his reaction, there is a much more significant factor—a factor that countless numbers of gay men experience daily. My client was feeling guilty, depressed, and suicidal for surviving AIDS. Though he and his friends shared everything for thirteen years, including very active sex lives with many different men, my client continued to test HIV-negative.

These feelings are highly conflictual for gay men. On the one hand, they are thankful to be alive. On the other, they feel tremendous guilt for surviving while so many of their friends have passed on. Many gay men, faced with such feelings, seek to alleviate them by actively trying to get infected with HIV.

These feelings refer to what is termed *survival guilt*. This is the guilt we feel for making it through a trauma or difficult circumstance when others did not. As Marion (1996) phrases it, survival guilt refers to grief about surviving. This is not just a phenomena of AIDS but rather, it is a very natural response on the part of all survivors. I remember working with families who lost their homes in the 1991 Oakland Hills fire. This fire ravaged through the hillside neighborhoods of Oakland and Berkeley, wiping out hundreds of homes. In a panic to get to a safer location, or in an effort to save their home from fire, many people died. This fire was driven by wind, which meant that it would literally skip homes. An entire block of homes would be totally destroyed, yet there would be one or two homes standing with little noticeable damage. Though those who lost their homes were highly traumatized, those whose homes remained felt guilt that their homes did not burn. Many were heard to say they wish their homes had burned too.

These same types of comments were heard from survivors after the Oklahoma City bombing, in which over 150 people died. Whereas walls crashed down and killed many, others were able to escape or be rescued with only some bruises or cuts. For them, they could not help asking, Why them? Why not me?

Inherent in the survival guilt that gay men feel is the recognition that the course of AIDS does not make rational sense. Just as the Oakland Hills fire jumped homes and trees that were as combustible and vulnerable as the surrounding ones that burned, some gay men find themselves infected with HIV while others are not. Men with histories of rampant and frequent sex test negative, while one client of mine who died of AIDS indicated he only had anal sex once. Does it make sense, logically? Of course not. Yet, many of us lose this perspective when we feel guilty for being alive.

### You Feel Guilty for Being Alive?

Inherent in survival guilt are feelings that we, too, should be HIV-infected, sick, or dead. It is the feeling that we got away with something that we should not have. In essence, we feel guilty for being alive.

When we feel guilty for being alive, we are likely to do things to punish ourselves. Though suicide is the most dramatic and profound form of punishment, most gay men are apt to punish themselves in more subtle ways. Examples of the way gay men who have survival guilt will punish themselves include the following:

- *Trying to get infected with HIV.* They believe that they, too, should be infected. Many will say that they do not feel like real gay men since all gay men get AIDS and die. Thus, to them, HIV infection equals being included instead of excluded. As one client of mine said, "The pain of being HIV positive is surely less than the pain of surviving while all my friends die."
- *Abuse of alcohol or drugs.* Just as gay men who feel bad or guilty for being gay will try to drown their feelings with alcohol or drugs, men with survival guilt will similarly try to find ways of neutralizing their pain. Substance abuse is often the most subtle, and accepted way, gay men punish themselves.
- *Failure in other areas of life.* Gay men who feel guilty will have difficulty achieving success in any area of life. Thus, to punish themselves for being alive, or for surviving while others do not, they will sabotage good things in their life. This might include ending a good or promising relationship, work-

ing below their potential, messing up at work in order to avoid a promotion, etc.

Just as I wrote in Chapter 2 that we need to stop feeling we have done something wrong because we are gay, we similarly need to stop feeling guilty for being alive in the age of AIDS. Many gay men do get AIDS, but this does not mean that all gay men will get AIDS. We know how to prevent further infection—to ourselves and to others—and we owe it to ourselves to stay healthy (Figure 7.1).

## AIDS AS TRAUMATIC STRESS

Most of us are probably able to identify one or two events in our life that we found fairly traumatic. For example, I remember almost being hit by a truck in Texas when I was twelve years old. I never saw the truck coming. All I remember is my mother yelling and the wind from the truck blowing my shirt away from my skin as it passed within six inches of my body. From your own childhood, you may remember being lost in a crowd of people, being unable to open a locked door, or falling off a bicycle. Though we all experience these types of events in our lives, most of us are still able to cross busy roads, enter rooms with locks on the doors, attend large events, and ride on bicycles or in cars.

There are some events, however, that are so traumatic we say that they are outside the range of normal human experience. This would include being kidnapped, having objects fall on you during an earthquake, being trapped by fire, being near a bomb blast, being in a place where there is random shooting going on, etc. What distinguishes these types of events from those mentioned is that most of us know that if we experience a near-miss auto accident or if we fall off a bicycle we can take steps to avoid this happening again. We may be fearful for a while, but generally we can reengage with things that caused us the potential of harm. With these latter examples, however, what makes them different are two main features:

1. You do not know when or if the event will end.
2. You are not sure until it is over that you will not die.

FIGURE 7.1. A look at the research: Why do some gay men continue to have unsafe sex?

In 1991 and 1992, researchers from several U.S. universities surveyed gay men in sixteen different cities about their sexual practices. The researchers, under the guidance of Jeffrey A. Kelly at the Medical College of Wisconsin, were primarily interested in surveying gay men living in or near smaller cities, those with populations of less than 180,000 people. They wanted to include gay men from small cities, rather than larger ones, since all other studies on gay male sexual behavior had been done in major metropolitan areas such as New York, Chicago, and San Francisco.

The researchers collected data from 5,939 men, with the average age of the sample being thirty-one years. Of these men, 1,943 indicated that they were in an exclusive relationship with another man and that they had no other sexual partner for the past year or longer. Therefore, these men were not included in the final analysis, leaving 3,996 men.

In addition to demographic data, each man was asked to complete a anonymous questionnaire that assessed the following:

- *Sexual behavior over the past two months.* The primary interest of the researchers was determining from these questions whether the respondent had engaged in unprotected anal intercourse with male partners in the past two months.
- *Safer sex social norm perception.* These questions were asked to assess the respondent's perceptions of peer group social norms concerning safe sex. A sample question was: "Do your friends always use condoms during intercourse?"
- *Personal risk estimation.* Respondents indicated their perceived personal estimate of risk for contracting HIV infection based on their behavior over the past two months.
- *Condom use behavioral intentions.* Respondents were asked how likely it is they would use a condom during their next intercourse occasion.
- *HIV testing history.* If and when they had tested.
- *Bar attendance:* Number of times in the past two months they visited a gay bar.
- *Conversations about safe sex.* The number of times in the past two months they had a conversation with a friend or acquaintance about safe sex.

Results

Twenty-seven percent of the sample reported engaging in unprotected anal intercourse as either the receptive or insertive partner, or both, during the two months before survey completion. The researchers found that men who engaged in unprotected anal intercourse were younger and had less education than their counterparts, and they more frequently patronized bars. Men who continue to engage in high-risk sexual behavior reported that safe sex is not as salient of a social norm within their own peer reference group as men who behave safely. The researchers note that, contrary to expectations, estimated perception of personal HIV risk was higher among men who continued to engage in unprotected anal intercourse, suggesting that these men were aware of their risk.

In my opinion, what most of us as gay men have been experiencing is stress related to trauma. Psychiatry has often used the term *post-traumatic stress disorder* to refer to symptoms associated with experiencing an event outside the range of normal human experience. However, as Marion (1996) points out, the stress associated with AIDS is not in our past. Rather, it continues and there is no end in sight. Thus, what many of us experience is a more active and *current* stress disorder.

One of the ways in which AIDS feels like a war—other than the high death toll—is how we hear of the deaths of others. For example, when one of my former supervisors suddenly died of AIDS, I was informed of this by a coworker in the hallway. I found out one client of mine died when he did not show for his session and I phoned his home and spoke with a family member. I have also learned of the death of people I knew from obituaries, news coverage, friends on the street, and even from clients. When this happens in life once or twice we can assimilate it. When it is repeated and frequent, knowing how to integrate this reality into our lives becomes increasingly difficult.

San Francisco psychiatrist Lenore Terr (1990), who based on her work with child victims of trauma, points out that traumatic stress reactions involve a variety of characteristics. These include the following: terror; rage; denial and numbing; shame and guilt; misperception; repeated dreams; and post-traumatic reenactment.

## Terror

The fright that results from traumatic stress is so unique that Terr says we do not even have a "right" word in the English language to describe it. Terror leads to a fear of fear itself. When it is over, most survivors of trauma are not even able to conceptualize that they have survived or escaped.

## Discussion

The terror many gay men have felt concerning AIDS covers so many different areas of life. From checking ourselves in the shower for the sudden appearance of skin blotches, to dreading the results from an HIV test, we have all found ourselves in a terrified state of mind because of AIDS many times over the past several years. One of the most difficult pieces for many gay men has been the fear of getting close to another man because of fear of infection or fear of losing him to AIDS. Many gay men have also dealt with the fear associated with losing an entire support network, while countless numbers of people with AIDS have confronted the terror of dying from a horrible disease. Most of us try to keep our own fears about AIDS at a manageable distance, but each of us can probably identify the ways in which fear has been a significant part of our experience with this disease.

### Rage

Terr points out that one of the earliest qualities humans develop is our autonomy. In traumatic situations we are robbed of our autonomy; we are totally helpless and we know it. Traumatic stress stirs up our fear and aggression, but rarely is there a suitable outlet for our feelings. So it stays inside of us and we remain angry.

### Discussion

From *Why him?*, to societal prejudice, to lack of government intervention in finding a cure for AIDS, the rage many of us feel is probably deeper and more intense than even we are aware of. Sometimes crying over our losses feels easy, but accessing the anger seems difficult. Yet, anger must be expressed. If it does not get discharged directly, anger will emerge indirectly. Indirect expressions of anger include depression, whereby the anger immobilizes us; identification with the aggressor, where we feel omnipotent to the effects of HIV and do not practice safe sex; or hostility, where we take our anger out on anyone who is around us by being mean, rude, disrespectful, or condescending.

### Denial and Numbing

Once disasters start piling up, we learn to deny the reality of this. We brace for more psychic shocks. We prepare. Eventually we begin to feel nothing and ignore what is going on. We guard against thinking about it. In essence, long-standing trauma makes us psychically dead.

*Discussion*

Some of the men I have seen in therapy would rather talk about any life event other than AIDS. For them, the toll the disease had on their lives and psyche left them void of energy for addressing the losses they experienced. Some report that others tell them of the recent death of a mutual friend with a neutral, casual style. Generally, they are shocked by this until they realize that their reaction to hearing the news is just as empty.

### Shame and Guilt

We do not want others to see that we were once vulnerable. So instead we refrain from talking about our traumatic experience. We want others to see us as people who are in control. When we find ourselves in circumstances we cannot control—and when others know this—we start to feel ashamed of ourselves and guilty for our helplessness.

*Discussion*

How many conversations have you had with friends about AIDS? When you talk about AIDS, do you focus on the number of friends you have lost, or do you also share the fear, anger, and sadness you have? Do you tell friends of the sexual risks you have taken since knowing how AIDS is transmitted? Do you think they have been honest with you in this area? If you have symptoms of survival guilt, with whom do you share this?

### Misperception

Trauma causes us to self-anesthetize ourselves. It is a protection we utilize to prevent ourselves from becoming totally overwhelmed. Yet when we are not fully paying attention, we misread what is going on around us. Our memories of what actually happened can therefore change over time.

## Discussion

One of the hazards of anesthetizing ourselves is the method(s) we use to achieve this. If we rely upon denial, we take the risk of forgetting to practice safe sex every time. If we rely upon substances, we risk developing an addiction. It is difficult to stay conscious of all our feelings about AIDS and loss. Yet we must not lose sight over what our experience with this disease has been.

### Repeated Dreams

Psychic trauma leads us to have dreams of the exact event itself, dreams in which the event is modified, dreams in which the traumatic event is disguised, and dreams that are so terrifying that we cannot remember them. Each leaves us, upon awakening, feeling uncomfortable and nervous.

## Discussion

Dreams represent a form of communication. They help us know what feelings or conflicts we have about different areas of our lives. What have been your dreams involving AIDS-related themes? Do you dream of getting sick, of seeing friends who have died? Try to remember these dreams. It can be very informative for you if you write your dreams down and review what you have written periodically.

### Post-Traumatic Reenactment

Terr tells the story of Alfred Hitchcock's father sending him to the police station with a note after he had done something his father thought wrong. The police officer read the note and subsequently locked the young boy in a jail cell. Not knowing how long he would be in jail, he was obviously disturbed and traumatized by this event—so much so, writes Terr, that most of Hitchcock's films have themes of fear or prison and confinement and the fear of pursuit by the law.

## Discussion

The most hazardous form of reenactment we can do is to practice unsafe sex. We may defiantly believe we are not vulnerable to infection, or we may act careless in an attempt to get infected. By doing these things, we risk retraumatizing ourselves.

## DEALING WITH AIDS
## IN THE HERE AND NOW

One basic tenet of psychotherapy is that you never ask a client to work on issues that you, the psychotherapist, have not fully addressed yourself. For me, it has been a struggle trying to sort out how much of my own grief process I have addressed in my personal life. Sometimes I think I am doing a fine job of coping with the amount of loss I have experienced, and then I hear or read something that catches me off guard and I am back to feeling vulnerable, angry, and devastated by the impact of AIDS in my life.

Given the ways in which AIDS has affected our lives and our identity as gay men, it is not realistic to think of an end point for our grieving process. If AIDS had entered our lives when it did and then ended sometime thereafter, the situation would be different. As I wrote, AIDS is a disastrous event that has not ended and we can expect it to be here for quite some time.

Therefore, one of the greatest challenges for each of us is to maintain recognition and awareness of AIDS without becoming so overwhelmed that we cannot function. To do this takes effort and support from others. Here are some ways we can maintain our psychological health given the reality of AIDS in our lives:

- *Do not deny that AIDS is here.* When you pretend that AIDS does not exist, you deny one of the most important—albeit painful—realities of being gay. AIDS is in our lives. There will be more of our brothers who will die from the disease. We owe it to them and to ourselves not to ignore the tragedies of this disease.
- *Help out in whatever way you can.* A client of mine, upon learning of his AIDS diagnosis, reported to me that his friends told him they could not be there for him. They said they had lost too many friends to AIDS and could not endure the process one more time. He told me he understood this since he felt the same. Many gay men feel unable to help others who are

dying of AIDS. Yet, you do not have an obligation or duty to devote all your energy toward the AIDS crisis. There are many ways you can make a difference: Reach out to a friend with AIDS in whatever way you can, volunteer for an AIDS service organization, donate money to AIDS charities, educate your family and friends about AIDS.

- *Keep addressing grief in your life.* Allow time in your life for acknowledging those people you have known who have died from AIDS. Attend AIDS memorial marches, burn a candle on the anniversary of their deaths, plant a tree in memory of them, visit the NAMES Project Memorial Quilt, record your feelings in a journal, etc.

- *Have safe sex every time.* It only takes one unsafe sexual encounter to become infected with HIV. Maintain a commitment to yourself and to your community not to put yourself at risk for becoming infected with HIV. You cannot end AIDS altogether, but you can prevent yourself from getting the disease if you are currently uninfected.

- *Remember other survivors.* Check in with your friends who have lost people to AIDS—particularly if you know someone who lost his lover. Ask them how they are doing, even if the death was long ago. Try to be extra supportive during the holidays, anniversaries, etc.

- *Do not let others forget.* Do not hide from others what your experiences with AIDS have been. Share your stories, losses, and feelings. If you know nongay people who have not lost friends to AIDS, let them know what it has been like for you. When you share your experiences with others, you help your own grief process, keep the memory of your loved one alive, and remind yourself and others that your life has been significantly affected by this disease.

# Exercises

## AIDS IN YOUR LIFE: TAKING STOCK

This exercise is designed to help you examine your experiences with AIDS over the course of the epidemic. I encourage you to take your time with this exercise, as many of the questions require you to think back to earlier times and experiences. You can expect that strong, and sometimes painful, memories and feelings will arise as you do this exercise. This is OK; it is part of your grieving process. You may want to record any feelings that arise during this exercise in your journal or discuss them in therapy.

### Early Memories of AIDS

How old are you now?_____

How old were you in 1981?_____

The difference between the two is how many years?_____

What significant events (e.g., grade school, college, divorce, major illness, new relationship, new job) were happening in your life in 1981? Include as many as you can remember:_____

_____

_____

Write about where you were in your gay development in 1981; that is, were you out as a gay man? Were you sexually active? If so, in what ways (with a lover, with a roommate, going to the baths, etc.)? Did others know you were gay? Did you have gay friends or a lover? How active were you in gay activities (politics, bars, parties, parades)?_____

_____

_____

_____

If you were not out as a gay man in 1981, describe what feelings or experiences, if any, you had that helped to shape your identity as a gay man. What were your beliefs about gay men at this time?_____

_____

_____

_____

When did you first hear about AIDS? Remember that AIDS was originally called GRID (Gay-Related Immune Disorder) and later, in 1983, HIV (Human Immunodeficiency Virus). Describe this in as much detail as you can. What or who was the source? What was being said? Do you recall what you were feeling?_____

_____

_____

_____

_____

What do you remember as your first—or one of your first—feelings in response to AIDS? (e.g., fear, indifference, disbelief, curiosity, etc.)? Describe: _____

_____

_____

_____

_____

Regardless of when you first heard of AIDS, write about your earliest memories about the disease. What can you recall hearing from teachers, friends, the media, other gay men, etc., about AIDS? What were your feelings and reactions to hearing this? _____

_____

_____

_____

_____

### Safe Sex Practices

When do you recall first hearing about safe sex and/or condoms for gay men? How did you hear this information? What was your reaction to hearing this information? _____

_____

_____

_____

_____

When was the first time you practiced any kind of safe sex? Who were you with? What did you do? Was it you or your partner who introduced the idea of practicing safe sex? _____

_____

_____

_____

Did you ever think that the safe sex guidelines did not apply to you? If YES, describe why: _____

_____

_____

_____

Describe the way(s) in which AIDS has altered or changed your sexual activity and behavior. Be specific: _____

_____

_____

_____

Were there ever times that you thought or feared you might have AIDS? If YES, describe why you thought you had AIDS and what your reaction(s) were: _____

_____

_____

_____

When did you first take the HIV test? _____
• What were your feelings leading up to this decision? _____

_____

_____

• How did you react to hearing the test results? _____

_____

_____

• How has your sexual behavior changed since receiving your test result?

_____

_____

_____

Think back to when you first heard about safe sex for gay men. Now think about the time(s) since then that you have had high-risk sex with no protection (e.g., anal intercourse, oral sex with ejaculation). Answer the following:

• Why do you think you did not practice safe sex after learning about it?

_____

_____

_____

• What thoughts or feelings do you recall having during these sexual encounters about AIDS and HIV? _____

_____

_____

_____

• Were there times that you had unsafe sex because you were afraid or reluctant to bring up the topic with a partner? If YES, describe your feelings:

_____

_____

_____

• How have your sexual partners reacted to your wanting to practice safe sex?

_____

_____

• Have you ever had sex with someone after he told you he did not want to practice safe sex? If YES, why did you have sex with him? Describe your feelings and thoughts during this encounter? _____

_____

_____

_____

• Have you ever had unsafe sex with someone you knew to be HIV positive? If YES, describe why you had unsafe sex with him. _____

_____

_____

### AIDS Loss

What is your estimate of the number of close friends you have lost to AIDS? _____
Write down the names of some or all of the people you knew who have died of AIDS:

_____    _____    _____

_____    _____    _____

_____    _____    _____

_____    _____    _____

_____    _____    _____

_____    _____    _____

How was it for you writing down these names? _____

_____

_____

Did you easily remember the names of those persons you knew who died of AIDS or did you have to strain to remember? _____

_____

_____

_____

Are you finding now that there are people you once knew who died of AIDS but you cannot remember their names?   YES   NO
• If YES, what are your thoughts' and feelings about this? _____

_____

_____

_____

Write down the names of people you know who are HIV positive who are still alive:

_____   _____   _____

_____   _____   _____

_____   _____   _____

_____   _____   _____

_____   _____   _____

_____   _____   _____

- How do you feel as you write down these names? _____

_____

_____

Who was the first person you knew who was HIV positive? _____
- What was your relationship to this person? _____
- Were you ever afraid of catching AIDS from this person?   YES   NO
- If YES, describe: _____

_____

_____

- Has this person died?   YES   NO
- If YES, when did this person die? _____
- Were you with him shortly before his death?   YES   NO
- Did you attend a memorial service?   YES   NO
- Did you make a quilt or other memorial to him?   YES   NO
- How often do you find yourself thinking of this person? Describe:

_____

_____

_____

- What do you miss the most about this person? _____

_____

_____

If you have lost more than one friend, lover, or family member to AIDS answer the following:

• Which loss has been the most difficult for you? Describe: _____

_____

_____

_____

• Do you ever have nighttime dreams about any of these people? If YES, describe. Write down the content of one or more of these dreams:_____

_____

_____

_____

_____

• Describe a happy memory you have about any of these persons' illness and/or death:_____

_____

_____

_____

• What physical reminders (photograph, belonging) do you still have that helps keep the memory of any of these people alive for you? What meaning do these hold for you?_____

_____

_____

• Do you commemorate the anniversary of any of these deaths? If YES, how?_____

_____

_____

• If NO, would you like to?   YES   NO
• If YES, how could you begin doing so?_____

_____

_____

Do you find yourself thinking of former gay friends or lovers, wondering if they are alive? If YES, write the name(s) of those you think about:

_____      _____

_____      _____

_____      _____

- What prevents you from trying to contact them or others who would know of their whereabouts?

_____

_____

_____

What has your experience with death and loss to AIDS taught you about life, death, God, religion, meaning, illness, and/or being gay?_____

_____

_____

_____

### Other Losses

What other losses have you experienced because of AIDS? For example, what changes have you made, in response to AIDS, in meeting men, going to bars or baths, etc.?_____

_____

_____

_____

How has this felt for you? _____

_____

_____

_____

### Continuing to Live

What do you do now that helps you cope with the losses you have experienced because of AIDS? This includes journal writing, talking to friends, going to a psychotherapist, praying, etc._____

_____

_____

_____

How do you discharge or express the following feelings you might have about AIDS?

• Anger:_____

_____

_____

• Sadness:_____

_____

_____

• Fear:_____

_____

_____

• Guilt: _____

_____

_____

Describe the most profound experience you feel you have had because of AIDS:

_____

_____

_____

_____

• What has this experience taught you about coping in the midst of loss?

_____

_____

_____

_____

What can or do you do to help others cope with the realities of AIDS?

_____

_____

_____

_____

_____

## *PHOTOGRAPHS AND STORYTELLING*

For this exercise you will need two things:

1. One or more photographs of loved ones who have died from AIDS.
2. A friend, therapist, or family member who will listen to you tell your story.

Tell your friend or therapist that you would like to bring your photograph(s) of your friend(s) who have died from AIDS with you the next time the two of you get together. If you are doing this with a friend, he or she can bring photographs also. On the designated day, choose a photograph and place it where you both can see it. Tell your friend or therapist that you would like to tell him or her about this person and what he or she meant to you in your life. You can say as little or as much as you would like. Consider including in your story answers to the following questions:

- How did you and this person meet?
- How long did the two of you know one another?
- What is your best memory of this person?
- What is your worst memory of this person?
- What is a funny story you have about this person?
- What has this person taught you about life?
- How did you deal with his or her death?
- What is missing from your life with him/her gone?
- How do you keep your memories of him/her alive?
- What, if anything, do you think happened to him/her after death?
- What would yours and his/her life be like today if this person were still alive?
- What is the most difficult part of him or her being gone?

## *IF YOU ARE HIV-INFECTED*

When did you find out you were HIV-infected? _____
How did you find this out?_____

_____

_____

If you found out you were HIV positive by taking the HIV test, did you think the results would turn out?   NEGATIVE    POSITIVE
- If you thought you would test HIV negative, what was it like hearing you are HIV positive? _____

_____

_____

- If you thought you would test HIV positive, in what ways did you and did you not react to this news as you thought you would? _____

_____

_____

What has surprised you the most about your reactions to dealing with being HIV positive?_____

_____

_____

How long after receiving the news of your HIV status did it take for the impact of this information to set in with you? _____

_____

_____

- Who was the first person you told about being HIV positive?_____

_____

- How did this person respond to hearing this news?

_____

_____

- Did your relationship with this person change after you told them you are HIV-infected?  YES   NO
- If YES, describe:_____

_____

_____

Who was it most difficult for you to tell you are HIV-infected?_____
- Explain why this was: _____

_____

_____

- How has your relationship with this person changed since telling them?

_____

_____

- Did you have a lover when you found out you are HIV positive? YES NO
- If YES, how did you feel about telling him?_____

_____

_____

- Did he react as you thought he would? Describe: _____

_____

_____

- How do you feel being HIV positive has affected this relationship?_____

_____

_____

Describe how your sex life and/or sexual feelings changed after finding out you are HIV positive:_____

_____

How long was it before you were able to be sexual with someone after finding out you are HIV positive?_____

Describe what it was like for you having sex for the first time after finding out you are HIV positive:_____

_____

_____

Did this person know you are HIV-infected?_____
- If YES, how did he know this?_____

_____

- If NO, how did you feel about this? _____

_____

_____

What has it been like for you telling sexual partners you are HIV-infected?

_____

_____

_____

- What has been your best experience in telling sex partners you are HIV positive?_____

_____

_____

_____

- What has been your worst experience in telling sex partners you are HIV positive?

_____

_____

_____

Discuss how much thought you give to your HIV status when you have sex with someone: _____

_____

_____

_____

_____

- How has this changed since you first found out you are HIV positive?

_____

_____

_____

Do you ever blame yourself for being HIV positive?  YES   NO
- If YES, describe and cite examples:_____

_____

_____

Who or what do you get the most angry at when you think of being HIV-infected? Describe and cite examples: _____

_____

_____

_____

What decisions have you made in life since knowing you are HIV positive that you probably would not have made otherwise? Describe and cite examples:_____

_____

_____

_____

Name four good things that have happened to you because of being HIV positive:

1._____

2._____

3._____

4._____

How has being HIV positive affected your religious or spiritual belief system? _____

_____

_____

_____

How do you maintain hope in light of being HIV positive? _____

_____

_____

_____

What do you see as your greatest challenges in your life given that you are HIV-infected? _____

_____

_____

_____

_____

# Chapter 8

# The Aging Gay Man:
# Lessons and Challenges
# in Development

Having satisfied the requirements of First Adulthood, now what? Surprise! Look at all the time left. Today there is not only life after youth, but life after empty nest. There is life after layoff and early retirement. There is life after menopause. There is life after widowhood. There is life after coronary. There is likely to be life after cancer. Another life to find a dream for, to plan for, to train for, to invest in, to *anticipate now.*

Gail Sheehy
*New Passages: Mapping Your Life Across Time*

## *INTRODUCTION*

As we prepare for the turn of the century there is a great deal of focus in the media on the large number of persons who are entering their forties and fifties. The U.S. Bureau of the Census estimates a 60 percent increase in those entering their fortieth year by the year 2000. At the same time we hear of the increase in life expectancy for both men and women. The average adult male can now expect to live an average of seventy-five years, and researchers believe there is little reason to doubt that we can live well beyond this age. Physician and author William Regelson has even gone so far as to say, "Aging is not a normal life event but a disease."

This means that most of us will have to make a mental shift from previously held notions about the aging process. Whereas we used to think of persons who are sixty-five years of age as elderly, and thus limited in their potential and capacity, many people this age are leading active, productive, and healthy lives. We, too, can look forward to a better quality of life as we age than was necessarily true for our parents and grandparents.

Yet, even with these hopeful statistics, many in our society fear getting older. Some actively attempt to fight the aging process. Through the use of skin creams, surgical procedures, hormonal treatments, hair transplants, and newly developed laser techniques, many people strive to stop or reverse any visible effects of aging. For some, this becomes an obsession borne out of desperation.

As gay men, we are not immune from feeling sensitive about our appearance and sharing with others feelings of dread or anxiety about getting older. In some respects, gay men often feel more vulnerable about aging due to the emphasis the gay subculture places on beauty, youth, and sexual attractiveness. Coupled with this is the stereotype many hold about the "depressed, lonely, rejected by family, spurned by younger men, oversexed, and thereby, also disgusting" older gay man (Ehrenberg, 1996).

A theme I have noticed in my work with gay men is the acknowledgment by many of those who are over age forty to feel *old*. In some respects, they present with panic as they report feeling that their age snuck up on them. In fact, many feel younger than their chronological age, feel more identified with men younger than themselves, and worry about time running out. It sometimes feels as if I am talking with a thirty-year-old athlete—past his potential in the sports world—than with a man with thirty-five or more years still ahead of him. One client of mine, for example, would never date someone his own age (forty-seven) because of his belief that they are too old. In his mind, he did not look or act as most forty-seven-year-old men do, and thus he felt identified with a younger generation.

## WHY DO WE FEAR GROWING OLDER?

It has been shown that stereotypes, myths, and negative attitudes toward aging gay men do exist (Kelly, 1980). Unfortunately, these stereotypes come from both within and outside of gay subculture. Our challenge is to ask ourselves why we believe or buy into such myths. Some people perpetuate the myth that gay men molest children. Yet, we know—from personal experience and from research (Jenny, Thomas, and Kimberly, 1994)—that this is not true. Why can't we similarly dismiss unfounded notions about older gay men?

Part of the problem is that, until recently, most of us did not know any gay men older than forty-five or fifty. Men of these generations had a more difficult time coming out as gay, and it is likely that many maintained closeted lives. Lately, however, there are more openly gay men who were in their twenties when gay liberation was initiated in the late 1960s. Also, as opportunities for meeting other gay men increase, we each may come into contact with gay men from all ages and backgrounds.

For some gay men, particularly if they are single, there is the concern that they will not be able to attract a lover after a certain age. A client of mine in his forties placed a relationship ad in a gay newspaper. Whenever a respondent asked his age, he would avoid the question and defensively defend his youthful looks, interests, and activities. Even gay men in long-term relationships report their own concerns about the aging process, however, suggesting that the concern is about more than obtaining new sexual partners.

As evidenced by the rise in men's health magazines, books on longevity, and the large number of skin products geared toward older adult males, fixation about aging is not limited to gay men. In fact, the concerns we have about aging are concerns shared by many men. However, we have the added burden of how others perceive gay men as a group, and it is difficult feeling disadvantaged in yet another realm. Perhaps our best source of data on how older gay men feel is to ask them directly. So for now let us take a look at the research on gay men and aging.

## WHAT DO WE KNOW ABOUT GAY MEN AND AGING?

In 1977, James Kelly published a pioneering study of 241 gay men between the ages of sixteen and seventy-nine. He concluded that the typical aging gay man does not fit the popular stereotype of someone who is socially isolated or who fears he has lost his physical attractiveness. Instead, Kelly found that older gay men are quite satisfied with their lives—including their sex lives—and that they have good relationships with men their own age. He also found that gay men did not withdraw from involvement with the gay community. Additionally, a full 83 percent of the respondents over age sixty-five reported being sexually satisfied.

Another researcher (Berger, 1982) interviewed 112 midwestern gay men between the ages of forty-one and seventy-seven by questionnaire and selected ten of these for an extensive interview. The men in his study were not lonely or isolated, and most felt that age brought them new freedom. They maintained their earlier level of sexual activity, although with fewer sexual partners.

Others (Kimmel, 1978; Lee, 1987; Grube, 1990) have interviewed gay men over age forty and found good psychological adjustment. These researchers found that most gay men adapt to changes as they grow older, with high levels of self-acceptance and life satisfaction.

Siegal and Lowe (1995), in their book on life passages of gay men, note the resiliency of most older gay men. They write that many older gay men have had to confront some difficult circumstances in their lives, and thus are better able to tap into their inner strength and resources:

> For the most part, gay men growing up under circumstances in which there was no emotional support draw on their monumental strength and have found the self-validation that they've needed to survive. Since they have challenged the negative stereotypes for their whole lives, they are in a perfect position to observe, gauge, and act on what might be the best way to assist younger or more fragile men in freeing themselves from their own struggles. (pp. 222-223)

Acknowledging that most heterosexual men rely on their wives to organize their family and social lives, Siegal and Lowe write that older gay men have likely developed a strong support system in addition to being better able at attending to their own needs. A good support system is important to us at any age, but particularly necessary as we grow older and face new challenges.

## ADULTHOOD AS TRANSITION:
## OUR FORTIETH YEAR AND BEYOND

Most men, be they gay or not, were raised believing that it is important to succeed and achieve. For some men, they were raised to believe that these goals should be attained at all costs. Thus, for them, success often meant having to sacrifice values, compromise personal needs, and at times, exploit others. Large numbers of gay men, because of feeling we have to prove ourselves, have generally been quite successful. No event made this more obvious than AIDS, as the illness brought to the attention of the world the homosexuality of highly talented actors, superb sportsmen, skilled politicians, and masterful writers, artists, and businessmen.

Daniel Levinson (1978) observed that many men sacrifice important relationships in their twenties and thirties, placing professional growth and development above the needs of their spouse and children. For gay men, we too have traditionally put more energy toward our careers than in other aspects of life. As one client, a successful businessman in his forties, told me, "I have made it professionally; now I am finally ready for a relationship."

Levinson (1978) found that the consequence to the men who made their careers a priority over their families was that their spouse and children learned to manage without them. How this became apparent was in the finding that most men, as they enter their fortieth year, feel emotionally barnkrupt. As men enter their forties they develop a need for emotional connectedness (Sheehy, 1995). The meaning of life also becomes more important to men at this time. Levinson found a natural tendency of the men he studied to turn their attention back toward their families. However, by this time their children were grown and their wives, if they stayed in the marriage, had friends, activities, and interests of their own. This is why, he maintains, many men have better and closer relationships with their grandchildren than they did with their own children.

This is the time of life Gail Sheehy (1995) calls Second Adulthood. She defines the time of life after our forties as a transition from survival to mastery. She elaborates:

> In young adulthood we survive by figuring out how best to please or perform for the powerful ones who will protect and

reward us: parents, teachers, lovers, mates, bosses, mentors. It is all about proving ourselves. The transformation of middle life is to move into a more stable psychological state of mastery, where we control much of what happens in our life and can often act on the world, rather than habitually react to whatever the world throws at us. Reaching this state of mastery is also one of the best predictors of good mental and psychological functioning in old age. (p. 142)

Popular psychology used to refer to this time of transition as a "midlife" crisis. The word crisis was used because of the emphasis placed on loss. Though for some people midlife is a time of crisis, for others it is a time of growth and opportunity. Much of it depends on your perspective as you enter these middle years. The risky point of view is that the good times are over, that aging may be good for some, but not for others. Viorst (1986) reflects this view when she writes:

But before we can come to some positive view of the other side of the mountain, we need to acknowledge that middle age is sad, because—not all at once, but bit by bit and day by day—we lose and leave and let go of our young self. (p. 267)

Sheehy (1995) developed a different conceptualizatlon of the midlife crisis. What she found, in her research and interviews, was that this time of life is better framed as a *meaning crisis* (p. 148). Because we are growing and changing, we need to adjust our expectations and goals and adapt to life's changes. Those who are better prepared for life's changes naturally do better when these adjustments occur. Sheehy concludes:

The most strikingly consistent result to come out of my surveys and focus groups with men is the evidence of a clear and finite change in the poles of the battery sometime between ages 45 and 55. The happiest men move from devoting most of their energy to competing and sexual conquest to devoting more and more of their energy to finding emotional intimacy, trust, and companionship and community with others. I see this as the essential task for men in middle life: to move from competing to connecting. (p. 274)

## BODILY CHANGES IN MEN

Men can take comfort in one piece of the aging process; it occurs much slower for us than it does for women. Whereas women must confront a sudden loss of reproductive function and the accompanying changes, men experience more gradual changes. Some have tried to introduce the concept of *male menopause*, though there remains no medical substantiation for it. Yet, even though there is no equivalent of menopause for men, there are changes in men's bodies. These can be summarized as follows:

- *Brain Function.* Concentration and language skill do not change much with age. Our ability to store and retrieve information declines steadily from the early twenties on, but not substantially.
- *Vision.* By age fifty, lifelong thickening of the lens causes a noticeable loss of night vision focus on close objects.
- *Body Fat.* Between the ages of twenty-five and seventy-five the amount of fat in proportion to the body's composition doubles. Much of that growth occurs in muscles and organs.
- *Hair Loss.* The number of hair follicles on the scalp decreases as men age, and the hair that is left grows at a slower rate.
- *Hearing.* Eardrums thicken and the ear canal atrophies, making pure tones and high frequencies harder to hear, especially in the late fifties.
- *Muscles and Bones.* Eventually muscles get smaller and weaker, but those changes can be offset by exercise. Bone loss, a universal aging trait, occurs at individual rates.

## THE PSYCHOLOGY OF MEN AND AGING: THE WORK OF DANIEL LEVINSON

A major developmental task of the Mid-Life Transition is to confront the Young and the Old within oneself and seek new ways of being Young/Old. A man must give up certain of his former youthful qualities—some with regret, some with relief or satisfaction—while retaining and transforming other qualities that he can integrate into his new life. And he must find positive meanings of being "older."

Daniel Levinson
*The Seasons of a Man's Life*

## Men in Their Thirties

In the late 1960s and early 1970s, Daniel Levinson began a study of forty men who were between thirty-five and forty-five years of age, equally distributed among four major occupational groups. The aim was to portray an individual life as it evolves over the years, and to quantify major themes associated with this time of life. Such research draws from the developmental theories of Erik Erikson, Carl Jung, and Sigmund Freud, all of whom believed that children and adults progress through a series of developmental stages, each with its own tasks, qualities, and challenges.

Levinson found that men face certain developmental challenges in their early to mid-thirties. How well these challenges are mastered has a direct effect on how a man copes and adjusts with the realities of being in his forties and fifties.

For example, Levinson found that in early adulthood, a powerful factor in the lives of men is the development and pursuit of the Dream. More than a vision or fantasy, the Dream provides men with one of the most central pieces of meaning in his early adult years. Levinson writes:

> The Dream is a vague sense of self-in-adult-world. It has the quality of a vision, an imagined possibility that generates excitement and vitality. . . . It may take a dramatic form as in the myth of the hero, the great artist, business tycoon, athletic or intellectual superstar performing magnificent feats and receiving special honors. . . . Whatever the nature of his Dream, a young man has the developmental task of giving it greater definition and finding ways to live it out. (p. 91)

The other challenge for men in their thirties, according to Levinson, is to find a mentor relationship. Much broader than a teacher, advisor, counselor, or lover, the mentor–typically male–guides the man toward the fulfillment of his Dream. Rather than being a defined role someone plays, the mentor relationship functions more in terms of the "character of the relationship and the function it serves." Levinson adds:

> Serving as a sponsor, he may use his influence to facilitate the young man's entry and advancement. He may be a *host and guide*, welcoming the initiate into a new occupational and social world and acquainting him with its values, achievements and a way of living, the mentor may be an *examplar* that the protege can admire and seek to emulate. He may provide counsel and moral support in time of stress. (p. 98)

Mentors tend to be older by roughly eight to fifteen years, and the young man feels himself appreciative of the guidance, direction, and support he receives from his mentor. Mentoring relationships usually last anywhere from two to ten years, and end in a variety of ways. However, regardless of how the relationship ends, Levinson found that most mentor relationships end with conflict or bad feelings by both persons. "The mentor who only yesterday was regarded as an enabling teacher and friend has become a tyrannical father or smothering mother." The young man, by this time, has internalized the mentor's qualities as his own, and he is now better able to listen to his own voice.

### Men in Their Forties

By now, most men have done the necessary exploring and have established themselves as adults. Men at this point feel more of an urgency to settle down and be responsible. Levinson refers to this period as the Mid-Life Transition. The central challenge for men at this time of life is coming to terms with both their past and their future.

Most men, Levinson believes, look back on their past at this stage and ask themselves the following questions:

- What have I done with my life?
- What do I want for myself?
- What do I want for other people?
- What are my values?

- What are my talents?
- What have I done with my dream?

Naturally, the examination of these questions cannot be an intellectual pursuit. Rather, many men experience much emotional turmoil as they struggle with these questions, and, as can be expected, most men do not like their answers to these questions.

Certainly, there are some men who do very little questioning or searching at this time of life. For them, life may feel fairly stable, and questions of value and meaning do not surface. However, Levinson believes that these men may be working on these questions unconsciously. "If not, they will pay the price in a later developmental crisis or in a progressive withering of the self and a life structure minimally connected to the self." Thus, denying or ignoring that your life must change is one of the greatest hazards of growing older.

Men also become more aware of their sense of aging after forty. In addition to becoming aware of physical limitations, men in their forties find themselves more in tune with the fact that at some point they are going to die. This has a direct effect on the questions men ask themselves about their lives, particularly as they assess what effect they have had in life. Sheehy (1995) believes that men have an easier time in their fifties than their forties since by that point they find that their fears about dying were unwarranted.

Levinson found that being a mentor to a young adult is one of the most significant relationships available to a man in middle adulthood. Levinson writes the following:

> Mentoring utilizes the parental impulse, but it is more complex and requires some degree of mid-life individuation. As he gains a stronger sense of self, and of his own continuing development in middle adulthood, a man is more able to foster the development of other adults.

By becoming a mentor to a younger adult, a man maintains his connection with the forces of youthful energy and vitality, both in himself and in the world as a whole. Levinson summarizes his findings in the following:

If a man creates a new form of self-in-world, late adulthood can be a season as full and rich as the others. Some of the greatest intellectual and artistic works have been produced by men in their sixties, seventies, and even eighties. Examples abound: Picasso, Yeats, Verdi, Frank Lloyd Wright, Freud, Jung, Sophocles, Michelangelo, Tolstoy. (pp. 36-37)

## *Commentary on Levinson's Research*

Levinson offers little on the subject of homosexuality, and what he does include is a bit naive and old-fashioned. Though five of the forty men he interviewed admitted to dealing with issues of homosexuality at some point in their life, they probably did not feel they had many options available to them regarding their sexuality given the era in which this research was conducted.

Still, I believe there is much of Levinson's research that applies to us as gay men. One crucial point is the focus Levinson places on mentoring. Though for him, most mentoring relationships are placed in the context of being related to a man's occupation, I feel that it is important to examine the issue of gay mentors/role models in our lives. This issue is explored in more depth in Chapter 2, so I will not give a detailed explanation here. However, many gay men rely upon older gay men to model healthy homosexuality, offer stable relationships to look up to, and at times, initiate us sexually in our coming out process.

Additionally, there is the broader role of the older mentor for the younger adult. Though this conjures up stereotypes of older gay men seeking younger gay men for sexual pursuit, there are ways in which older gay men can be role models and provide support for younger gays. This can include being active in one's local gay community, providing financial support to gay youth organizations, having gay men of all ages in your friendship network, and sharing your own experiences as a gay man with younger generations. As Siegal and Lowe (1995) write:

> The older gay man deserves the respect and honor due his hard-earned achievements and wealth of experience, and like the older heterosexual—man or woman—he wants to share them. (pp. 223-224)

Another major point Levinson raises is the evaluation each of us do about our past during times of transition. In addition to those questions set forth by Levinson, gay men in their forties may also ask the following:

- How might my life had been different if I had come out sooner?
- Who has been hurt because of my being gay? Could this have been prevented?
- How do I feel I have managed the gay side of my life?
- What have I done to promote the well-being of other gay men?
- How have I perpetuated or changed peoples' stereotypes about gay men?
- How do I feel about lovers and relationships in my past?
- How does being gay affect my life as I grow older?
- How do I feel about having survived this long when many other gay men have not?

## SEX AND MOOD AS WE AGE

### Sex and the Older Gay Man

Due primarily to lower levels of sex hormones, many men experience less sexual desire as they age. However, this does not translate into a total lack of sexual interest or erection capacity, and research suggests that it certainly does not translate into no sex life at all for older men.

Kelly's (1980) research on aging gay men found that most older gay men are satisfied sexually:

> Concerning the degree of sexual satisfaction within the gay population, 87 percent of the total questionnaire respondents indicated that they were on the satisfactory side of the continuum. By comparison, among a group of predominantly heterosexual men who responded to the *Psychology Today* questionnaire on sex, only 69 percent rated their sexual satisfaction as adequate. (p. 184)

McWhirter and Mattison (1984), in their study of long-term male couples, found that even though couples reported a decline in the frequency of sex over time, there still was an overall satisfaction with their sex together. For many gay couples, they found that sex may be less frequent, but there is still a high need for affection, tenderness, and closeness.

What many men find problematic as they age is the first time they experience difficulty getting or sustaining an erection. Though this occurrence may just be a natural response, some men fear that it is the beginning of the end of their sexual capacity. Only with assurance from their physicians do they realize that it is common to experience problems with erections or ejaculation at all stages of life, but rarely is it permanent.

During the late 1980s, researchers (Sheehy, 1995) examined 1,700 Boston-area men between the ages forty and seventy. They found that older men's impotence was almost always linked to vascular conditions. This research, and other studies on male potency, have found that there are some factors that consistently correlate with erectile difficulties in older men. These include the following:

- Elevated stress levels
- Smoking
- Alcohol abuse
- Hypertension (especially with accompanying medications)
- Diabetes
- Heart disease

Basically, the message is *take care of your body.* Men who remain healthy and relatively physically fit report active sexual lives into their seventies and eighties.

## DEPRESSION AND AGING

At no time is the connection between mental and physical health greater than in our forties and beyond. For a variety of reasons, we are more resilient when confronted with stress, conflict, or depression when we are in our twenties or thirties than we are when we are older. But for many of the reasons discussed thus far, the aging process can take a tremendous psychological toll on some people. One consequence of this is depression.

Depression is both a medical and psychological term. It refers to more than the periodic blues we feel at times. Depression usually manifests when we feel like we have lost or are losing what feels like life's struggle. Sometimes we do not even know we are depressed. Friends may sense that we are depressed, but may not always tell us. Usually our first clues are when we engage in self-destructive habits, experience a decline in our effectiveness at work or in relationships, or exhibit some of the following features.

## Warning Signs of Depression

- Lack of energy
- Difficulty sleeping or excessive sleeping
- Loss of sex drive
- Self-deprecation or feelings of guilt
- Not eating enough or eating too much
- Irritability or sadness
- Uncontrollable crying
- Feelings of worthlessness
- Bodily complaints
- Increased use of alcohol and/or drugs
- More frequent illness or slow recovery from illness
- Loss of interest in usual activities
- Thoughts of suicide

One of the main contributors to feelings of depression in older adults is the recognition of loss. The effects are particularly strong when the loss is cumulative. Loss can occur for a variety of reasons, and may involve many different types. Examples of loss that affect older adults include the following:

## Losses That Can Cause Depression

- Loss of a job (even retirement)
- Loss of health
- Loss of lovers or friends (especially in large numbers as with AIDS)

- Loss of a sense of power
- Loss of a sense of meaning
- Loss of income
- Loss of a relationship
- Loss of energy
- Loss of hope

Estimates of depression vary from 5 to 10 percent in those over age sixty-five. There is an increased rate for those over eighty, the poor, and for single persons. The onset of most depression occurs between ages fifty-five and sixty-five in men. Further, depression in men is often a silent phenomena in that, for many men, they are unaware of being depressed. This is a result of our socialization that tells us it is not OK for men to have feelings—particularly painful or distressing feelings. The risk, however, is too great for us not to be aware of when we are experiencing depression.

### Suicide

Most studies have concentrated on the high incidence of suicide in adolescents and the elderly. Yet, the majority of men who commit suicide are about forty years old. Even as we are living longer, and having more productive years in midlife, the high rate of suicide by midlife men is expected to continue.

Suicide can be thought of as the ultimate in developmental stagnation. It is also the final stage of depression. As Maris (1981) points out, some midlife males simply cannot negotiate the midlife transition. Some midlife men kill themselves because they do not believe it is possible to change their youth-oriented lifestyle and become viable middle-aged adults. Others may find it overwhelming to deal with declining health, loneliness, or regret about their lives. Financial struggles can also present a high level of difficulty for men.

Robins, West, and Murphy (1977) point out that the distinctive traits of midlife male suicides include the following:

- Loss of spouse
- Years of heavy drinking
- Reaching the age of high depression risk

- Personal experience with other suicides
- Facing debilitating old age without psychological compensations

Loss of occupational status and isolation are also two major contributors to midlife suicide by men.

Though women make more suicide attempts than men, men are two times as likely to be successful at suicide. Mainly this is because men choose more violent means of suicide such as weapons or hanging. Women, on the other hand, are more likely to attempt suicide by overdosing on medication.

Depression is not just a psychosocial phenomena, however, nor is suicide. Both suicide and depression run in families. Thus, if family members of yours were depressed and/or committed suicide, you may be at high risk for the same. I encourage you to take a look at the genogram you did in the exercise in Chapter 1 to see if you can identify themes of depression or suicide in your family. If you see this pattern, it is very important that you pay attention to your own mood and how you cope with feelings of depression.

## MANAGING DEPRESSION

It is very likely that most of us will experience moments of depression as we get older. Though the studies referenced in this chapter identify the happiness and well-being many older adults feel, this is achieved only after periods of grieving, letting go, and evaluating aspects of our past. However, if you are able to identify any of the warning signs from the previous list, or if loved ones tell you they think you might be depressed, consider the following recommendations.

### Talk About It

You do not necessarily have to tell another person that you are depressed, but it can be helpful to share with another some of your worries, concerns, or fears about life. Many men feel shame when they think of sharing with another their financial concerns, regrets about life, things they feel guilty of, etc. Yet, if you can open up and share your feelings with a friend, lover, or family member, you will probably feel a lot better. If your feelings are related to growing older, share this too. You are not alone. If you do not feel that you can talk to the people in your life, consider hiring a psychotherapist. Sometimes even four or five sessions in psychotherapy can be beneficial enough when you are feeling depressed.

## Exercise

Studies consistently show that our mood is tied to our energy levels. To help keep your energy level up, you need to eat right and do some type of exercise. Even walking a few blocks two or three times a week is extremely beneficial at keeping your body in shape, your muscles firm, and your aerobic capacity functioning well. Walking, bike riding, or other activities also provide you with the opportunity to think through or talk about your problems on your own or with another person.

## Alcohol

Alcohol is a drug. It is also a depressant. If you find yourself depressed, you may be drinking too much. If you are depressed, you are also more likely to use alcohol as a way of escaping your problems, but it does not work. The health risks from excessive alcohol consumption, especially in our later years, are too high. Examine how much alcohol you drink. The exercises in Chapter 3 can help you take a critical look at alcohol use in your life.

## Medications

There are many new antidepressant medications that have few side effects. Most people experience beneficial effects from medication after one to two weeks. It does not have to be a permanent option. Sometimes you may just need some help from medication for a few months or so. Talk to your doctor; he or she is trained to understand the benefits of taking medication for depression.

## CONCLUSION

Ultimately, our capacity for dealing with aging and the accompanying life changes is a continuation of how we live the earlier parts of our life. Certainly, we gain wisdom and new strengths as we age, and we learn how resilient we really are. As gay men we have learned how to master several challenges in life, and there is no reason why we cannot age successfully and with happiness. We have experienced firsthand the unfortunate early deaths of friends, lovers, and others in our community. We are fortunate to be alive and to live as long as our bodies and circumstances permit. Let each of us make the most of it.

# Exercises

### *A LOOK AT YOUR OWN AGING PROCESS*

There are so many factors that contribute to successful aging. Part of aging well is giving up stages of the past and welcoming new developmental stages and challenges. This exercise is designed to help you identify the developmental stages of your current life.

### *Questions*

How old are you now? _____
What age group do you feel most emotionally connected to?

    Early Adulthood (Age 20-39) _____
    Middle Life Transition (Age 40-50) _____
    Middle Adulthood (Age 50-60) _____
    Late Adulthood Transition (Age 60-65) _____
    Late Adulthood (Age 65 and above) _____

To what age group do you actually belong?

    Early Adulthood _____
    Middle Life Transition _____
    Middle Adulthood _____
    Late Adulthood Transition _____
    Late Adulthood _____

What group do you think your friends see you most reflective of ?

    Early Adulthood _____
    Middle Life Transition _____
    Middle Adulthood _____
    Late Adulthood Transition _____
    Late Adulthood _____

Is there a disparity between the group you feel emotionally connected to and the age group you belong to?   YES   NO
If yes, cite reasons and examples for this. Be honest: _____

_____

_____

_____

_____

_____

What has the been the most difficult part of growing older for you? Cite examples:_____

_____

_____

_____

_____

If your age places you in the Middle Adulthood Transition category or above, what do you miss the most from or about earlier developmental periods (e.g., Early Adulthood). Cite more than one example:

_____

_____

_____

• Continuing from the previous question, what makes it hard for you to have at this time of life what you miss from the earlier developmental period?

_____

_____

_____

• Is this something you wish could change?  YES    NO
• Is this something that can change?  YES    NO
• If it cannot change, how do you feel about this fact?

_____

_____

_____

_____

What do you need to do to feel more at peace with your aging process? How much of this are you currently doing in your life? _____

_____

_____

_____

_____

## *WHAT DO YOUR GENES SAY?*

Family history is one of the best predictors for what you can expect in terms of longevity, illness, etc., as you age. By answering the following questions, you can get an idea of what preventive measures you can take with regard to your health.

How old is your mother _____; or
How old was your mother when she died? _____
If your mother is deceased, how did she die: _____

How old is your father _____, or
How old was your father when he died? _____
If your father is deceased how did he die: _____

How old is your maternal grandmother _____; or
How old was your maternal grandmother when she died? _____
How did she die? _____

How old is your paternal grandmother _____; or
How old was your paternal grandmother when she died? _____
How did she die? _____

How old is your maternal grandfather _____; or
How old was your maternal grandfather when he died? _____
How did he die? _____

How old is your paternal grandfather _____; or
How old was your paternal grandfather when he died? _____
How did he die?_____

If your mother or father died of a physical illness (cancer, diabetes, heart attack, stroke, etc.), did anyone else within two generations of them die the same way? Specify:_____

_____

_____

What illnesses run in your family. Think of your parents, grandparents, aunts, uncles, brothers, sisters, nephews, nieces: _____

_____

_____

Do you know if you have any of these illnesses? YES NO If yes, which one(s):_____

_____

Are any of the above illnesses potentially life-threatening? If yes, list: ___

_____

If you answered yes, what preventive measures can you take to minimize your risk of either contracting or exacerbating the illness(es)? _____

_____

_____

Do you smoke cigarettes? YES   NO
Do you have more than four alcoholic drinks per week? YES   NO
Do you exercise less than three times a week? YES  NO
Do you eat a diet high in fat? YES   NO
Are you significantly overweight? YES  NO

(Answering YES to more than one of the above may mean that you are putting your health at substantial risk and thereby reducing your chances for good health in your later years.)

Have any members of your family attempted or committed suicide?
YES   NO
If YES, who:

_____

_____

_____

_____

_____

If more than one person in your family has attempted or committed suicide you may be at risk for depression. Suicide tends to run in families. If anyone in your family has attempted or committed suicide, it is extremely important that you monitor your own stress, depression, and coping mechanisms. This is also information your therapist and/or physician should be aware of.

When was the last time you had a physical examination by a physician? As we age, we need to see our doctor more frequently. If you are over forty and have not had a physical examination in the last two years, it is in your best interest to make an appointment with your doctor.

## *BEING A MENTOR*

If one of the developmental challenges of growing older is to be a mentor to a younger person, perhaps you can reflect on your role as mentor. A mentor can be one who teaches, guides, supervises, or in other ways shows a younger person "the way." This can be done with someone at work, in one of your classes, at church, or even one of your clients or patients. You can even be a mentor to a family member, perhaps a nephew.

### *Questions*

Do you see yourself as a mentor? YES  NO

If yes, is this to one person or a group of persons?_____

To whom are you a mentor? _____

For you, what are the three most important parts of your mentor role?

    1._____

    2._____

    3._____

How did it turn out that you are a mentor to this person or group?

_____

_____

_____

_____

How is your role as mentor likely to end?

_____

_____

_____

_____

Who were your mentors when you were younger?

    1._____

    2._____

    3._____

Do you think of him/them often? If YES, describe: _____

_____

_____

If you are not currently a mentor to someone, are there ways you could make this happen? YES   NO

If YES, explain:_____

_____

_____

_____

## QUESTIONS TO ASK AT MIDLIFE

There are many questions we ask ourselves at midlife about our past. Below are some examples of common questions. In this exercise, you are encouraged to read the question, spend some time thinking about it, and then write your answer down. Take your time. These are important questions, and it may require doing some thoughtful reflection about earlier times in your life.

Choose one question at a time. Take your time reflecting on the question. In your journal, or on a pad of paper, write out your thoughts, feelings, and reflections about each question. Give yourself permission to be open and honest with yourself.

- What have I done with my life?
- What do I want for myself?
- What do I want for other people?
- What are my values?
- What are my talents?
- What have I done with my dream?
- How might my life have been different if I had come out sooner?
- Who has been hurt because of my being gay? Could this have been prevented?
- How do I feel I have managed the gay side of my life?
- What have I done to promote the well-being of other gay men?
- How have I perpetuated or changed peoples' stereotypes about gay men?
- How do I feel about lovers and relationships in my past?
- How does being gay affect my life as I grow older?
- How do I feel about having survived this long when many other gay men have not?
- What *tasks* or *duties* do I feel are left for me to do in this life?

## *INTERVIEWING AN OLDER ADULT*

I emphasized in this chapter that much of what we know about aging, by both gay and nongay persons, comes from extensive research with older adults. Talking with older adults about their life is a good way to learn firsthand how they see their lives, how they feel about their past, and how aging has affected their self-image.

In this exercise, you are encouraged to identify at least one older adult who will be willing to speak with you about their life. Preferably, I would like you to interview a gay man who is over fifty years of age. However, you can still find benefit in this exercise by interviewing parents, friends, or co-workers. Consider tape-recording the interview. You can develop your own questions. However, here is a sample of questions you may consider including in your interview.

- What do you consider your greatest achievement in life?
- Talk about how you were different in your thirties than now. What contributed to some of the changes?
- How do you feel about your current age? Do you miss being younger?
- Discuss some of the regrets you have about your life.
- How has your sense of self changed over the years?
- Which years of your life were most difficult?
- What would you do different in your life if you could?
- What advice do you have for younger gay men?
- What does being gay mean to you at this point in your life?
- What fears did you have about growing older? Did they come true?
- At what point in your life were you the happiest? What contributed to this?
- How you feel about death?
- What kinds of fears do you have at this time of your life?
- How do you deal with problems and crises that arise in your life?
- Did you have a mentor growing up? Do you feel you were ever a mentor?
- How do you derive intimacy and closeness in your life?
- What has been the impact of AIDS on your life?
- What was the best and worst about being gay in your life?
- What is your best and worst memory in life?
- How do you feel about your parents? How has this changed over the years?
- How do you want to be remembered after you die?

## *ASSESSING DEPRESSION IN YOUR LIFE*

Our risk for feeling depressed increases as we grow older. Much of this is because of the amount of loss we experience as we age. This brief screening measure will help you identify whether or not depression is something you may be currently struggling with. Answering YES to some of the following questions does not guarantee that you are clinically depressed. Rather, you may be tired, fatigued, or preoccupied with some concern, which is not resulting in depression. Still, if you answer YES to more than three of the following questions, it may be in your best interest to obtain a more thorough evaluation from a physician or psychotherapist.

Within the past two weeks, have you experienced any of the following:

|     |                                                              | YES | NO |
|-----|--------------------------------------------------------------|-----|-----|
| 1.  | Poor appetite                                                | ___ | ___ |
| 2.  | Loss of sexual interest or pleasure                          | ___ | ___ |
| 3.  | Crying easily                                                | ___ | ___ |
| 4.  | Feelings of loneliness                                       | ___ | ___ |
| 5.  | Excessive worrying                                           | ___ | ___ |
| 6.  | Disinterest in things that usually give you pleasure         | ___ | ___ |
| 7.  | Feelings of guilt                                            | ___ | ___ |
| 8.  | Feelings of worthlessness                                    | ___ | ___ |
| 9.  | Difficulty concentrating                                     | ___ | ___ |
| 10. | Difficulty falling asleep                                    | ___ | ___ |
| 11. | Feeling low in energy                                        | ___ | ___ |
| 12. | Feel easily irritated, annoyed, or angrier than usual        | ___ | ___ |
| 13. | Thoughts of death, dying, or ending your life                | ___ | ___ |
| 14. | Hopeless about your future                                   | ___ | ___ |
| 15. | Waking up early in the morning and unable to get back to sleep | ___ | ___ |

Scoring:
    5 or less:  Slightly depressed or fatigued
    5 or more: Significant likelihood of depression

# References

Alexander, C. (1996). *Gay and lesbian mental health: A sourcebook for practitioners.* Binghamton, New York: The Haworth Press, Inc.

Aldrich, H. (1996). Closet violence. *Santa Fe Reporter*, May 8-14, 15-20.

Baum, M.D., and Fishman, J.M. (1994). AIDS, sexual compulsivity, and gay men: A group treatment approach. In *Therapists on the front line.* S.A. Cadwell, R.A. Burnham, and M.F. Forstein, eds. Washington, DC: American Psychiatric Press.

Beatty, R. (1983). "Alcoholism and adult gay male populations of Pennsylvania." Master's thesis. University Park, Pennsylvania State University.

Berger, R.M. (1982). *Gay and gray: The older homosexual man.* Boston, Massachusetts: Alyson.

Bernstein, B.E. (1990). Attitudes and issues of parents of gay men and lesbians and implications for therapy. *Journal of Gay and Lesbian Psychotherapy*, 1(3), 37-53.

Berzon, B. (1988). *Permanent partners: Building gay and lesbian relationships that last.* New York: Plume Books.

Bradshaw, J. (1988). *Healing the shame that binds you.* Deerfield Beach, Florida: Health Communications, Inc.

Bryant, S.A., and Demian (1994). Relationship characteristics of American gay and lesbian couples: Findings from a national survey. *Journal of Gay and Lesbian Social Services*, 1(2), 101-117.

Byrne, D. (1996). Clinical models for the treatment of gay male perpetrators of domestic violence. *Journal of Gay and Lesbian Social Services*, 4(1), 107-116.

Chessick, R.D. (1985). *Psychology of the self and the treatment of narcissism.* New Jersey: Jason Aronson, Inc.

Ehrenberg, M. (1996). Aging and mental health: Issues in the gay and lesbian community. In *Gay and lesbian mental health: A sourcebook for practitioners.* C. Alexander, ed. Binghamton, New York: The Haworth Press, Inc.

Ekstrand, M.L., and Coates, T.J. (1990). Maintenance of safer sexual behaviors and predictors of risky sex: The San Francisco Men's Health Study. *American Journal of Publich Health*, 80, 973-977.

Elliott, P. (1996). Shattering illusions: Same-sex domestic violence. *Journal of Gay and Lesbian Social Services*, 4(1), 1-8.

Engel, L., and Ferguson, T. (1990). *Imaginary crimes.* Boston, Massachusetts: Houghton Mifflin Company.

Farley, N. (1996). A survey of factors contributing to gay and lesbian domestic violence. *Journal of Gay and Lesbian Social Services*, 4(1), 35-42.

Friedman, R.C. (1988). *Male homosexuality: A contemporary psychoanalytic perspective*. New Haven, Connecticut: Yale University Press.

Gil, E. (1988). *Treatment of adult survivors of childhood abuse*. Walnut Creek, California: Launch Press.

Gonzales, M.H., and Meyers, S.A. (1993). Your mother would like me: Self-presentation in the personals ads of heterosexual and homosexual men and women. *Personality and Social Psychology Bulletin*, 19(2), 131-142.

Grube, J. (1990). Natives and settlers: An ethnographic note on early interaction of older homosexual men with younger gay liberationists. *Journal of Homosexuality*, 12, 139-152.

Harvey, A. (1994). Rebirth through the wound. In *Gay soul: Finding the heart of gay spirit and nature*. M. Thompson, ed. San Francisco, California: Harper-Collins.

Hershberger, S. (1996). Categorization of lesbian, gay and bisexual suicide attempters. In *Gay and lesbian mental health: A sourcebook for practitioners*. C. Alexander, ed. Binghamton, New York: The Haworth Press, Inc.

Isay, R. (1989). *Being homosexual*. New York: Avon Books.

Isensee, R. (1990). *Love between men: Enhancing intimacy and keeping your relationship alive*. New York: Prentice-Hall, Inc.

Jenny, C., Thomas, R.A., and Kimberly, P.L. (1994). Are children at risk for sexual abuse by homosexuals? *Pediatrics*, 94(1), 41-47.

Kelly, J. (1980). Homosexuality and aging. In *Homosexual behavior: A modern reappraisal*. J. Maimor, ed. New York: Basic Books.

Kelly, J.A., St. Lawrence, J.S., and Brasfield, T.L. (1991). Predictors of vulnerability to AIDS risk behavior relapse. *Journal of Consulting and Clinical Psychology*, 59, 163-166.

Kelly, J., Sikkema, K., Soloman, I.L., Heckman, T., Stevenson, Y., Norman, A., Winett, R., Roffman, R., Perry, M., and Desiderato, I.L. (1995). Predicting continued high-risk behavior among gay men in small cities: Psychological, behavioral, and demographic characteristics related to unsafe sex. *Journal of Consulting and Clinical Psychology*, 69(6), 1166-1172.

Kimmel, D.C. (1978). Adult development and aging: A gay perspective. *Journal of Social Issues*, 34, 113-130.

Lazur, R.F. (1987). Identity integration: Counseling the adolescent male. In *Handbook of counseling and psychotherapy with men*. M. Scher, M. Stevens, G. Good, and G.A. Eichenfield, eds. Newbury Park, California: Sage Publications.

Lee, J.A. (1987). What can gay aging studies contribute to theories of aging? *Journal of Homosexuality*, 13, 43-71.

Letellier, P. (1996). Twin epidemics: Domestic violence and HIV infection among gay and bisexual men. *Journal of Gay and Lesbian Social Services*, 4(1), 69-82.

Levinson, D. (1978). *The seasons of a man's life*. New York: Ballantine.

Marion, M. (1996). Living in an era of multiple loss and trauma: Understanding global loss in the gay community. In *Gay and lesbian mental health: A source-*

*book for practitioners.* C. Alexander, ed. Binghamton, New York: The Haworth Press, Inc.

Maris, R.W. (1981). *Pathways to suicide.* Baltimore, Maryland: Johns Hopkins University Press.

Martin, J.I. and Knox, J. (1995). HIV risk behavior in gay men with unstable self-esteem. *Journal of Gay and Lesbian Social Services,* 2, 21-41.

Masterson, J.F. (1988). *The search for the real self: Unmasking the personality disorders of our age.* New York: The Free Press.

McWhirter, D.P. and Mattison, A.M. (1984). *The male couple.* Englewood Cliffs, New Jersey: Prentice-Hall, Inc.

Modrcin, M.J. and Wyers, N.L. (1990). Lesbian and gay couples: Where they turn when they need help. *Journal of Gay and Lesbian Psychotherapy,* 1(3), 89-104.

Monette, P. (1994). On becoming. In *Gay soul: Finding the heart of gay spirit and nature.* M. Thompson, ed. San Francisco, California: HarperCollins.

Nardi, P.M. and Sherrod, D. (1994). Friendship in the lives of gay men and lesbians. *Journal of Social and Personal Relationships,* 11, 185-199.

Nord, D. (1990). Assessing the negative effects of multiple AIDS-related loss on the gay individual and community. *Journal of Gay and Lesbian Social Services,* 4(3), 1-34.

Perkins, D.O., Leserman, J., Murphy, C., and Evans, D.L. (1993). Psychosocial predictors of high-risk sexual behavior among HIV-negative homosexual men. *AIDS Education and Prevention,* 5(2), 141-152.

Pollak, M. (1993). Homosexual rituals and safer sex. *Journal of Homosexuality,* 25, 307-317.

Prendergast, W.E. (1991). *Treating sex offenders in correctional institutions and outpatient clinics.* Binghamton, New York: The Haworth Press, Inc.

Rando, T.A. (1984). *Grief, dying, and death: Clinical interventions for caregivers.* Champaign, Illinois: Research Press Company.

Robins, L.N., West, P.A., and Murphy, G.E. (1977). A high rate of suicide in older white men. *Social Psychiatry,* 12, 1-20.

Roscoe, W. (1994). The geography of gender. In *Gay soul: Finding the heart of gay spirit and nature.* Mark Thompson, ed. San Francisco, California: Harper-Collins.

Ross, H. and Milgram, J. (1982). Important variables in adult sibling relationships: A qualitative study. In *Sibling relationships: Their nature and significance across the life-span.* M.E. Lamb and B. Sutton-Smith, eds. Hillsdale, New Jersey: Lawrence

Satir, V. (1972). *Peoplemaking.* Palo Alto: Science and Behavior Books.

Schwartz, M. (1996). Gay men and the heath care system. *Journal of Gay and Lesbian Social Services,* 5(1), 19-32.

Sheehy, G. (1995). *New passages: Mapping your life across time.* New York: Ballantine.

Siegel, S. and Lowe, E. (1994). *Understanding the life passages of gay men.* New York: Penguin Books.

Siever, M. (1996). The perils of sexual objectification: Sexual orientation, gender, and socioculturally acquired vulnerability to body dissatisfaction and eating disorders. In *Gay and lesbian mental health: A sourcebook for practitioners.* C. Alexander, ed. Binghamton, New York: The Haworth Press, Inc.

Sinclair, H. (1990, May). "Not her, him." Paper presented to the San Francisco District Attorney's Office and General Works, San Francisco, California.

Sleek, S. (1996). Research identifies causes of internatlized homophobia. Monitor: The American Psychological Association, 27(10), 57.

Terr, I.L. (1990). *Too scared to cry.* New York: Basic Books.

Tewksbury, R. (1995). Adventures in the erotic oasis: Sex and danger in men's same-sex, public, sexual encounters. *The Journal of Men's Studies,* 4(1), 9-24.

Thompson, M. (1994). *Gay soul: Finding the heart of gay spirit and nature.* San Francisco, California: HarperCollins.

Trimble, S. (1993). The people. Santa Fe: School of American Research Press.

Viorst, J. (1986). *Necessary losses.* New York: Simon and Schuster.

Wegscheider, S. *Another chance: Hope and health for the alcoholic family.* Palo Alto, California: Science and Behavior Books.

World Service Office. (1986). *Am I an addict?* Van Nuys, California: Author.

Wurmser, L. (1987). Shame: The veiled companion of narcissism. In *The many faces of shame.* D.L. Nathanson, ed. New York: The Guilford Press.

# Index

# Order Your Own Copy of
# This Important Book for Your Personal Library!

## GROWTH AND INTIMACY FOR GAY MEN
## A Workbook

_____ in hardbound at $49.95 (ISBN: 0-7890-0153-5)

_____ in softbound at $22.95 (ISBN: 1-56023-901-8)

COST OF BOOKS_____

OUTSIDE USA/CANADA/
MEXICO: ADD 20%_____

POSTAGE & HANDLING_____
(US: $3.00 for first book & $1.25
for each additional book)
Outside US: $4.75 for first book
& $1.75 for each additional book)

SUBTOTAL_____

IN CANADA: ADD 7% GST_____

STATE TAX_____
(NY, OH & MN residents, please
add appropriate local sales tax)

FINAL TOTAL_____
(If paying in Canadian funds,
convert using the current
exchange rate. UNESCO
coupons welcome.)

☐ **BILL ME LATER:** ($5 service charge will be added)
(Bill-me option is good on US/Canada/Mexico orders only;
not good to jobbers, wholesalers, or subscription agencies.)

☐ Check here if billing address is different from
shipping address and attach purchase order and
billing address information.

Signature_____

☐ **PAYMENT ENCLOSED: $**_____

☐ **PLEASE CHARGE TO MY CREDIT CARD.**

☐ Visa   ☐ MasterCard   ☐ AmEx   ☐ Discover
☐ Diners Club
Account # _____

Exp. Date _____

Signature _____

Prices in US dollars and subject to change without notice.

NAME _____

INSTITUTION _____

ADDRESS _____

CITY _____

STATE/ZIP _____

COUNTRY _____ COUNTY (NY residents only) _____

TEL _____ FAX _____

E-MAIL_____
May we use your e-mail address for confirmations and other types of information? ☐ Yes   ☐ No

*Order From Your Local Bookstore or Directly From*
**The Haworth Press, Inc.**
10 Alice Street, Binghamton, New York 13904-1580 • USA
TELEPHONE: 1-800-HAWORTH (1-800-429-6784) / Outside US/Canada: (607) 722-5857
FAX: 1-800-895-0582 / Outside US/Canada: (607) 772-6362
E-mail: getinfo@haworth.com
PLEASE PHOTOCOPY THIS FORM FOR YOUR PERSONAL USE.

BOF96